SHONEN JUMP MANGA

NARUTO
VOL. 16
EULOGY

STORY AND ART BY
MASASHI KISHIMOTO

CHARACTERS
Sasuke
サスケ
Naruto
ナルト
Guy ガイ
Sakura
サクラ
Neji ネジ
Rock Lee
ロック・リー
Tenten
テンテン
Kiba & キバ&
Akamaru 赤丸
Hinata
ヒナタ
Itachi
イタチ
Shikamaru
シカマル
Shino シノ
Ino いの
Choji
チョウジ

Third Hokage
火影

Orochimaru
大蛇丸

Kankuro
カンクロウ
Gaara 我愛羅

Temari
テマリ

Kakashi
カカシ

Jiraiya
自来也

The Story So Far...

Twelve years ago a destructive nine-tailed fox spirit attacked the ninja village of Konohagakure. The Hokage, or village champion, defeated the fox by sealing its soul into the body of a baby boy. Now that boy, Uzumaki Naruto, has grown up to be a ninja-in-training, learning the art of ninjutsu with his teammates Sakura and Sasuke.

Naruto and company take on the Chûnin Selection Exams but suffer a sudden attack from Orochimaru in the Forest of Death. Orochimaru leaves a curse mark on Sasuke's body and vanishes…

During the finals of the Chûnin Exams, Orochimaru, disguised as Kazekage, takes the Hokage hostage and erects a barrier shield. *Operation Destroy Konoha* is underway! Meanwhile, Naruto and his friends have been chasing after Sasuke and Gaara, who is undergoing a terrifying transformation. Now, to save Sasuke and Sakura, Naruto must face off against this monstrous new version of Gaara.

NARUTO

VOL. 16
EULOGY

CONTENTS

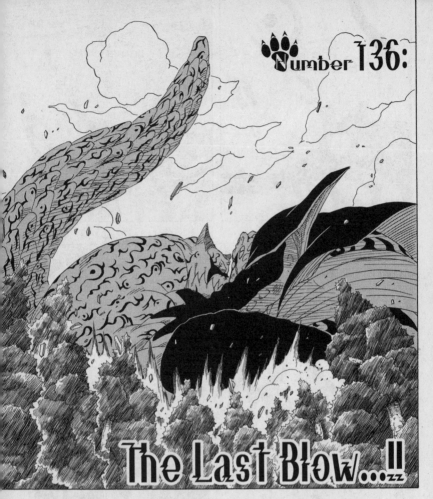

Number 136: The Last Blow...!!

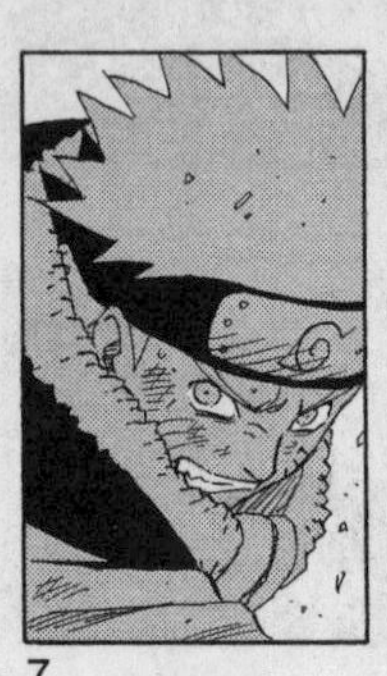

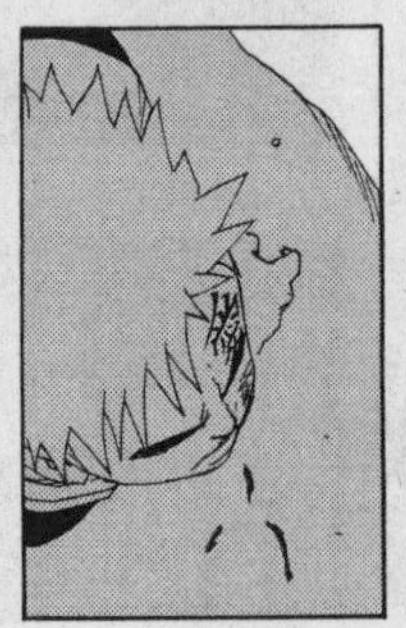

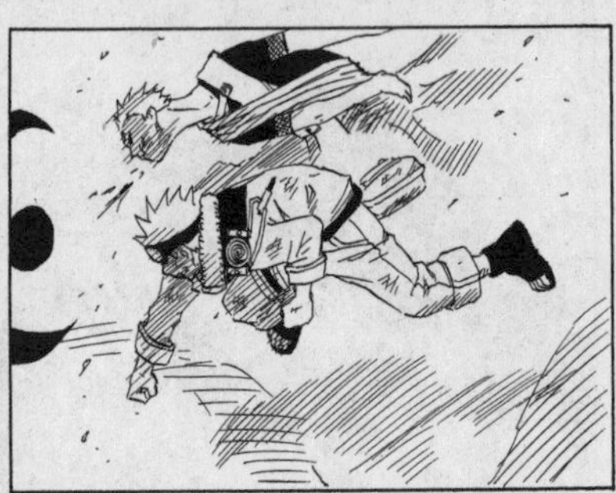

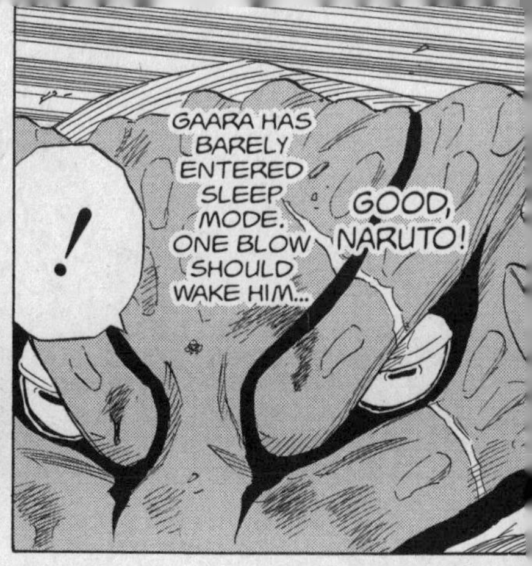
GOOD, NARUTO!
GAARA HAS BARELY ENTERED SLEEP MODE. ONE BLOW SHOULD WAKE HIM...
!

!!
THEY BLOCKED MY JUTSU!!
UGH!
FAP

I DON'T WANT TO GO BACK IN!
AAARGH!!

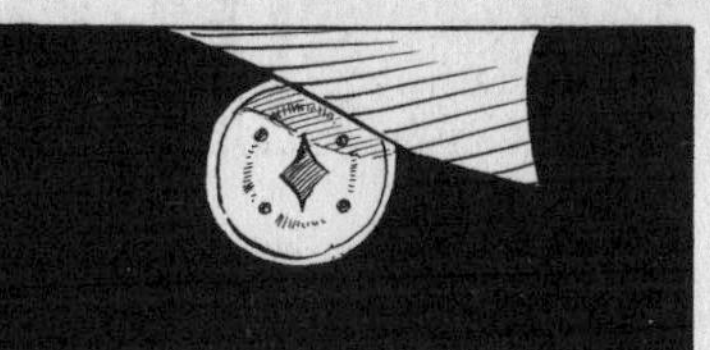

WE STOPPED HIS JUTSU! WHY IS HE STILL SO STRONG?!
KREEE
SKRUD

FZT

FUMP
GAH...
SHFFF
!
SHWOOM
YAAAAH!!

SQUELCH
!
URK...
!!
ZWIRL
PA!!

!!
FAWP
SLAM
...THIS IS THE CHIEF'S TONGUE ...!
DON'T YOU MOCK ME...
HUF
RRRRR
HUF
!!

SLTTTH
SLTTTH

UGH!

GRRR...

SHFFF!

UGH!
JUST HOW MUCH STRENGTH DOES THIS ONE HAVE...?!
SHWUMP

READ
THIS
WAY

NOT GOOD...!
NARUTO AND I HAVE BOTH COMPLETELY USED UP OUR CHAKRA!!
HUF

...
HUF
HUF

SHFFF...
SNAP
SNAP SNAP

!
SAKURA!!

SHFFF
SNAP SNAP

I SHALL KILL YOU.
I WILL NOT CEASE TO EXIST.

I'VE GOT TO STOP THIS TANUKI MONSTER.

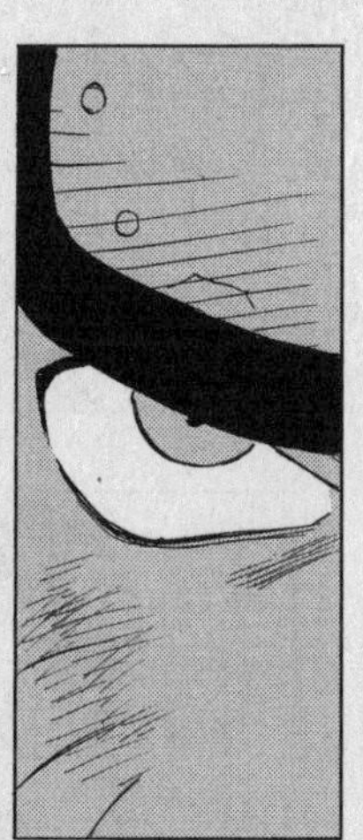

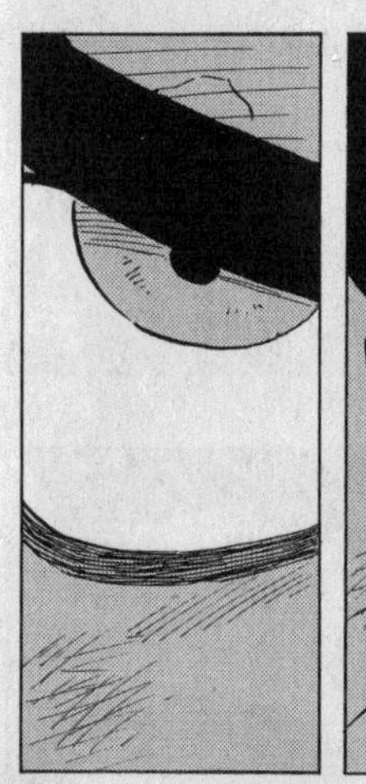

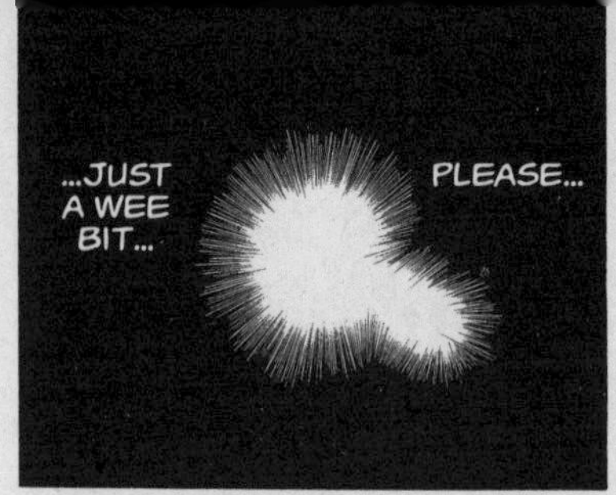
PLEASE...
...JUST
A WEE
BIT...

FWUUUH

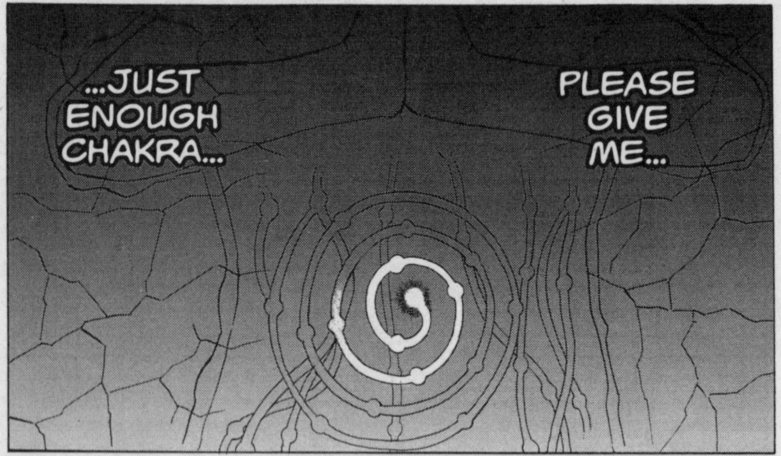
PLEASE
GIVE
ME...
...JUST
ENOUGH
CHAKRA...

...TO PROTECT
EVERYBODY!!

RRRRROAR!!

SNAP
POP
ZIZZLE

READ THIS WAY

SHUP

DIE!
HERE I COME!! YOU DUMB TANUKI!!
SHOOO
ZOOM

KAROOSH
!

YOU...

... BRUTE !!!

WHAM

PLIP

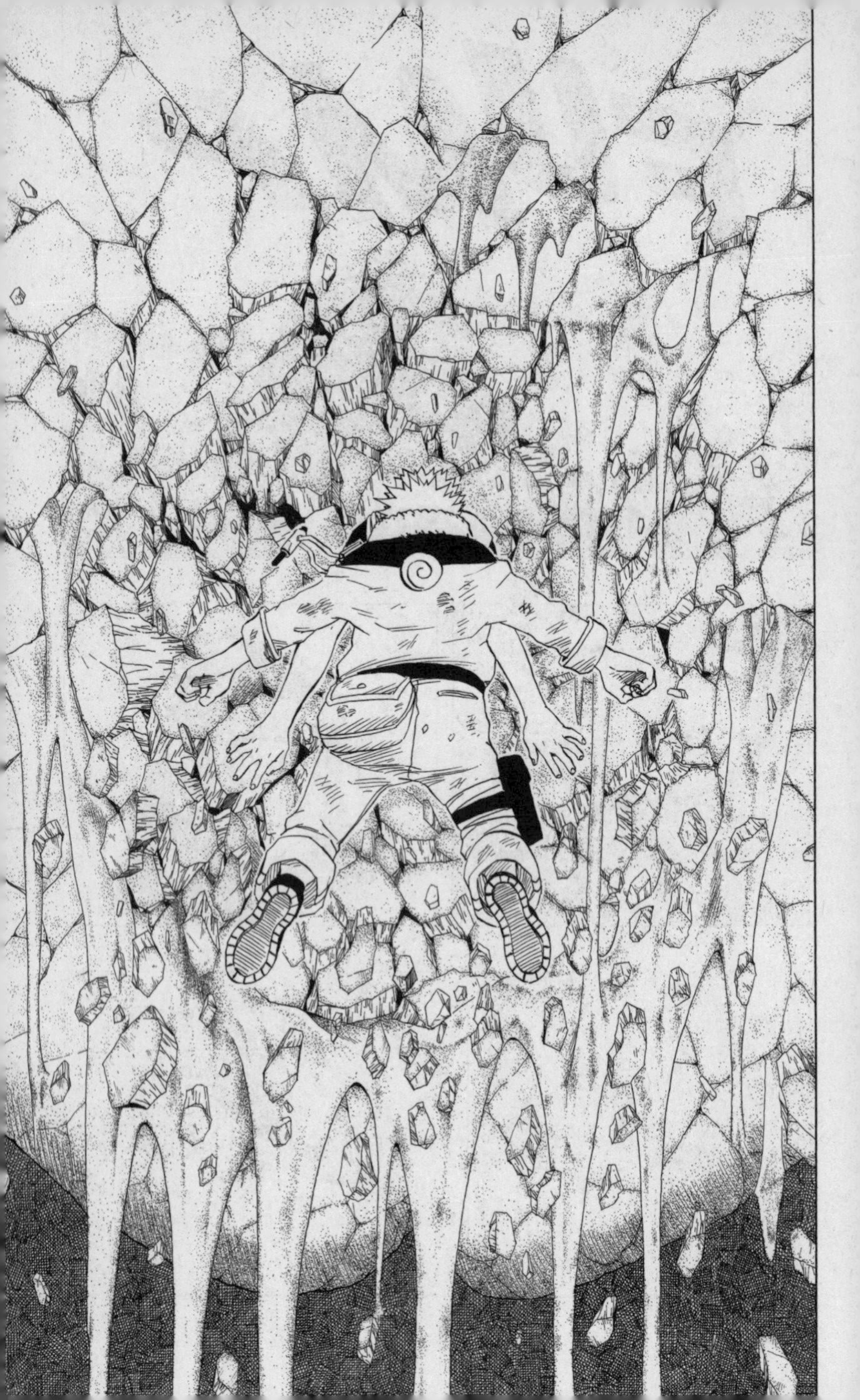

FUMP

...!
DID HE WIN?!

A SIMPLE HEAD BUTT... HIS FIGHTING STYLE MAY BE COARSE AND UNPOLISHED, BUT...
HE CAN DRAW SO MUCH CHAKRA...

I'VE NEVER SEEN SUCH A BUMBLING NINJA BEFORE, BUT HE'S CERTAINLY AN EXTRAORDINARY BOY!

I REGRET NOT BEING ABLE TO STAY TO WATCH IT TO THE END, BUT...
I'M GETTING TO MY LIMIT AS WELL...
SHK...

WE'RE HEADING HOME, GAMAKICHI!
SURE THING, PA!

POP

UGH!

WHOA!

HUF
HUF
HUF
HUF
HUF
HUF

...THIS TIME I'M REALLY... COMPLETELY EMPTY...
YOU TOO, RIGHT...?!
HUF
HUF
...ONE MORE PUNCH IS ALL I'VE GOT LEFT...

WE'RE BIRDS OF A FEATHER...
LET'S MAKE THIS IT!!

HUF
...
HUF
HUF

I'M SHOCKED THAT NOT JUST SOUND... BUT SO MANY SAND JÔNIN WOULD TRY TO INFILTRATE OUR VILLAGE...!

WELL... THINK ABOUT IT...
THAT'S WHY THEY CALL IT WAR.

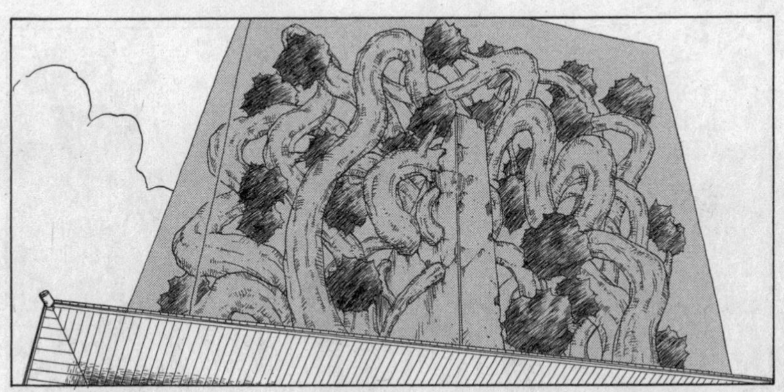

THIS FIGHT HAS BEEN GOING ON FOREVER...

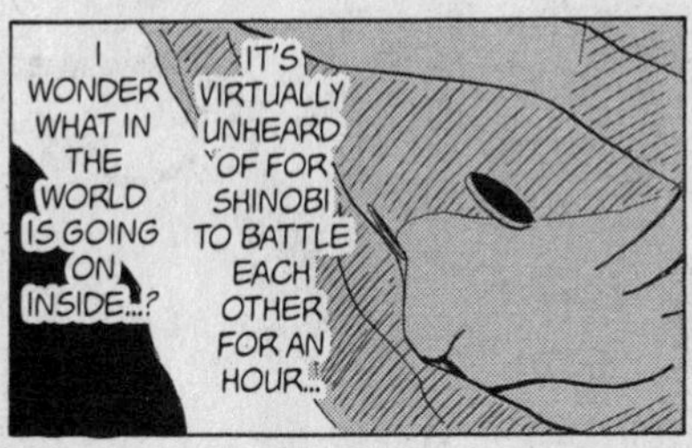
IT'S VIRTUALLY UNHEARD OF FOR SHINOBI TO BATTLE EACH OTHER FOR AN HOUR...
I WONDER WHAT IN THE WORLD IS GOING ON INSIDE...?

READ THIS WAY

HUF
IT SEEMS...
...I DON'T HAVE ENOUGH STRENGTH LEFT TO DRAG OUT ALL OF YOUR SOUL.
HUF

HUF
HUF
THEN BY ALL MEANS, PLEASE DIE...
... MASTER SARUTOBI!

PAK

HOW-EVER...
...!

HUF
HUF
...I SHALL PUT AN END TO YOUR PLANS...
...HERE AND NOW!!

THE WORLD OF KISHIMOTO MASASHI
MY PERSONAL HISTORY, PART 23

IN MY SECOND YEAR OF COLLEGE, I GOT SERIOUS AND DECIDED TO SUBMIT MANGA FOR REAL, TARGETING SHONEN MAGAZINES. "NOW! WHAT SHALL I DRAW..." I STARTED OFF IN HIGH SPIRITS, BUT THEN IMMEDIATELY RAN INTO A BLOCK. THE STORY I HAD THOUGHT UP HAD TOO MANY PLOT POINTS, AND I COULDN'T FIT EVERYTHING INTO THE PAGE LIMIT. EARLY ON IN ONE'S CAREER, ONE OFTEN BECOMES OVERENTHUSIASTIC AND GREEDY, TRYING TO SQUEEZE ALL OF ONE'S IDEAS INTO A SINGLE PIECE. I WAS LIKE THAT TOO. THE STORY OFTEN BECOMES CLUNKY AND UNWIELDY, AND THERE ARE SO MANY CHARACTERS THAT NO ONE CHARACTER ENDS UP STANDING OUT AS THE MAIN CHARACTER.

THUS! I USED THE PAGE LIMIT AS MY CLEAR-CUT SOLUTION. I SHAVED OFF WHATEVER PLOT POINTS I FELT WERE EXTRANEOUS, AND GOT RID OF A BUNCH OF CHARACTERS. WHEN I FINALLY FELT I COULD TELL THE STORY WITHIN THE PAGE LIMIT, I SAT DOWN AND STARTED DRAWING IN EARNEST. ...HOWEVER, IT'S NOT LIKE THE STORY COULD STAY COMPLETELY THE SAME, SO A **FEW MINOR DIFFICULTIES** AROSE. ...BUT... THEY WEREN'T HUGE DIFFICULTIES! JUST THAT PLOT-WISE, I HAD ORIGINALLY WANTED TO TELL THE TALE OF A **NATIONAL** DILEMMA STARRING A MAIN CHARACTER POSSESSING NATIONAL POWER, WITH GRAND SPECTACLE (!). BUT IN THE END, IT WAS A SMALL-SCALE STORY INVOLVING "SMALL-TOWN FOLK" THAT I SOMEHOW MANAGED TO WORK UP... IT'S LIKE THE FEW MINOR DIFFICULTIES THAT WOULD CROP UP IF ONE FORGED AHEAD AND FILMED A SCI-FI MOVIE EVEN KNOWING ONE WOULDN'T BE GIVEN ANYTHING NEAR AN ADEQUATE BUDGET. THAT'S WHAT'S KNOWN AS "A NEWCOMER'S COARSENESS SHOWING THROUGH HIS INABILITY TO SNUGLY CONTAIN THINGS"!

...IN ANY CASE! WHAT I AIMED FOR WAS *WEEKLY SHONEN JUMP*'S HOP☆STEP AWARD, WITH ITS PRIZE MONEY OF 500 THOUSAND YEN [ROUGHLY $5000] (TAKE-HOME)... OR RATHER... I WON!!!

THE TITLE OF THAT MANGA WAS "KARAKURI" [MECHANISM]. "KARAKURI" IS A POPULAR NAME FOR A SUPER-STRENGTH ANDROID OR ROBOT. I HAD ALWAYS THOUGHT THAT JAPANESE NAMING SCHEMES WERE COOL, SO I DECIDED I WOULDN'T USE ANY WEIRD WESTERN TERMS OR NAMES. THAT'S WHY I WENT WITH THE JAPANESE "KARAKURI" INSTEAD OF "CYBORG"! AND IT TURNS OUT THAT THIS STAND-ALONE STORY, "KARAKURI," WOULD GREATLY CHANGE MY DESTINY. BUT OF THAT, THE YOUNG KISHIMOTO WAS STILL UNAWARE.

Number 137:
The Shinobi of Konoha...!!

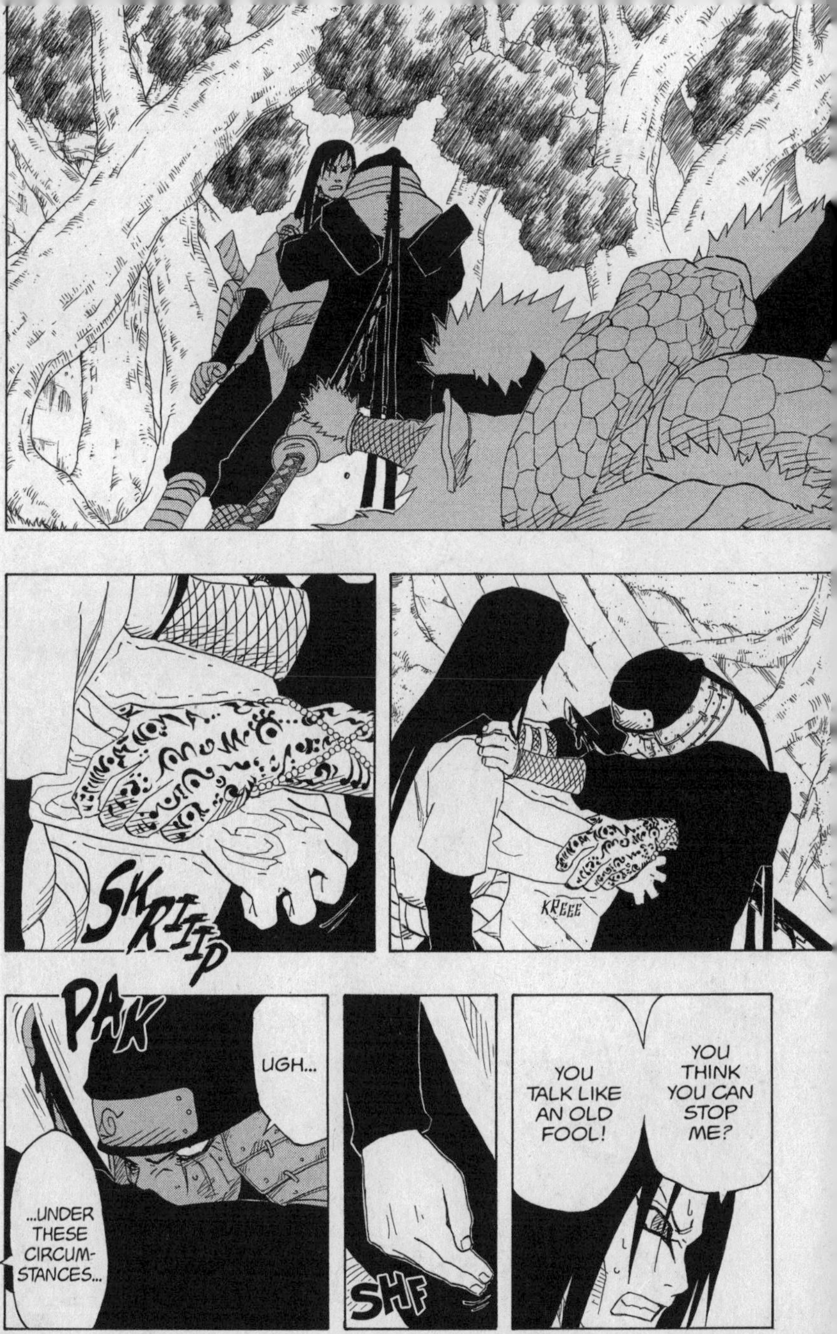

KREEE

SKRIIIP

YOU THINK YOU CAN STOP ME?
YOU TALK LIKE AN OLD FOOL!

SHF

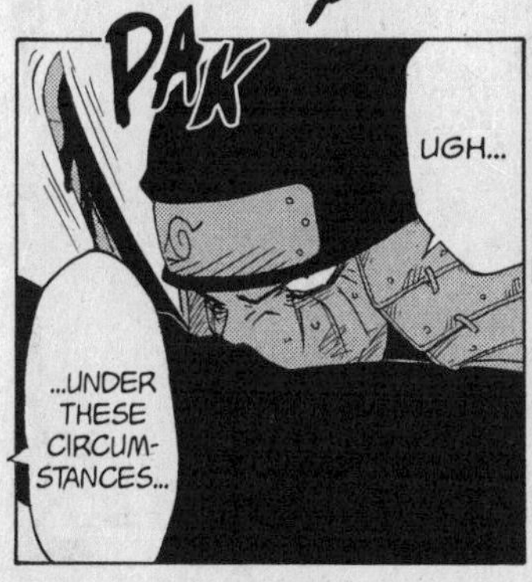
DAK
UGH...
...UNDER THESE CIRCUM-STANCES...

UGH...
MY ARMS
ARE STILL
TRAPPED...
...I CAN'T
CAST ANY
JUTSU...

LET ME
GO!
GRIND
GRIND

UGGH...
I CANNOT BE STOPPED!
YOU WILL DIE HERE!!
UGH... I WILL NOT ALLOW YOU TO DESTROY THIS VILLAGE...!

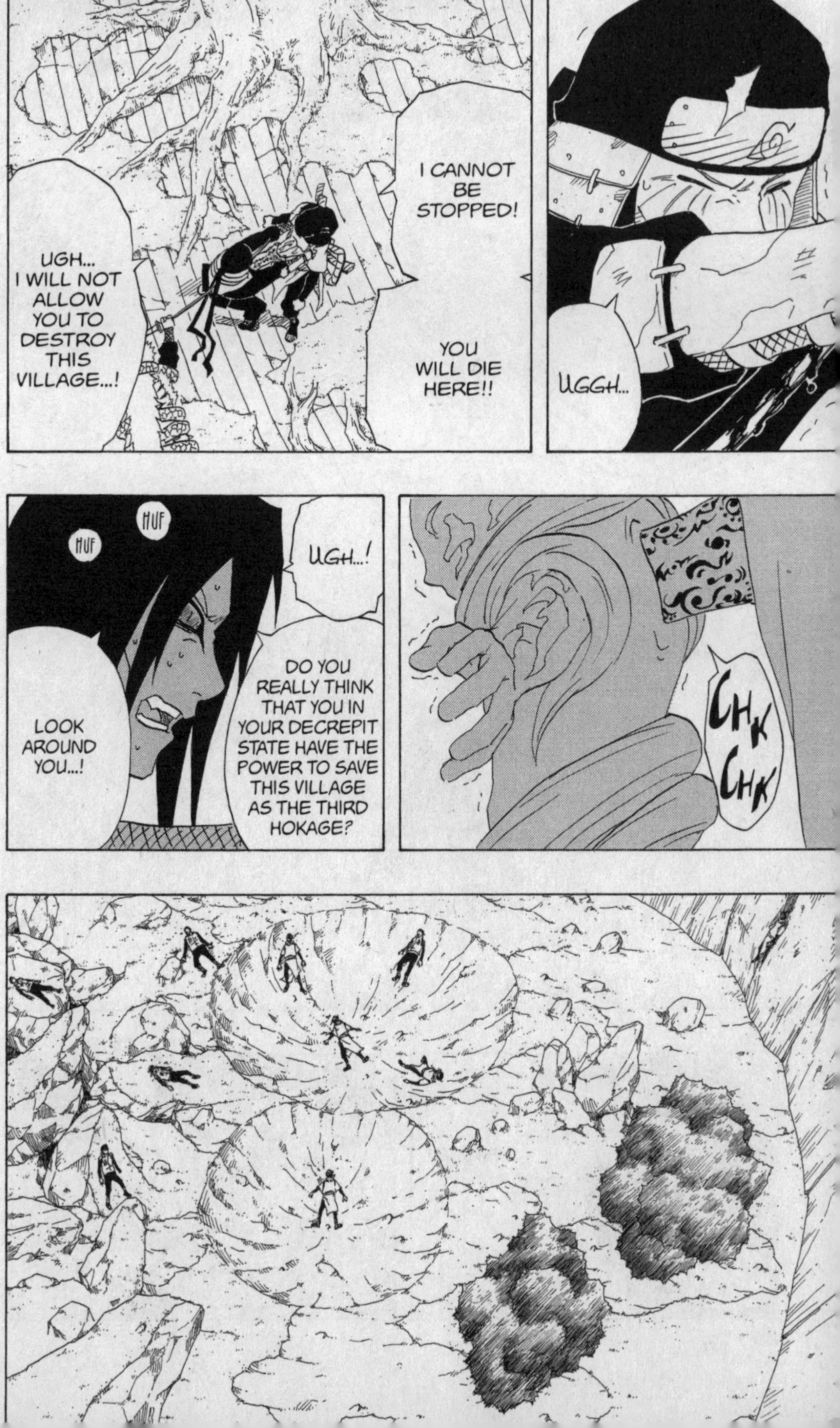

CHK CHK

HUF
HUF
UGH...!
DO YOU REALLY THINK THAT YOU IN YOUR DECREPIT STATE HAVE THE POWER TO SAVE THIS VILLAGE AS THE THIRD HOKAGE?
LOOK AROUND YOU...!

READ
THIS
WAY

HUF
IN ADDITION TO MY FOLLOWERS...
...SUNAGAKURE SHINOBI HAVE INVADED THIS VILLAGE AS WELL, YOU KNOW.
HUF

ALL KONOHA SHINOBI...
HUF
...WILL BE ANNIHILATED, WOMEN AND CHILDREN INCLUDED...

OPERATION DESTROY KONOHA SHALL BE FULFILLED!
HUF
HUF

...

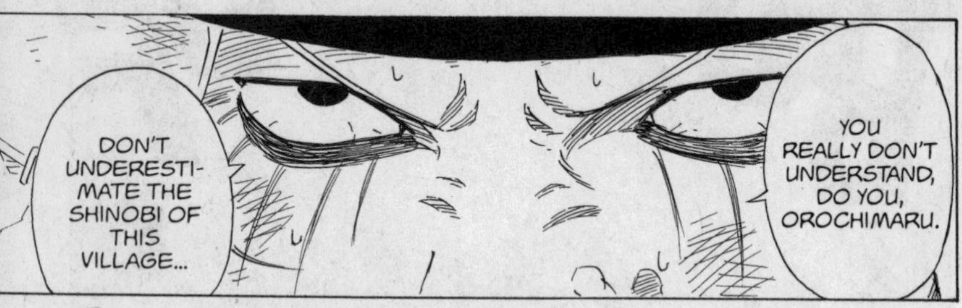
YOU REALLY DON'T UNDERSTAND, DO YOU, OROCHIMARU.
DON'T UNDERESTIMATE THE SHINOBI OF THIS VILLAGE...

HUF

HUF
HUF

FUMP

FUMP

BOOF

READ
THIS
WAY

I SWEAR TO AVENGE YOU.

SLLLP

LET'S GO!
ROGER!!

(*Gravestone: the names of Konoha's fallen heroes.)

うつほ　ミソノあさげ
のたいが　梅星にぎり
ジナ　月光ハヤテ
WHOOSH WHOOSH WHOOSH WHOOSH WHOOSH

AAARGH!
HYUGA IS THE MOST POWERFUL CLAN IN KONOHA...
REMEMBER IT WELL!
BAIKA NO JUTSU! THE ART OF EXPANSION!!
FWIP
SWELL
WAAAH!!
ARGH!!

TWITCH
TWITCH
QUIVER
QUIVER

...CAN'T MOVE!!

IS THIS YOUR FIRST TIME...
...EXPERIENCING KONOHA'S SECRET ART OF SHADOW PARALYSIS?
FWUP

WELL THEN... AS AN ADDED BONUS...
HERE'S KONOHA'S SECRET ART OF SUFFOCATING DARKNESS!
SLTTHH
SLTTHH

FWIP
SHINRANSHIN NO JUTSU! ART OF MIND DESTRUCTION!!

HEY... STOP IT!!
WHAT'S WRONG WITH YOU?!
ZOOM
MY BODY'S MOVING ON ITS OWN...!!

IT SURE BRINGS BACK MEMO-RIES!
AAARGH!!
THE INO-SHIKA-CHO TRIO REUNITED!
CLOMP

...!
...THE POISON'S DISPELLING...

DON'T MOVE, SHINO.
I'VE SENT PARASITIC BEETLES IN... THEY'RE DRAWING OUT THE POISON.

FATHER...

...!

LET'S GO, KURO-MARU!
ARF!

HUF
HUF
HUF

READ THIS WAY

THE SHINOBI OF KONOHA, IN ORDER TO DEFEND THEIR VILLAGE...
HUF
...WILL ALL FIGHT WITH EVERY-THING THEY'VE GOT!
HUF

...!
HUF
HUF

IN THIS WORLD, TRUE STRENGTH...
...ARISES NOT FROM HONED NINJUTSU.

I THOUGHT I HAD TAUGHT YOU THIS, ONCE...
...

...

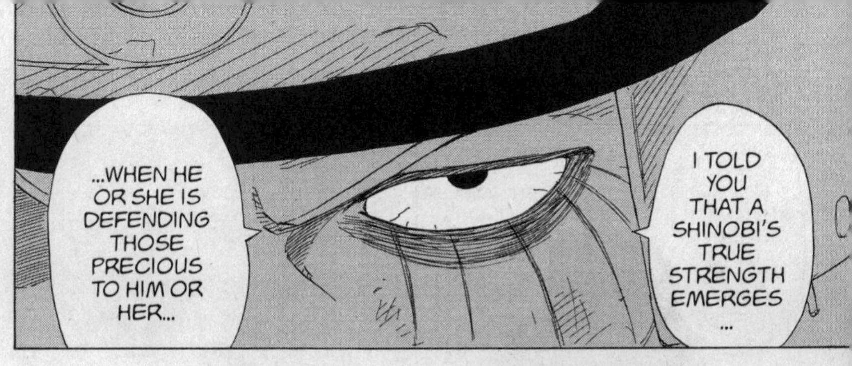
I TOLD YOU THAT A SHINOBI'S TRUE STRENGTH EMERGES...
...WHEN HE OR SHE IS DEFENDING THOSE PRECIOUS TO HIM OR HER...

SPARE ME THE LECTURE...

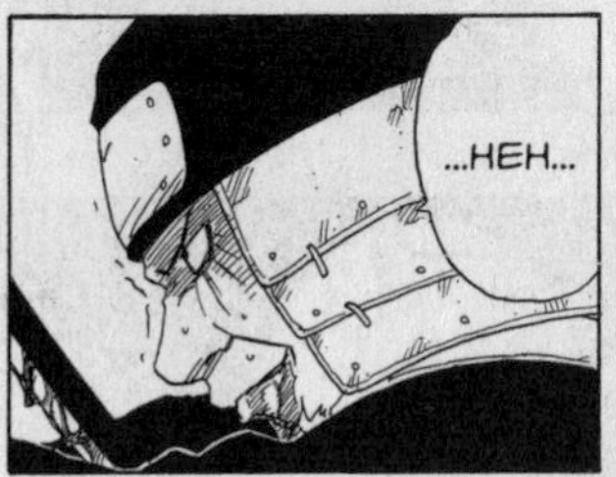
...HEH...

WELL, NO MATTER.
...IT'S NOT LIKE I INTEND TO FORGIVE YOU AT THIS POINT, ANYWAY.
TO YOU WHO IS SO ADDICTED TO FALSE PRIDE...
...THERE IS NO GREATER OR MORE APPROPRIATE PUNISHMENT.

I SHALL TAKE ALL YOUR JUTSU WITH ME!!

!
WHAT?!

RRRRROAR!!

SHOOF

SKRIIID

ZZZF

DON'T TELL ME...!

NO!!

SEAL!!

UGH!
MY ARMS, THEY'RE PARALYZED...

NOW, YOU CAN NO LONGER USE EITHER ARM...
AND THUS, YOU CAN NO LONGER WEAVE SIGNS...
HUF
HUF
HUF

YOU HAVE NO NINJUTSU LEFT TO USE.
SHLP

HUF
HUF
HUF
HUF
SWING
SWAY

SLURP
OPERATION DESTROY KONOHA IS OVER...

YOU USELESS OLD MAN! GIVE ME BACK MY ARMS!!

NOW WHO IS THE FOOL, OROCHIMARU?
IT'S A SHAME I CAN'T TAKE YOU WITH ME, BUT...

...MY DEAR DISCIPLE, LET US MEET AGAIN ONE DAY IN THE AFTERLIFE.

SLURP

YOU OLD FOOL!
HOW DARE YOU! HOW DARE YOU TAKE MY JUTSU...!

WHERE TREE LEAVES DANCE... ONE SHALL FIND FLAMES...

THE FIRE'S SHADOW WILL ILLUMINATE THE VILLAGE...

...AND ONCE AGAIN TREE LEAVES SHALL BUD ANEW.

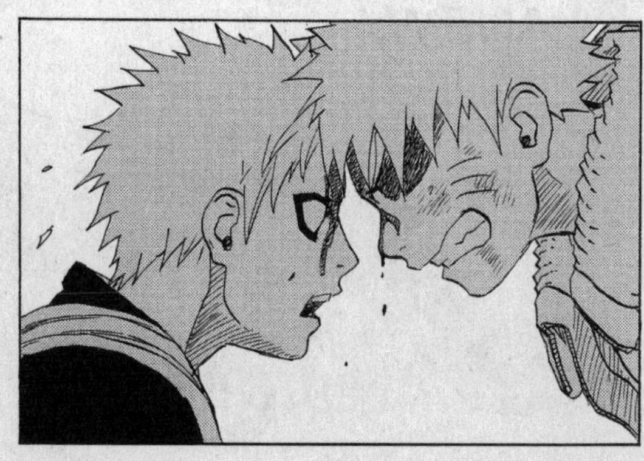

Number 138:
Operation Destroy Konoha, Terminated!!

WHOOSH
SHPAP
CRASH CRASH
KTHUD
THUD
WH... WHY...
(HUF)
(HUF)
(HUF)
(HUF)

READ
THIS
WAY

SWAY

...!!

...Y...

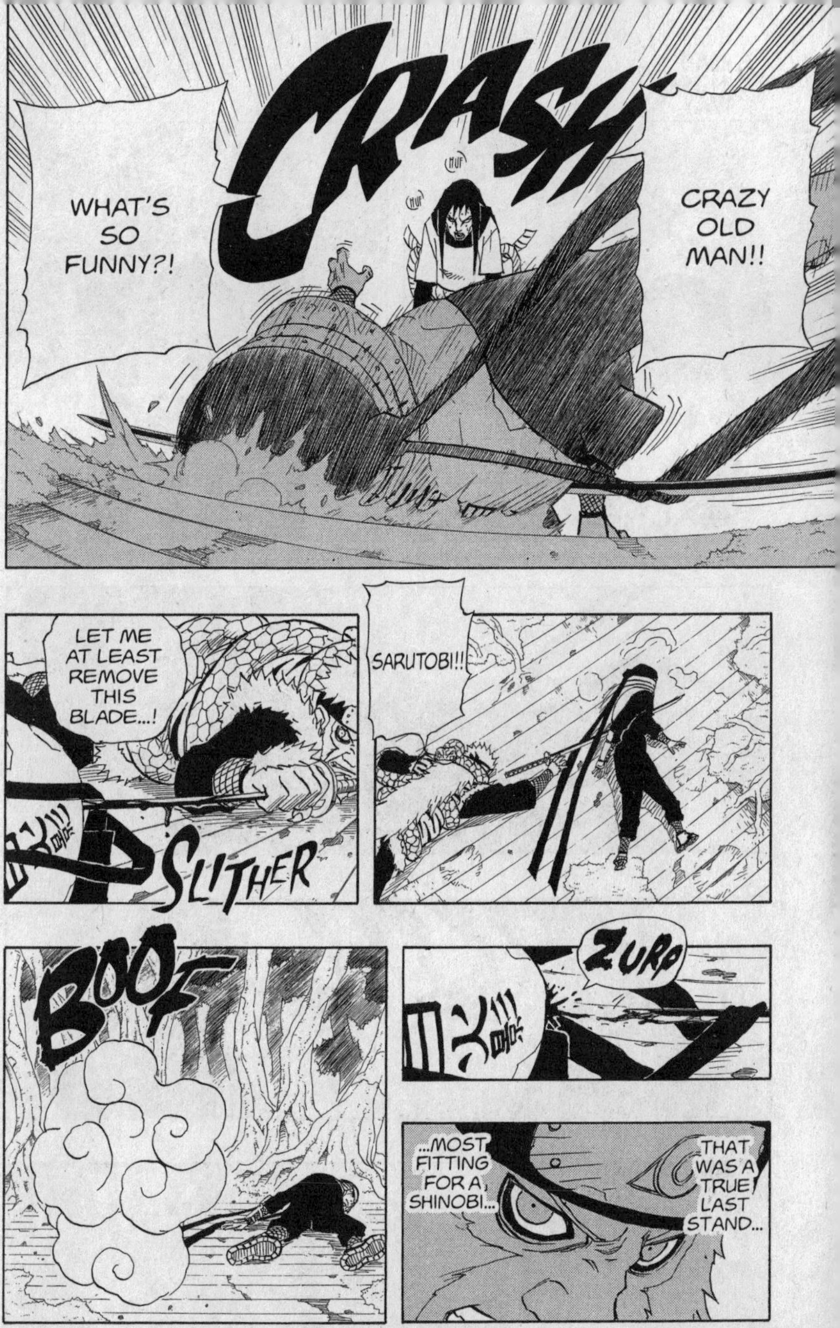

WHAT'S SO FUNNY?!

CRASH

HUF HUF

CRAZY OLD MAN!!

LET ME AT LEAST REMOVE THIS BLADE...!
SLITHER

SARUTOBI!!!

BOOF

ZURP

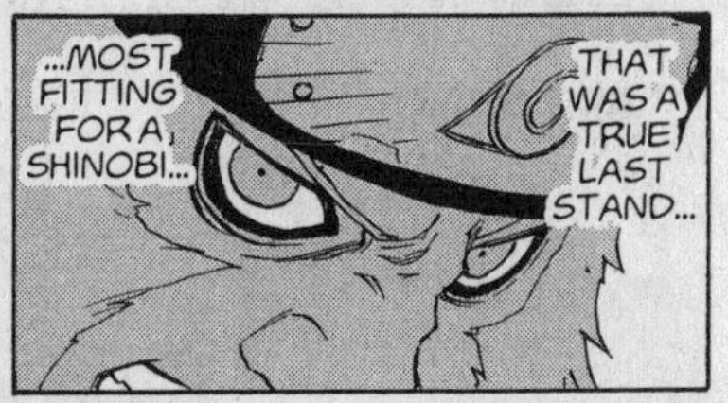
THAT WAS A TRUE LAST STAND...
...MOST FITTING FOR A SHINOBI...

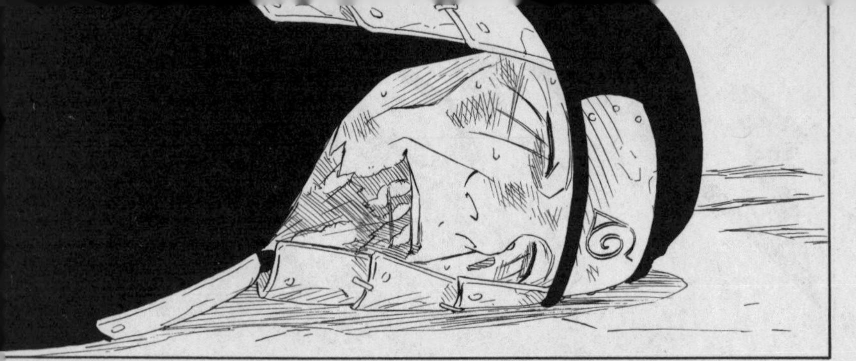

AAARGH!!
MY ARMS FEEL LIKE THEY'RE ON FIRE...

LORD OROCHI-MARU!!

UGGH... WE'RE DONE FOR NOW...
YOU MAY TAKE DOWN THE SHIELD...
WE'RE GOING HOME...

YES, SIR!

VROOSH

!
!

ZOOM
LET'S GO!!
ZOOM
ZOOM

!
...

ZOOM
SPROO

YOU'RE NOT GETTING AWAY!!

FWIP
NINJA ART!
KUMOSHIBARI! SPIDER WEB NET!!
SPURT
!
!
CHAK
UGH!!
STICKY THREADS INFUSED WITH CHAKRA...!

SMACK
KAKASHI! THEY'RE ON THE MOVE.
SHOULD WE CHASE AFTER THEM?!
NO, WAIT, GUY!

LET'S NOT BE HASTY. IF WE RUSH IN...
...WE'LL ONLY GET SNARED IN THE ENEMY'S TRAPS.

I'M WELL AWARE OF THAT.
BUT WHETHER THERE ARE TRAPS WAITING OR NOT, I CAN'T LET ENEMIES GET AWAY... IT'S JUST MY NATURE AS A KONOHA SHINOBI.

...SO...
ALL YOU ENDED UP DOING WAS WATCHING...
KABUTO ...

CLMP

SO YOU KNEW...

READ THIS WAY

RUNNING AWAY FROM ME AGAIN?
FOR NOW, YES...
I NO LONGER WISH TO SHOW YOU MY JUTSU SO YOU CAN JUST COPY IT.

HEY...
SO WHAT'S THE PLAN?
I THINK WE SHOULD RETREAT ...

ALTHOUGH... IT DOES SEEM LIKE YOU HAVEN'T MASTERED THAT EYE AS COMPLETELY AS A MEMBER OF THE UCHIHA CLAN COULD HAVE...
...

WELL THEN.

BOOF

...

TEMARI
...

SKITTER SCATTER

!

KANKURO!!

TAK

TOTTER

HUF
SHMP
HUF

TAP
UGH...!

HEY!!
ZOOM

TAKE CARE OF HER...
HUF
HUF

HUF
HUF
...WHY ... IS HE SO STRONG...?!
...
HUF
HUF

GRRR

HUF

KREEE...

HUF

...I WILL NOT CEASE TO EXIST ...!

I WON'T !!

I REFUSE !!

UGH...

READ THIS WAY

I TOLD YOU NOT TO TALK TO HIM!

WHOA! SOMETHING SURE IS STINKY!

HEY! THERE HE IS!
SO THAT'S HIM, HUH...
HE DOESN'T HAVE A FAMILY!
GO AWAY!

FREAK!

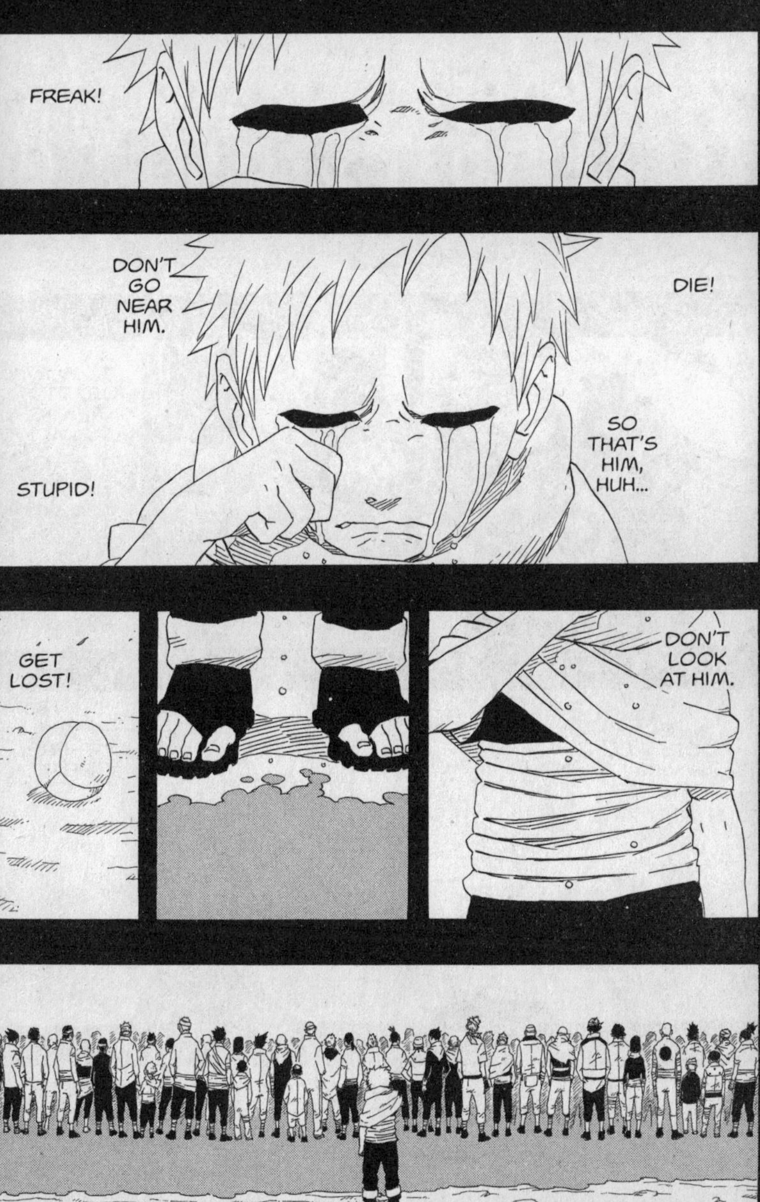
FREAK!
DIE!
SO THAT'S HIM, HUH...
DON'T GO NEAR HIM.
STUPID!
DON'T LOOK AT HIM.
GET LOST!

TO THEM... I AM NOW A RELIC OF THE PAST THAT THEY WISH TO ERASE AND FORGET.

SO... FOR WHAT PURPOSE DO I EXIST? WHY AM I ALIVE?

SKRIIIP

AND THEN IT CAME TO ME... I KNEW WHAT I WAS... AND I WAS FORCED TO ACCEPT IT.

THAT WAS THE MOST PAINFUL THING...

UGH...!

SKRIIIP

...ACCEPTING THAT I WAS ALONE IN THE WORLD...

HUF

HUF

...SUPERFLUOUS. UNWANTED. SHUNNED...

SKRIIIP
D...DON'T COME NEAR ME!!
ZAP
UGH...!
SKRIIIP

...THAT PAIN... OF BEING ALL ALONE...
...IT'S NOT TRIVIAL...
...THE WAY YOU FEEL... I DUNNO WHY, BUT... I UNDERSTAND IT SO WELL... THE HURT...

HUF
HUF
BUT... I'VE GOT PEOPLE WHO CARE ABOUT ME NOW...
PEOPLE THAT ARE IMPORTANT TO ME... I WON'T LET YOU HURT THEM...
HUF
HUF

...

HUF
EVEN IF I HAVE TO KILL YOU...
I WILL STOP THIS...
HUF

...
WHY...

UGH...
SKRIIISH

WHY SHOULD YOU CARE ABOUT OTHERS...?

THEY SAVED ME FROM MY PIT OF LONELINESS...

AND THEY UNDERSTAND ME...I COULDN'T LIVE WITHOUT THEM...

I LOVE THEM.

...
...LOVE...
...THE FEELING THAT MAKES YOU WANT TO STRIVE FOR AND PROTECT THOSE AROUND YOU WHO ARE PRECIOUS TO YOU...

SO THAT'S WHY HE'S SO STRONG...

UGH...
SKRIIIP
CLOMP
YOU CAN STOP NOW, NARUTO...

SAKURA'S SAFE.
!
GAARA'S USED UP ALL HIS CHAKRA. THE SAND AROUND SAKURA HAS GONE...
HUF
HUF
HUF

...OH, GOODY...
SMILE

!!!
HUF
HUF
SWOOP
SWOOP

IT'S ALL RIGHT... I QUIT.
...UZUMAKI NARUTO...

...GAARA'S NEVER SEEMED SO EXHAUSTED.
HUF
HUF
HUF

ZOOM
ZOOM
HUF
HUF

HUF HUF
ALL RIGHT ...
RUF

...
HUF
HUF

...

PERHAPS...
...MAYBE SOMEDAY...

READ THIS WAY

...

I'M SO SORRY...
!
!

TEMARI, KANKURO...
愛

UH, WELL, IT'S OKAY, I GUESS...

ZOOM
ZOOM
UGH...!
ZOOM
ZOOM

THE WORLD OF KISHIMOTO MASASHI
MY PERSONAL HISTORY, PART 24 CHAPTER 1

I SOMEHOW MANAGED TO FINISH DRAWING THE 31 PAGES OF THE STAND-ALONE "KARAKURI", AND THE DAY I HAD TO MAIL IT IN TO *JUMP* FINALLY ARRIVED. IF I REMEMBER CORRECTLY, IT WAS RIGHT AT THE END OF FEBRUARY, AND MY EXAMINER WAS ARAKI HIROHIKO* SENSEI.

I WENT TO THE POST OFFICE, NERVOUSLY HANDED OVER MY MANUSCRIPT, AND PUT MY HANDS TOGETHER SAYING "PLEASE LET ME WIN!" I WAS PRAYING TO THE GODS ONLY WHEN CONVENIENT, AS USUAL. BUT ALWAYS WITH UTMOST SINCERITY, OF COURSE! I WOULD CLOSE MY EYES AND WISH FERVENTLY FROM THE BOTTOM OF MY HEART. I PROBABLY REPEATED MY WORDS, OFFERING THEM TO THE HEAVENS, 20 TIMES. I WAS PRAYING SO EARNESTLY THAT I DIDN'T NOTICE AT FIRST, BUT WHEN I CAME TO, THE POSTAL WORKER WAS FROZEN IN PLACE, ENVELOPE IN HAND, WITH AN INCREDIBLY COLD LOOK IN HIS EYES.

NOT THAT I BLAME HIM, FOR IF SOMEONE HANDS YOU AN ENVELOPE AND IMMEDIATELY FALLS INTO FERVENT WORSHIP, ANYONE WOULD THINK "THIS FELLOW'S WEIRD...". FURTHERMORE, I HAD STARTED MUTTERING UNDER MY BREATH, LOOKING ALL SERIOUS. SO FORGET WEIRD, HE PROBABLY THOUGHT I WAS SCARY! BUT I DIDN'T CARE!! I WANTED TO WIN THE AWARD SO BAD, I COULDN'T HELP IT!!

AFTERWARDS, I HAD TO GO HOME AND WAIT THE LONG TWO MONTHS UNTIL THE WINNERS WERE ANNOUNCED. ...EVEN DURING FUN CONVERSATIONS WITH FRIENDS, OR IN THE MIDDLE OF CLASS, I COULDN'T STOP THINKING ABOUT IT. IT WOULD KEEP ME UP AT NIGHT IF I THOUGHT ABOUT IT RIGHT BEFORE BEDTIME. I WOULD SECRETLY PEEK BACK AT THE COPY OF MY MANUSCRIPT AND BE LIKE, "SHOOT! THIS WILL NEVER WIN!" OR, "HMM~! BUT MAYBE, JUST MAYBE, IT WILL PASS..." ...I BECAME MENTALLY FATIGUED. AND SIX DAYS BEFORE THE RESULTS WERE SUPPOSED TO BE ANNOUNCED, ONE OF MY FRIENDS TOLD ME SOMETHING OUTRAGEOUS!

THAT FRIEND WAS A HIGH SCHOOL FRIEND OF USUTA KYOSUKE* SENSEI. AND THIS IS WHAT HE TOLD ME.

(TO BE CONTINUED)

[NOTE: ARAKI HIROHIKO IS THE ARTIST OF *JOJO'S BIZARRE ADVENTURE*. USUTA KYOSUKE IS THE ARTIST OF *SEXY COMMANDO GAIDEN*.]

Number 139: Eulogy...!!

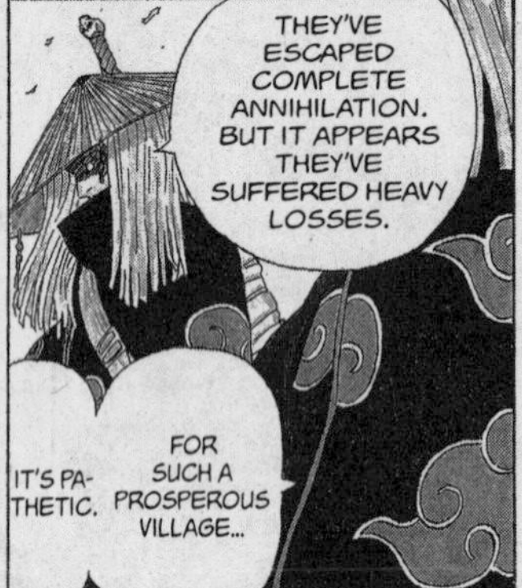
THEY'VE ESCAPED COMPLETE ANNIHILATION. BUT IT APPEARS THEY'VE SUFFERED HEAVY LOSSES.
FOR SUCH A PROSPEROUS VILLAGE...
IT'S PATHETIC.

...
THAT'S UNLIKE YOU...
SO YOU STILL HAVE LINGERING AFFECTION TOWARDS YOUR HOME-LAND? EVEN YOU HAVE NOSTALGIA ...?

NO...
NONE AT ALL.

Number 139:
Eulogy...!!

NARUTO
-ナルト-

SSSLURP
GRIN GRIN
一楽

TWO DAYS AFTER THE BATTLE.

...

...SOB... SOB...

...
SOB... SNIFF...
IT HAS ALREADY BEEN A YEAR, EH...
IT'S NOT EASY TO HIDE ONE'S GRIEF AND PRETEND TO LAUGH...
!
I HAVE HEARD FROM YOUR HOMEROOM TEACHER...
...THAT AT THE ACADEMY...
...YOU'RE THE BUTT OF EVERYONE'S JOKES...
HIC
HIC
...
...
I...I'M NOT SAD AT ALL!
IT IS HONORABLE FOR SHINOBI TO DIE IN THE LINE OF DUTY!!
...
BOTH PA AND MA...
...HELPED DEFEND THIS VILLAGE FROM THE FOX MONSTER AT THE COST OF THEIR LIVES...
THEY'RE HEROES!!
蝶野アゲハ
真白ネズミ
芋井工
あじヒラキ
霜降に

AND I AM THEIR SON!!
I'M NOT SAD BECAUSE I'M NEVER ALONE!!
AND THESE, THESE ARE TEARS OF JOY...
ENOUGH ...
A BOY HUGS HIS KNEES ONLY WHEN HE FEELS TRULY ALONE...
SQUEEZE
!
...
...HOWEVER, AS YOU SAY, YOU ARE NOT ALONE...
!
FOR ALL OF KONOHA'S SHINOBI...
...CARRY THE WILL OF FIRE WITHIN THEM.
...
...WILL OF FIRE?

THE BURNING DESIRE TO DEFEND THIS VILLAGE.
...
...SO LONG AS ONE BEARS THIS WILL OF FIRE, EACH AND EVERY ONE OF THOSE WHO LIVE IN THIS VILLAGE ARE FAMILY...
...MY DEAR IRUKA... DO YOU POSSESS IT...?
...
伊賀シノビ
蝶野アゲハ
真白ネズミ
あじヒラヤ
霧ハサミ
目空ウロコ
YEAH!
SMILE...

SOB... SOB...

SHF

...

THAT FOR HAYATE ...?

THE THIRD LORD'S FUNERAL SERVICE HAS ALREADY STARTED...
YOU BETTER HURRY...

AND YOU, KAKASHI? PAYING RESPECTS TO OBITO...?
INSTEAD OF CONSTANTLY INVENTING NEW EXCUSES FOR WHY YOU'RE LATE, WHY DON'T YOU JUST COME HERE EARLIER?

...

...I DO... FIRST THING IN THE MORNING...
...!

...IT'S JUST THAT ONCE I GET HERE...
...I CAN'T STOP THINKING ABOUT WHAT AN IDIOT I USED TO BE...

HEH.

THERE ARE TWO BELLS.

THE FACT THAT THERE ARE ONLY TWO MEANS...

...ONE STUDENT WILL END UP TIED TO THE STUMP...?

GOOD GUESS, OROCHIMARU.

JINGLE JINGLE

ALL RIGHT!! I'M UP FOR IT!!

JINGLE

HA HA HA... JIRAIYA, I WIN THE BET!

YOU'RE THE ONE ON THE STUMP, LIKE I GUESSED!

SHUT UP, TSUNADE! YA TOMBOY FREAK!!

READ THIS WAY
WHAT DIDJA SAY, YOU EGGHEAD PERV?!!
ALL RIGHT, ALL RIGHT! BREAK IT UP NOW...
TSUNADE, YOU AND OROCHIMARU CAN GO HOME.
YES, SIR--♡
KWF
SHOOF
...HEH.
...
POUT...
...SHEESH...
IT'S DOWNRIGHT EMBARRASSING FOR A NINJA TO FALL FOR SUCH OBVIOUS TRAPS OVER AND OVER AGAIN!!
BUT...

YOU COULD LEARN A THING OR TWO FROM OROCHIMARU!
GRRR
...
MASTER SARUTOBI, YOU'RE **ALWAYS** "OROCHIMARU THIS" AND "OROCHIMARU THAT"!
BUT FOR WHEN I GO RESEARCHING, I USE TRANSPARENCY JUTSU!
I HAVEN'T BEEN CAUGHT YET!
...
... SHEESH ...
ALL RIGHT, LET'S SEE JUST HOW GOOD THESE SPYING JUTSU OF YOURS ARE...
I'M GOING WITH YOU NEXT TIME...
...?!
...
...
YOU OLD PERV, MASTER SARUTOBI ...

MASTER
IRUKA...
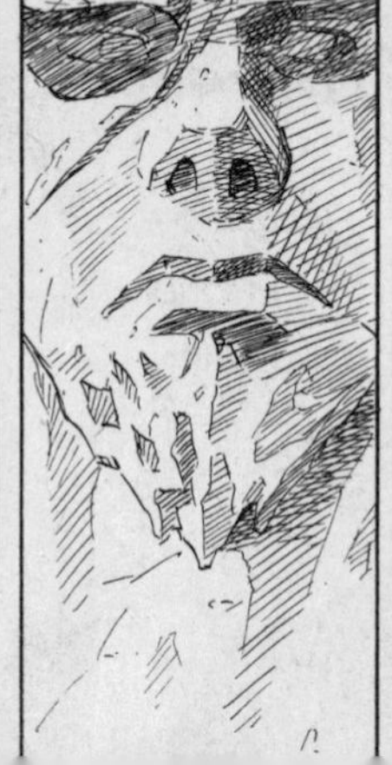

!

...WHY DO PEOPLE...
...RISK THEIR OWN LIVES FOR THE SAKE OF OTHERS...?

...

WHEN ONE HUMAN DIES... THEY PASS AWAY.
ALONG WITH THEIR PAST, THEIR CURRENT LIFE, AND THEIR FUTURE...
MANY PEOPLE DIE ON MISSIONS OR THROUGH WAR.
AND WHEN THEY DIE, IT HAPPENS STARTLINGLY QUICKLY... AND SIMPLY.

HAYATE IS ONE SUCH EXAMPLE...

THOSE WHO DIE HAVE DREAMS AND GOALS... BUT THEY ALL HAVE SOMETHING ELSE JUST AS IMPORTANT.

READ THIS WAY

PARENTS, SIBLINGS, FRIENDS, THEIR FELLOW VILLAGERS, PEOPLE WHO ARE IMPORTANT TO THEM...
BONDS FORM BETWEEN THEM AND THOSE WHO ARE PRECIOUS TO THEM FROM THE TIME THEY ARE BORN, THROUGH TRUSTING AND HELPING EACH OTHER...

THESE STRINGS THAT CONNECT THEM, AS TIME PASSES...
...GROW THICKER AND STRONGER...

THERE'S NO LOGIC OR REASON TO IT! PEOPLE JUST DO THINGS LIKE THAT...
...BECAUSE THEY HAVE PRECIOUS THINGS TO PROTECT...

...
YEAH... I THINK I'M STARTING... TO GET THAT NOW...

BUT... IT'S PAINFUL TO DIE, TOO.

WELL, THE THIRD HOKAGE DID NOT DIE IN VAIN.
HE DID LEAVE ALL OF US SOMETHING IMPORTANT...

?
WELL, DON'T WORRY... YOU'LL UNDERSTAND EVENTUALLY.

HEY...!
GIVE ME SOME CREDIT— I UNDERSTAND!

READ
THIS
WAY

WELL THEN, MASTER IRUKA!
YEAH.
KWF

SHOO

THIRD HOKAGE... ...IT SEEMS ALL THE LITTLE TREE LEAVES OF KONOHA...
...HAVE SPLENDIDLY INHERITED THE WILL OF FIRE OF WHICH YOU SPOKE...

...THOSE LITTLE EMBERS THAT ALIGHT UPON THE TREE LEAVES WILL EVENTUALLY BLAZE STRONG AND FIERCE...
...AND WILL COME TO LIGHT AND PROTECT THIS VILLAGE ONCE MORE...

...WITH A NEW HOKAGE...

Number 140: Contact...!!

EH-HEH HEH.

YOU STILL ENGAGE IN SUCH FOOLISH ACTIVITIES...?
CRUNCH
TECHNI-CALLY, IT'S RESEARCH!

IF IT ISN'T OLD MAN HOMURA AND MISTRESS KOHARU...
AND JUST WHAT BUSINESS DO THE CHIEF COUNSELORS HAVE WITH ME?

UGH...!
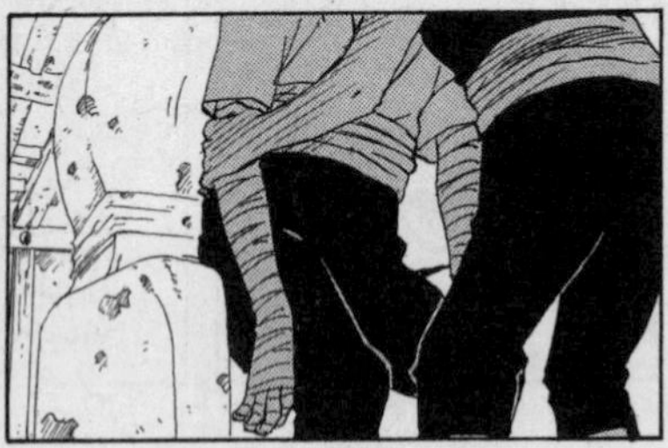

FWUMP
SARU-TOBI... YOU...!
CREAK

WELL, WE KNEW IT WASN'T GOING TO BE EASY.
AFTER ALL, WE DID TAKE ON THE HOKAGE FULLY KNOWING HIS REPUTATION AS THE STRONGEST LEADER OF THE FIVE PRINCIPAL TERRITORIES.

BESIDES, YOU DID EXTREMELY WELL.
EVEN SUMMONING TWO OF THE FIVE SHADOWS ...

...!

I WON'T BE PATRONIZED, DO YOU UNDERSTAND ME...?

I WILL KILL YOU...

...

...THAT WAS NOT MY INTENTION, OF COURSE...

FOR SURE, PERHAPS WE WERE NOT ABLE TO TAKE DOWN THE VILLAGE, BUT...

IN TERMS OF OUR OTHER GOAL, UCHIHA SASUKE...

YOU DID DECORATE HIM WITH YOUR COLLAR...

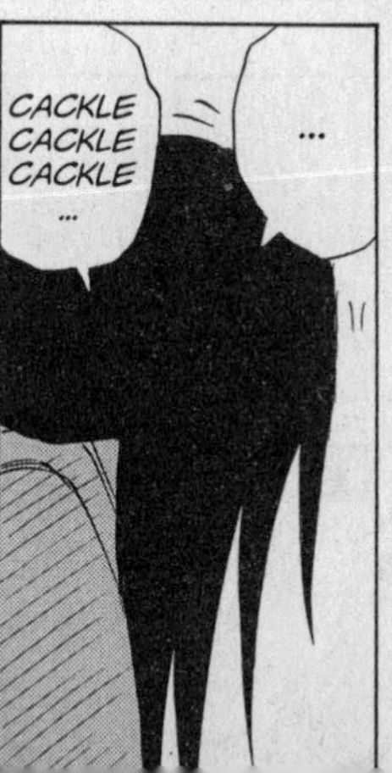
...
CACKLE CACKLE CACKLE ...

AT THE COST OF THESE ARMS AND ALL MY JUTSU...

...

THIS ALL WOULD NOT HAVE BEEN NECESSARY IF WE HAD BEEN ABLE TO ROPE IN UCHIHA ITACHI FROM THE BEGINNING...
BUT THAT DREAM HAS DIED...

HE IS STRONGER THAN I...

...

THAT'S WHY... I BROKE AWAY FROM THAT ORGA-NIZATION...

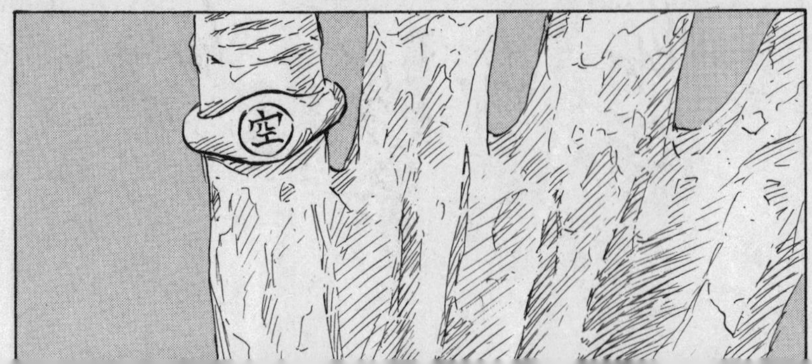

TWEEE
TWEEE
TWEEE
WHAP
WHAP
WHAP
WHAP
WHAP

READ THIS WAY

THIS WAY!

TMP
TMP

!!
TH... THAT'S!

THE BODIES ARE DECAYED...
...I SUSPECT THEY WERE KILLED BEFORE THE START...

...GAH...

I SEE... SO THAT'S WHAT HAPPENED, HUH...
...BLAST HIM...

OROCHIMARU...

AFTER LORD KAZEKAGE'S ASSASSINATION, OROCHIMARU... OR PERHAPS KABUTO... ASSUMED HIS IDENTITY...
WE WERE CARELESS.

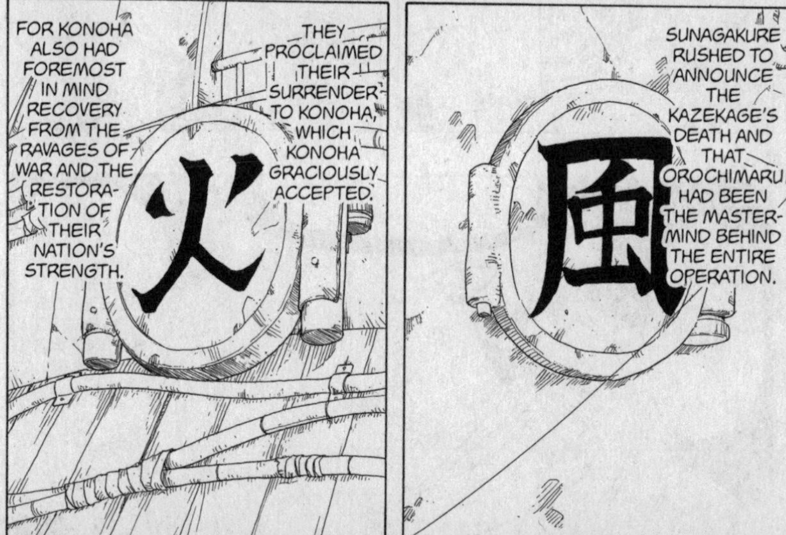

SUNAGAKURE RUSHED TO ANNOUNCE THE KAZEKAGE'S DEATH AND THAT OROCHIMARU HAD BEEN THE MASTERMIND BEHIND THE ENTIRE OPERATION.
THEY PROCLAIMED THEIR SURRENDER TO KONOHA, WHICH KONOHA GRACIOUSLY ACCEPTED.
FOR KONOHA ALSO HAD FOREMOST IN MIND RECOVERY FROM THE RAVAGES OF WAR AND THE RESTORATION OF THEIR NATION'S STRENGTH.

READ THIS WAY

WHAT BUSI-NESS, YOU SAY...?
YOU OUGHT TO KNOW, WITHOUT ME HAVING TO SPELL IT OUT!

...

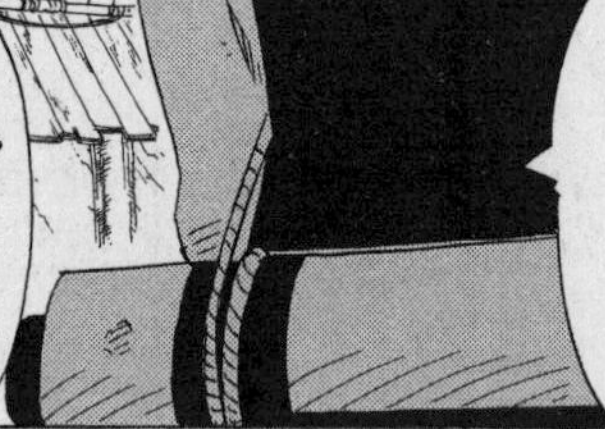
WHY SUCH GRIM FACES? I HEARD THE TALKS WITH SAND WENT WELL.

...AT THIS POINT, OUR RELATIONSHIP WITH SUNAGAKURE IS NOT AN URGENT MATTER.

RIGHT NOW, KONOHA-GAKURE'S STRENGTH IS AT A FRIGHTFUL LOW...
UNDER THESE CIRCUMSTANCES, OUR NUMBER ONE PRIORITY MUST BE TO ANTICIPATE AND PREPARE FOR ANY FURTHER CRISES.

...WE DON'T KNOW WHEN OR IF ANY OF OUR NEIGHBORS WILL MAKE A BOLD MOVE...
THEREFORE, UNTIL THE VILLAGE HAS RESTORED ITS STRENGTH, WE HAVE DECIDED TO GATHER THE TOP NINJA FROM EACH CELL AND ASSEMBLE AN EMER-GENCY EXECUTIVE COUNCIL TO HANDLE THE SITUATION.
...BUT FIRST...

WE NEED A STRONG, TRUSTWORTHY LEADER.

...AT THE PRESENT TIME, THERE ARE SEEDS OF TROUBLE SCATTERED ALL ABOUT...
OROCHIMARU ISN'T OUR ONLY PROBLEM.
UNDERSTAND THIS... ONE FUNDAMENTAL POLICY WE CANNOT IGNORE...

WE NEED OUR FIFTH HOKAGE AS SOON AS POSSIBLE!

AND SO YESTERDAY, IN AN EMERGENCY MEETING WITH THE RULER OF THE LAND OF FIRE... JIRAIYA...
...IT WAS DECIDED THAT IT WOULD BE YOU.

SORRY, BUT NO THANKS.
I'M NOT SUITED FOR SUCH A...

READ
THIS
WAY

THE DECISION HAS ALREADY BEEN MADE.
BESIDES, IF YOU—TOUTED AS ONE OF THE THREE GREAT SHINOBI OF KONOHA LEGEND—ARE NOT SUITED FOR IT, THEN WHO IS?!
IF IT'S ONE OF THE THREE GREAT SHINOBI YOU'RE AFTER, THERE'S STILL ONE OTHER...

...

TSUNADE...

...SHE MAY INDEED BE AN APPRO-PRIATE CANDIDATE, BUT...
WE DO NOT KNOW HER WHERE-ABOUTS AT ALL.

I'LL TRACK HER DOWN AND BRING HER BACK.
WOULD THAT BE ACCEPT-ABLE?

... HOWEVER ...

AS OPPOSED TO UN-WILLING, APATHETIC ME...
THE SHARP, GO-GETTING PRINCESS TSUNADE IS MUCH BETTER SUITED FOR HOKAGE.

...

...
ALL RIGHT... WE'LL PUT IT UNDER CONSID-ERATION IMMEDI-ATELY...
HOWEVER, WE SHALL ATTACH THREE ANBU BLACK OPS TO YOU FOR YOUR TSUNADE SEARCH PARTY...

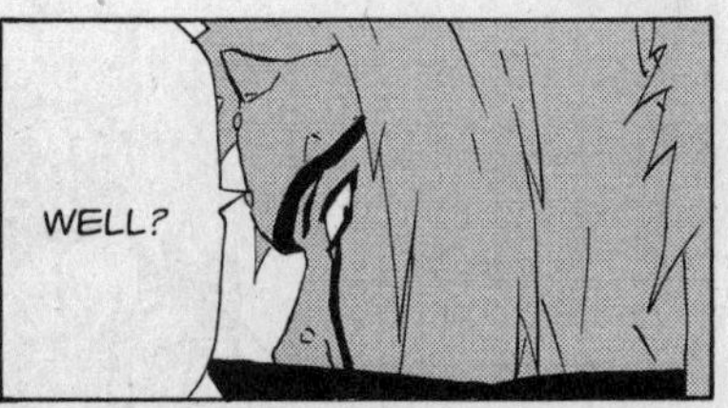
WELL?

DON'T WORRY, I SWEAR I WON'T RUN AWAY.

I DON'T NEED CHAPERONES.

JUST... THERE IS ONE FELLOW I'D LIKE TO TAKE WITH ME ON MY TRAVELS.

I'D LIKE TO SEE WHAT HE CAN DO.

だんご

IT'S BEEN A WHILE SINCE YOU LAST RETURNED HOME, RIGHT...? WELL, SHALL WE HAVE SOME TEA BEFORE WE GO LOOKING FOR WHAT WE SEEK...?
...YEAH... SURE...

!

YO! HEY THERE, YOU TWO... YOU'RE SO CHUMMY...
ARE YOU ON A DATE?

FOOL. ANKO ASKED ME TO BUY HER SOME DANGO.
WHAT ABOUT YOU, WHAT ARE YOU DOING HERE? I THOUGHT YOU DIDN'T LIKE SWEETS...

WELL... I CAME TO BUY SOME-THING TO PUT ON A GRAVE, SO I FIGURED I'D JUST MEET UP WITH SOMEONE HERE WHILE I WAS AT IT.

SASUKE, ACTUALLY.

...

THAT'S A RARE SIGHT, FOR **YOU** TO BE WAITING FOR SOMEONE...

CLUNK

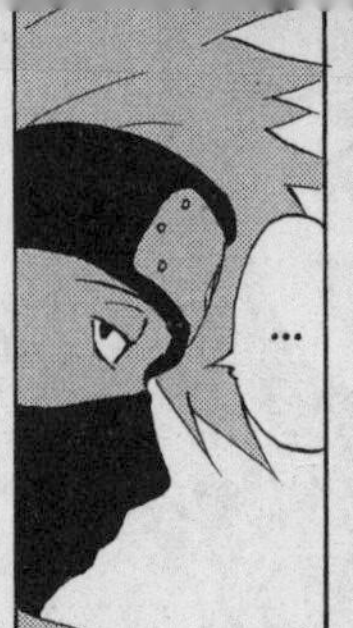
...

WHOA, KAKASHI... YOU SHOWED UP BEFORE ME?
TMP
TMP
SHF
WELL! I CAN BE ON TIME, ONCE IN A WHILE...

!

I DON'T LIKE NATTO OR SWEET THINGS.
OH... REALLY.

...
HUNH

NOD
NOD

!
FWOOO
FWOOO

ラ
一楽

IT'S JUST AS I HAD HEARD... YOU REALLY DO EAT NOTHING BUT RAMEN, HUH...
!
ZAP

SSSLURP
GRIN GRIN

VWO! PFERFY PFAGE!

CRUNCH

IT'S BEEN SO LONG...
ASUMA... KURENAI...

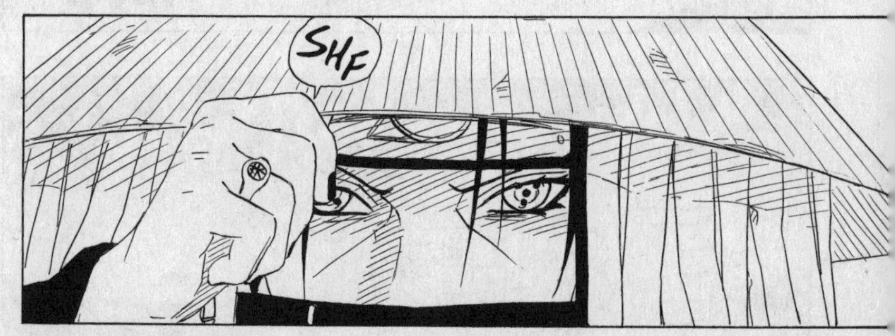
SHF

YOU'RE NOT FROM THIS VILLAGE...
WHAT'S YOUR BUSINESS HERE...?

YOU COULD ONLY KNOW OUR NAMES...
...IF YOU WERE SHINOBI OF THIS VILLAGE.

!!

Y... YOU'RE?!

THE WORLD OF KISHIMOTO MASASHI
MY PERSONAL HISTORY, PART 24 CHAPTER 2

MY FRIEND TOLD ME, "USUTA SENSEI WAS CONTACTED BY THE EDITORIAL DEPARTMENT ABOUT ONE WEEK AGO"!

"WHAT!" MEANS WHAT? AND WHAT DOES IT MEAN THAT I HAVEN'T BEEN CONTACTED YET, THEN!? DON'T TELL ME I DIDN'T MAKE IT?!! I FELT DEFLATED, TOOK OFF FROM SCHOOL, GOT SULKY, AND PLAYED VIDEO GAMES. HOWEVER, WHILE I WAS PLAYING VIDEO GAMES, IN THE BOTTOM OF MY HEART... BUT IF WHOEVER WON IS CONTACTED TOO EARLY AND OUT OF BLIND ECSTASY POSTS HIS VICTORY ON THE INTERNET, EVERYONE WILL KNOW THE RESULT BEFORE IT'S ANNOUNCED IN *JUMP*! IF THAT WERE TO HAPPEN, THAT WOULD BE BAD! IT'S JUST NOT KOSHER! THAT'S PROBABLY WHY THEY DON'T CONTACT YOU UNTIL THAT DAY OR AT THE EARLIEST THE DAY BEFORE *JUMP* HITS THE BOOKSTORES! SURELY! I KEPT SILENTLY MAKING SUCH EXCUSES TO MYSELF AND PRAYED THAT I WOULD HEAR FROM THEM.

AND THEN, IT WAS FINALLY THE DAY BEFORE THE ANNOUNCEMENT! I ENDED UP STAYING HOME THE WHOLE DAY, THINKING THAT I MIGHT GET A CALL, BUT THE DAY ENDED WITHOUT ANY WORD. THAT NIGHT, I HAD TROUBLE FALLING ASLEEP, STAYING UP UNTIL MIDNIGHT ALL ANXIOUS. AND THEN, JUST AS I STARTED FEELING MYSELF NOD OFF... THE PHONE RANG...

I PICKED THE RECEIVER UP AND PUT IT TO MY EAR. MY HEART FELT LIKE IT WAS GOING TO BURST! "HELLO... THIS IS KISHIMOTO." THEN... "HELLO, THIS IS *WEEKLY SHONEN JUMP* CALLING..." "...YES?!" I IMMEDIATELY BLURTED... "WE WOULD LIKE TO INFORM YOU THAT YOUR "KARAKURI" HAS BEEN SELECTED AS THIS ROUND'S WINNER! CONGRATULATIONS!" WHEN I HEARD THAT, I SERIOUSLY THOUGHT MY HEART HAD BURST, IT **POUNDED!** SO HARD, AND THEN I WOKE UP...

...IT HAD ALL BEEN A DREAM. I'M DEAD SERIOUS!! I WAS SO BLUE ONCE I WAS COMPLETELY AWAKE!

AND THEN, FINALLY, ON THE ACTUAL MORNING OF THE ANNOUNCEMENT DAY, "I WISH THAT DREAM WAS A PORTENT"... I THOUGHT TO MYSELF, AS I HEADED TO THE CONVENIENCE STORE. I HAD ALREADY RESIGNED MYSELF TO THE WORST. I MAY NOT HAVE MADE IT... I WANTED TO JUST KNOW THE RESULT AND GET IT OVER WITH AND YET I DIDN'T... WITH THAT CONFLICTED FEELING, I ENTERED THE CONVENIENCE STORE, WHERE A MOUNTAINOUS PILE OF *WEEKLY SHONEN JUMP* LAY STACKED RIGHT NEXT TO THE REGISTER. I DON'T THINK MY HEART EVER POUNDED THAT HARD. I FELT LIKE IT WAS GOING TO JUMP OUT OF MY THROAT.

Number 141: Uchiha Itachi!!

... UCHIHA ITACHI.

Number 141: Uchiha Itachi!!

TUG

FLIP

... HUMPH.
THERE'S NO MISTAKE ...

POP
POP

READ THIS WAY

...
...

...ARE THEY ACQUAINTANCES OF YOURS, ITACHI-SAN?
RUF
I SUPPOSE... I SHOULD INTRODUCE MYSELF AS WELL.

...

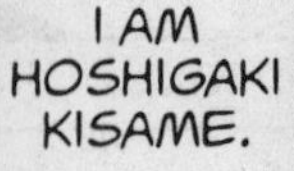
I AM HOSHIGAKI KISAME.
PLEASED TO MEET YOU, AND HOPE TO GET TO KNOW YOU LATER.

THERE'S NO LATER.

I'M GONNA TAKE YOU DOWN RIGHT NOW!

...ITACHI... IT SEEMS THAT YOU TOO ARE RATHER DETESTED IN YOUR HOME VILLAGE.

I'VE HEARD OF YOU...
HOSHIGAKI KISAME, A FORMER KIRIGAKURE SHINOBI...

AN OUTLAW SHINOBI CURRENTLY BEING SOUGHT BY THE LAND OF WATER...
...FOR CHARGES SUCH AS ASSASSINATION AND SUBVERSIVE MACHINATIONS AGAINST THE STATE.

...YOU TWO... ARE MAJOR FELONS THAT HAVE BINGO BOOK RANK S.

...

ITACHI ...
YOU'VE GOT GUTS TO STEP FOOT IN THIS VILLAGE AGAIN AFTER WHAT YOU DID...

...ASUMA, KURENAI...
PLEASE DO NOT INTERFERE... I DON'T WANT TO KILL YOU.

FOR SOMEONE WHO'S COMMITTED PARRICIDE, THAT'S AN ODD THING TO SAY.
BESIDES ...

...THERE'S NO WAY YOU WOULD JUST SHOW UP LIKE THIS, NONCHA-LANTLY...
...WEARING CLOTHES THAT DON'T LOOK RESPECTABLE, FOR ABSO-LUTELY NO REASON.

SO WHAT ARE YOU AFTER?

...

CLMP

HE BOTHERS ME.

SHALL I KILL HIM?

WELL, IT DOESN'T SEEM LIKE WE'LL BE ABLE TO JUST WALK OUT OF THE VILLAGE WITHOUT A FIGHT, SO...

JUST TRY NOT TO OVERDO IT.

YOUR MOVES TEND TO ATTRACT ATTENTION...

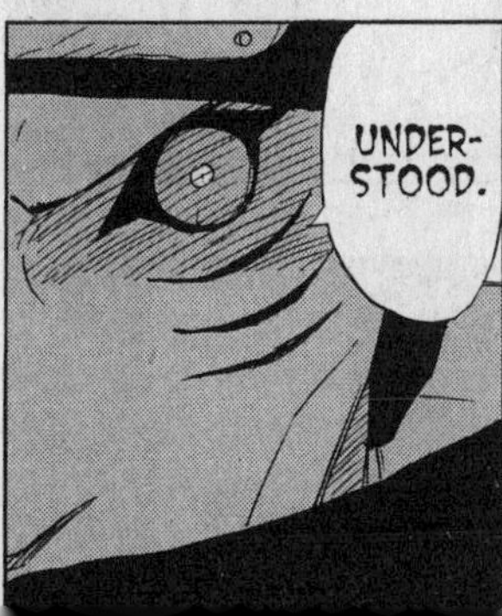
UNDER-STOOD.

TAP

KACHIINGG

SHWP
SHWP

...

ZAWP

THIS IS...

...GENJUTSU!

FZT

GRRR

HE'S KEEPING ME DOWN WITH JUST THE TIP OF HIS BLADE... SUCH STRENGTH!
TAP
RRRRR

SPURT
...!!

MY LONG SWORD IS CALLED SAMEHADA! IT MEANS SHARKSKIN! IT DOESN'T SLICE...

YAAAH!!!

SHOOF

SPLISH!
IT CUTS YOU TO RIBBONS!!

GAH!
...!!

SWING

...
KURENAI... WHAT'S TAKING YOU SO LONG?

!

SSSINK

WHIPPP

READ THIS WAY

CHAK

FOOSH

CLMP...

SHAAK
YOU'RE FINISHED.

A WEAK GENJUTSU HAS NO EFFECT ON ME...

!!

THIS IS... GENJUTSU-GAESHI! REFLECTION TECHNIQUE !!

SLIP

...

CHOMP

FLASH

READ
THIS
WAY

VOOSH
FWOOO
SHFFF
!!
SHAA
BAP
SPLASH
KURENAI
!!
!!
!
DON'T GET DISTRACTED.

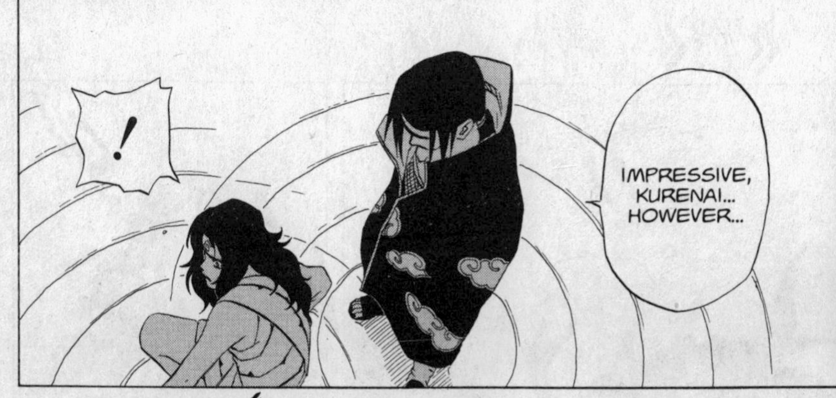
IMPRESSIVE, KURENAI... HOWEVER...
!

!
...IT ALL ENDS NOW.
FOR YOU, THAT IS.

VOOSH
VOOSH
ZIP

VOOSH
ZIP

READ THIS WAY

WHAT?!
SPURT

BZZ...

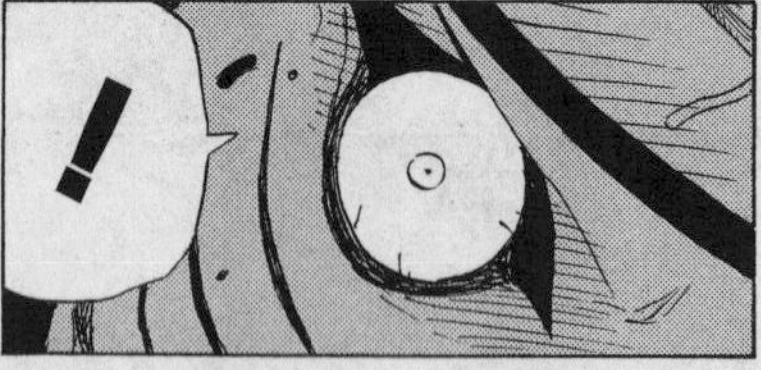
!

SHUP SHUP SHUP
WATER STYLE!

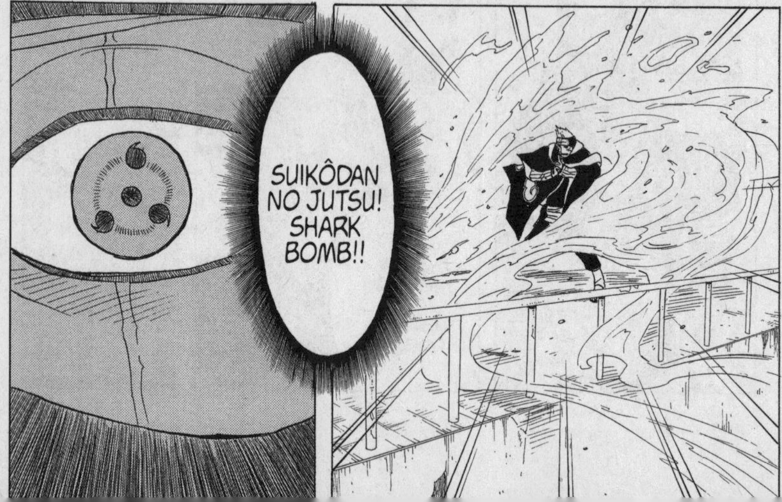
SUIKÔDAN NO JUTSU! SHARK BOMB!!

THAT'S MY JUTSU...!!

WHY ARE YOU HERE NOW?
I KNOW I ASKED YOU TO DO THIS FOR ME...

BUT I GUESS I GOT A LITTLE WORRIED...
SHADOW DOPPEL-GANGERS ...

SPLA

KAKASHI
...

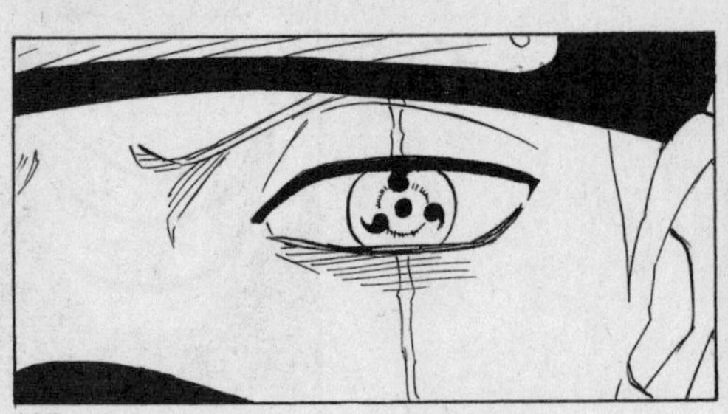

Number 142:
Kakashi vs. Itachi

HIS EYES HAVEN'T CHANGED A BIT...

...HE'S A TRUE SHARINGAN HEIR... I HAVE TO EXPECT THE WORST...

MY, MY, YOU'RE A SURPRISE ...
NO WONDER YOU STOPPED ME...

THERE IS ANOTHER WITH THE EYE...
...YOU MUST BE KAKASHI THE MIRROR NINJA, THEN...

I'M THE ONE WHO WAS SURPRISED...
...CATCHING THE SCENT OF SUSPICIOUS FOLK AT THE TEA HOUSE, AND WHO SHOULD IT BE, BUT...

I NEVER IMAGINED IT WOULD BE UCHIHA ITACHI...

...AND THE SCOURGE OF KIRIGAKURE, HOSHIGAKI KISAME.

WELL, WELL... YOU EVEN KNOW MY NAME.
WHAT AN HONOR.

...I SEE, SO THAT GIANT BLADE OF YOURS BELONGS TO ONE OF THE SEVEN NINJA SWORDSMEN OF THE MIST, SAMEHADA, THE SHARKSKIN.

HEH HEH.

...I HAD HEARD THAT YOUNG ZABUZA HAD SPARRED WITH YOU...?
YEAH...

READ THIS WAY

HEH HEH...
I'LL CUT YOU TO RIBBONS...
CLENCH

DROP IT...
KISAME.

!

!

!

...IF YOU SPAR WITH HIM HEAD-ON, YOU WON'T GET AWAY SCOT-FREE...
AND IF YOU TAKE TOO MUCH TIME, YOU'LL GIVE OTHER SHINOBI A CHANCE TO ARRIVE.
BUT...

DO NOT FORGET OUR PURPOSE...
YOU DID NOT COME HERE TO SUFFER INJURIES!

...AND PRAY TELL, WHAT MIGHT THAT PURPOSE BE...?
BOOOK

...

...

WE KNOW WHAT WE'RE LOOKING FOR IS HERE...

...
LOOKING FOR...?

AND WHAT MIGHT YOU BE LOOKING FOR?
...

...I, UNLIKE KISAME, WOULDN'T TAKE ANY TIME AT ALL.

CLICK
NINJA ART!
SUITON SUIJINHEKI! WATER STYLE WATER WALL!!
FWIP
FWIP
VOOSH
VOOSH
VOOSH
VOOSH

READ THIS WAY

WHAT SPEED...! I COULDN'T FOLLOW HIS SIGN-WEAVING AT ALL...
FURTHER-MORE, THAT HE WOULD USE THE SHURIKEN IN HIS RIGHT HAND AS A DECOY TO DISTRACT ME... WHILE LAUNCHING A SUITON ATTACK AT MY FEET. IMPRESSIVE.
SPLASH

TRUST YOU, KAKASHI, TO HAVE SUCH A SHARP SENSE OF PERCEPTION...

!!
...INDEED.
SKOOSH

A SHADOW DOPPEL-GANGER ?!!

HE'S SUPER-HUMAN...!!

...

HEH HEH... IMPRESSIVE, THAT THE MIRROR NINJA HAS MASTERED MY FORMER VILLAGE'S JUTSU SO WELL...
A WATER DOPPEL-GANGER?!!

SPLASH...

NICE... KAKASHI!!

!

CLMP

WHAT?!

THIS ONE'S THE SHADOW DOPPEL-GANGER...!
POP!
WATCH OUT, KURENAI!!

KABOOM

SPLAAASH
HIS DOPPEL-GANGER EXPLODED?!!
FWOOO

KAKASHI! KURENAI!!
!!

KRIK
UGH...
KAKASHI ...!

FOOSH

DON'T LET YOUR GUARD DOWN... HE'S SOMEONE WHO ROSE TO BLACK OPS SQUAD COMMANDER BY THE TIME HE WAS 13.
I CAN'T BELIEVE HE'S THIS GOOD...
SHUP

NO, ACTUALLY, HE'S BETTER. HE HASN'T EVEN BEGUN TO SHOW HIS TRUE STRENGTH.

VERY IMPRESSIVE, THAT YOU WHO ARE NOT EVEN OF UCHIHA BLOOD...
...HAVE MASTERED THE SHARINGAN THIS MUCH...
HOWEVER ...
...YOUR BODY, NOT BEING GENETICALLY ADAPTED...
...IS NO MATCH FOR THAT EYE.

THAT'S RIGHT...
IT GETS FATIGUED VERY QUICKLY...

LET ME SHOW YOU...
...MY CLAN'S TRUE STRENGTH!

DO YOU KNOW WHY THE UCHIHA CLAN HAS BEEN LAUDED AND FEARED AS THE MOST POWERFUL...?
BLINK

FWUUUH...

!!!
N...NO WAY!!

SHOOT!!

YOU TWO, DON'T LOOK HIM IN THE EYE!!

CLAMP
!

CLAMP
!

CLAMP

READ THIS WAY

LISTEN CLOSELY, BOTH OF YOU, DO NOT OPEN YOUR EYES, NO MATTER WHAT...
IF YOU MEET EYES WITH HIM RIGHT NOW, YOU'LL BE FINISHED.

ONLY ANOTHER SHARINGAN CAN HANDLE HIM NOW.

IF ONE POSSESSES THE SHARINGAN...

...ONE CAN RESIST THIS MANGEKYO TO SOME EXTENT.

BUT YOU CANNOT BREAK THIS SPECIAL SHARINGAN JUTSU...
...TSUKUYOMI, THE NIGHTMARE REALM!
ONLY SOMEONE WITH KEKKEI GENKAI AND A SHARINGAN CAN STOP ME!

... SASUKE ...
ZEEEE!!

!

SKOOSH

AARGH!!!

IN THE TSUKUYOMI DREAMSCAPE, I COMPLETELY CONTROL TIME, SPACE, AND EVEN ALL SUBSTANCE.

FOR THE NEXT 72 HOURS... YOU WILL BE CONTINUALLY STABBED OVER AND OVER AGAIN...
LOOM

AAAA ARGH...!!!
GOUGE

HUF
HUF
HUF
HUF

REEE
HUF
HUF
HUF
HUF

BUCKLE...
WHAT'S WRONG, KAKASHI...?
KEEP YOUR EYES SHUT!

WHAT'S GOING ON?!
ONE SECOND THAT GUY'S TALKING AND THE NEXT SECOND YOU HIT THE GROUND!!

HUF
HUF
UNH... I SEE... THREE DAYS IN THAT REALM AND LESS THAN A MOMENT PASSED IN THIS ONE....
WHY NOT JUST KILL ME? IF HE WANTED TO HE COULD...
UGH... IT'S STILL... AFFECTING ME...

HM... AFTER ALL THAT THE FOOL'S SPIRIT IS INTACT...
MEANWHILE YOU'VE OVERUSED THOSE EYES OF YOURS... YOU KNOW THAT'S DANGEROUS...
TMP

READ THIS WAY

HUF
HUF

UGH...
THIS THING YOU SEEK... IS IT SASUKE?
HUF
HUF

...

...
NO...

THE LEGACY OF THE FOURTH HOKAGE...

THE WORLD OF KISHIMOTO MASASHI
MY PERSONAL HISTORY, PART 24 CHAPTER 3

SO I IMMEDIATELY WENT TO BUY THE ISSUE OF *JUMP*, BUT MY HANDS WERE TREMBLING SO MUCH I COULDN'T HOLD ON TO IT VERY WELL. MY HEART WASN'T JUST POUNDING, IT WAS BOUNDING. I SOMEHOW MANAGED TO PAY FOR THE *JUMP*, AND I LOOKED FOR THE ANNOUNCEMENTS PAGE RIGHT AWAY. I SWEAR I ALMOST COLLAPSED!

WHICH IS IT?! DID I WIN?! DID I NOT WIN?! WHICH IS IT, DARN IT?! WITH SUCH IRRATIONAL TENSION, I EAGERLY FLIPPED THOUGH THE PAGES! (I BET I DIDN'T GET IT, DARN IT!!) AND SO, I FINALLY REACHED THE PAGE BEFORE THE ANNOUNCEMENT PAGE FOR THE FEBRUARY HOP☆STEP AWARD, AND I SLOWLY TURNED THE PAGE.

THIS ART LOOKS KIND OF FAMILIAR...

THAT WAS MY FIRST IMPRESSION. ...THEN, IT STARTED SINKING IN...

...THESE DRAWINGS... THEY'RE MY DRAWINGS... THEY'RE MY DRAWINGS! ...WHICH MEANS...

AND THEN, OBLIVIOUS TO ALL THE FOLK WHO WERE IN THAT CONVENIENCE STORE, I SUDDENLY CRIED OUT:

"WHOA, WHOA"

I SO COULDN'T SPEAK CLEARLY I MUST HAVE SEEMED LIKE A DERANGED LUNATIC WHO WAS CHANTING SOME WEIRD SPELL ...PROBABLY. AND THEN, I STARTED QUIVERING. I WAS SO ECSTATIC I THOUGHT I WAS GOING TO EXPLODE, AND I EXITED THE STORE. ...SUDDENLY, FOR NO EXPLAINABLE REASON, I VIOLENTLY THREW THE *JUMP* ACROSS THE ROAD. THE MAGAZINE FLEW THROUGH THE AIR, PAGES FLAPPING! I DON'T KNOW IF IT WAS A REMNANT SUBCONSCIOUS REFLEX FROM MY FORMER BASEBALL DAYS, BUT I DO REMEMBER RECEIVING QUITE A FEW COLD STARES FROM PASSERSBY. THEY WERE PROBABLY THINKING, (WHAT THE...! WHO IS THIS WHACKED-OUT GUY...?! WHAT A WEIRDO...!), BUT, YOU KNOW WHAT, I DON'T CARE AT ALL!! IT'S THE HAPPIEST MOMENT OF MY 21 YEARS OF LIFE, SO TOUGH!!

Number 143:
The Fourth Hokage's Legacy!!

HUF
THE FOURTH HOKAGE'S ...
HUF
...LEGACY, EH...
HUF

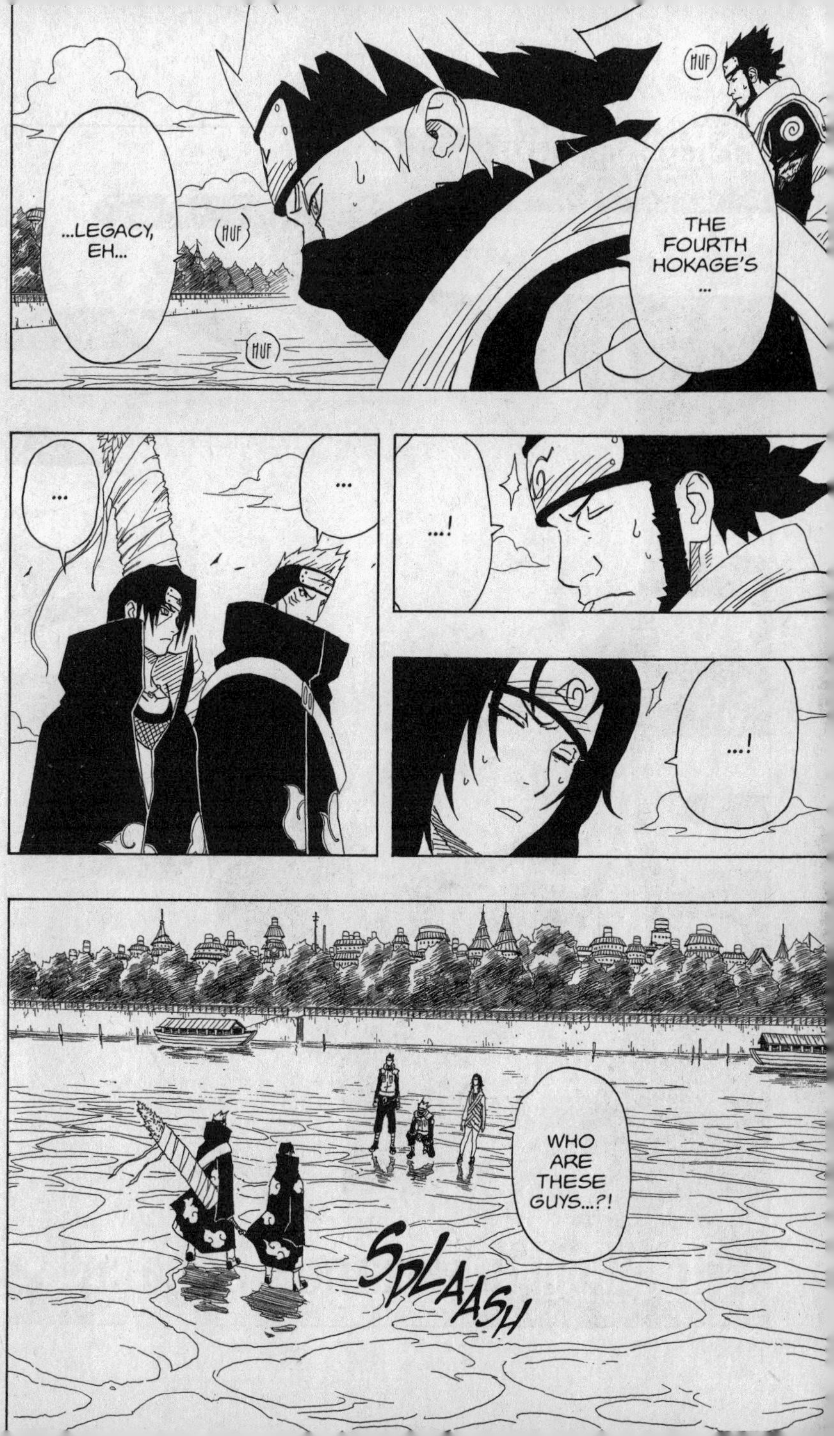

...!

...!

...
...

WHO ARE THESE GUYS...?!
SPLAASH

READ THIS WAY

HUF
...NARUTO, HUH...!
HUF

WHOOO

LONG TIME NO SEE...
HOW MANY YEARS HAS IT BEEN SINCE THE LAST TIME YOU WERE BACK?

...

KAKASHI...

...

I'LL TRAIN NARUTO FROM NOW ON...
...!
THE THIRD HOKAGE WAS WISE TO PLACE THE BOY UNDER YOUR SUPERVISION. HE'S BEEN WELL LOOKED AFTER.
BUT...EVEN SOMEONE OF YOUR REMARKABLE ABILITIES MIGHT NOT BE ENOUGH TO GET HIM READY...
...
WHATEVER DO YOU MEAN?
...
...I'VE BEEN KEEPING AN EYE ON OROCHIMARU EVER SINCE THE DAY HE FLED KONOHA...
FOR A LONG TIME HE KEPT MOSTLY TO HIMSELF... BUT THEN...
BECAUSE IT WAS EVIDENT HE WOULD RETURN...
...

READ THIS WAY
YES?
HE JOINED AN ORGANIZATION.
ORGANI-ZATION?
...
...WHAT ORGANIZATION?
I DON'T REALLY HAVE A LOT OF DETAILS, BUT IT SEEMS TO BE A SMALL SYNDICATE OF NINE SHINOBI THAT CALLS ITSELF THE AKATSUKI.
AT FIRST THEY STUCK TO SMALL-SCALE CLOAK AND DAGGER STUFF. NOTHING DRAMATIC. BUT YOU KNEW SOMETHING BIG WAS COMING...
...CONSID-ERING WHO THEY ARE.
?
ALMOST ALL OF THEM ARE LISTED IN THE BINGO BOOK...
...AS S-CLASS CRIMINALS!

...AND AMONG THEM IS ITACHI.
!!
WHEN NINE SHINOBI LIKE THAT GET TOGETHER IT'S NOT BECAUSE THEY WANT TO DO CHARITY WORK...
SO YOU SEE WHERE THIS IS GOING...?
...
RECENTLY THE GROUP STARTED SPLITTING UP... OROCHIMARU WENT OFF ON HIS OWN...
...WHILE THE OTHERS PAIRED UP AND DISPERSED ...
THEY'VE BEEN SEARCHING FOR NEW JUTSU... AMONG OTHER THINGS...

...ANY PROOF THAT ONE ITEM ON THEIR SHOPPING LIST HAS NINE TAILS?!
...IT'S A DISTINCT POSSIBILITY.
IT MAKES SENSE. THE NINE-TAILED FOX DOES HAVE ONE OF THE HIGHEST LEVELS OF CHAKRA...

KAKASHI...
SOONER OR LATER, NARUTO'S GOING TO HAVE TO DEAL WITH WHO AND WHAT HE REALLY IS...
THAT'S THE BOY'S DESTINY.

...

FOR NOW, FOCUS ON SASUKE...
IT'S UP TO YOU TO TEACH HIM HOW TO USE HIS SHARINGAN...
ESPECIALLY SINCE ITACHI'S PART OF THE ORGANIZATION.

AND I'LL KEEP AN EYE ON NARUTO. LEAVE HIS TRAINING TO ME.

HUF
YOU SEEK... THE NINE-TAILED FOX INSIDE NARUTO?

!
!

HUF
YOU'RE... NOT THE ONLY ONES, ARE YOU?
HUF
I KNOW ALL ABOUT YOU...
YOU CALL YOURSELVES THE AKATSUKI?

!

...!!

...?
THE AKA-TSUKI?

KISAME...! CHANGE OF PLANS: WE'RE TAKING KAKASHI WITH US.
MAKE THE OTHER TWO DISAPPEAR.

SHWIP

!

KRK

WH...
WHAT?!!
FAP

SH

!!

KONOHA GÔRIKI SENPÛ! SEVERE LEAF HURRICANE!!

SPLA

WHO ARE YOU?!

!

KONOHA'S NOBLE BLUE BEAST...
HUF
HUF
MIGHT GUY!!

...
WHAT DO WE HAVE HERE?
THE LEAF VILLAGE'S FIERCEST BEAST OF BATTLE?

DO NOT UNDERES-TIMATE HIM.

...IT'S HIM... ITACHI!

...UGH...
SPLAT

READ THIS WAY

GLUB GLUB GLUB

THAT HE COULD PUSH KAKASHI THIS FAR...
RUF

DON'T LOOK ITACHI IN THE EYE, GUY!!
HE'LL SNARE YOU IN HIS JUTSU!!

YOU DON'T HAVE TO TELL ME THE OBVIOUS!!
I'VE ALREADY MASTERED COUNTER-SHARINGAN BATTLE TECHNIQUES FROM ALL MY BOUTS AGAINST KAKASHI!

OPEN YOUR EYES, BOTH OF YOU!!

WHEN YOU GO UP AGAINST THE SHARINGAN, YOU ONLY NEED TO AVOID MEETING YOUR OPPONENT'S EYES!
JUST KEEP YOUR SIGHT ON THEIR FEET AT ALL TIMES, AND YOU CAN STILL READ THEIR MOVEMENTS AND REACT.

NOW THAT YOU MENTION IT, THAT DOES MAKE SENSE, BUT...
BLINK

YOU'RE PROBABLY THE ONLY ONE OF US... WHO IS ANY GOOD AT IT.
BLINK

I SUPPOSE SO... YOU SIMPLY NEED TO ACQUIRE THE KNACK FOR DISCERNING AN OPPONENT'S MOVE-MENTS JUST FROM THEIR FEET.

BUT IN THIS EMERGENCY SITUATION, WE DON'T HAVE THAT LUXURY.
YOU'LL JUST HAVE TO LEARN IT ON THE FLY!!

...

READ THIS WAY

SO WHAT'S THE PLAN?

KURENAI! GET KAKASHI TO THE MEDICS!!
ASUMA, YOU'RE GOING TO BE BACKING ME UP.

ALL WE NEED TO DO IS BUY SOME TIME...

...UNTIL THE ANBU BLACK OPS REINFORCEMENTS THAT I REQUISITIONED ARRIVE!!

YA GOT GUTS...

KISAME... I'M CALLING IT OFF.

!

WE DIDN'T COME HERE TO START A WAR...
TEMPTING AS IT IS, THIS IS NOT THE WAY TO DO THIS... LET'S GO.

...HMPH...

THEY DON'T KNOW HOW LUCKY THEY ARE...
FSH

...
...
GAH ...!

FWOOO
FWOOO

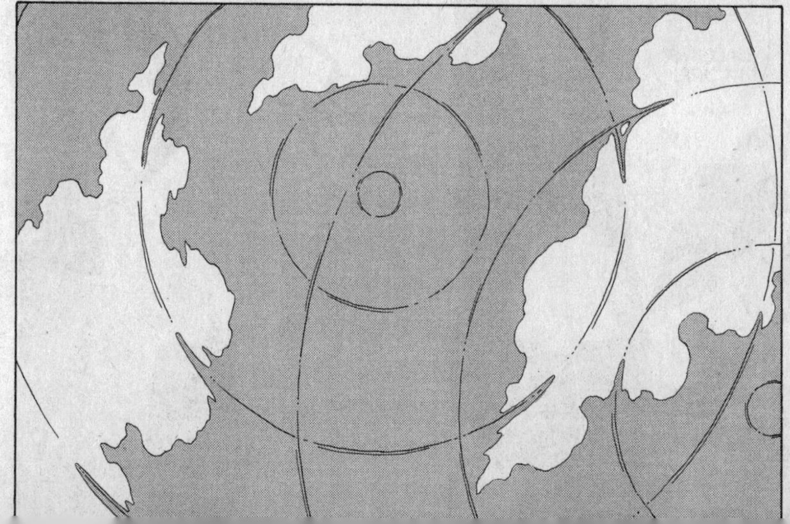

HOW COME I GET STUCK TAGGING ALONG WHILE YOU DO YOUR RESEARCH FOR ANOTHER ONE OF YOUR PERVY BOOKS?!
WHY?! WHY?!

WHAT?!!

I'VE GOT TO TRAIN... MASTER KAKASHI'S GOING TO TEACH ME ALL SORTS OF NEW JUTSU, LIKE THE CHIDORI!!
I DON'T HAVE TIME FOR THIS!
I SWEAR, MASTER KAKASHI'S BEEN PLAYING FAVORITES LATELY!
PLOD PLOD

THIS IS NO ORDINARY RESEARCH JAUNT, YOU KNOW.
THERE'S A PARTICULAR WOMAN I WANT TO COVER, SO WE NEED TO FIND HER.

LOOK PERVY SAGE, WHAT YOU DO ON YOUR TIME IS YOUR BUSI- NESS! BUT I'VE GOT MORE IMPORTANT THINGS TO DO THAN CHASE YOUR WOMEN!
NO, NO THANKS!!
SIGH... ...I KNOW THIS REAL COOL JUTSU... THAT'S SO MUCH MIGHTIER THAN THE CHIDORI...
OH WELL, MAYBE I'LL ASK SASUKE TO TAG ALONG.

WELL... UH... I DON'T KNOW HOW TO SAY THIS NICELY, BUT I DON'T THINK THAT YOU'RE CUT OUT FOR THAT MOVE...
BESIDES, THIS WOMAN, SHE'S A REAL LOOKER... I KNOW YOU'LL WANT TO MEET HER!

OH!
OH!
FAWIP
I'LL GO!
I'LL GO!!

JUST LET ME GO PACK SOME STUFF! I'LL BE RIGHT BACK...!
DON'T YOU DARE LEAVE WITHOUT ME, PERVY SAGE!!
WHIZZZ

...HEH HEH... KNUCKLE-HEAD...
STILL, YOU CAN'T HELP LIKING HIM...

READ THIS WAY

SNAP

ALL RIGHT--!! I'M GOING TO GO LEARN SOME NEW JUTSU AND BLOW SASUKE AND MASTER KAKASHI AWAY!
THEN SAKURA'LL FALL FOR ME TOO!! I BET...!!

LET'S GO!!!

UNNH...
KREEE...
YOU'RE A LITTLE TOO ENTHUSI-ASTIC, KID...
IT'S NOT LIKE WE'RE HOLING UP IN SOME MOUNTAIN FOR A FEW MONTHS...

MEET KISHIMOTO'S ASSISTANTS
PART SEVEN
YET ANOTHER NEW, YOUNG ASSISTANT HAS JOINED OUR NARUTO STAFF. AS ALWAYS, WE'LL BE INTRODUCING HIM HERE.
ASSISTANT NO. 7: OHKUBO AKIRA
PROFILE
• STILL FRESHLY SCRUBBED, YOUNG AND SPRIGHTLY.
• NO MATTER HOW STARTLED, MANAGES TO SAY "WOW" IN A NORMAL TONE OF VOICE.
• PRETTY SHARP-EYED.
• HAS BAGS UNDER HIS EYES.
• A SOCCER LAD WHO IS OBSESSED WITH SOCCER.
• MANLY IN A CASUAL WAY.
JOB: BETA [THE ARTIST THAT SPOTS THE SOLID BLACKS IN HAIR AND CLOTHING], TONING, AND BACKGROUNDS.

PLOD
PLOD

Number 144: The Pursuers

SO HEY! HEY! PERVY SAGE!
SO WHAT KIND OF AMAZING JUTSU ARE YOU GOING TO TEACH ME THIS TIME?!

...“PERVY SAGE” THIS, “PERVY SAGE” THAT...

HEY... YOU REALLY DON'T KNOW HOW DISTINGUISHED I AM, DO YOU...?

?

LISTEN UP...

THE TOAD SAGE IS JUST AN ALIAS! BUT NO MORE DISGUISES!

A LADIES' MAN THAT CAN HUSH EVEN A CRYING CHILD!

NORTH, SOUTH, WEST, EAST! I AM THE TOAD MASTER, THE WHITE-HAIRED PRODIGAL SON, ONE OF THE THREE GREAT SHINOBI!

“LORD JIRAIYA,” THAT'S ME!!

BAM

Number 144: The Pursuers

...
HUH...

...
PLOD
PLOD

CHIRP
CHIRP

HEY! HEY! SO...

...THE FACT THAT SUCH AN IMPRESSIVE PERVY SAGE ASKED ME TO BE HIS TRAVEL COMPANION MEANS SOMETHING, RIGHT?

I TOLD YOU, MY NAME IS JIRAIYA... SHEESH...

IT MEANS I'VE GOT SOME INCREDIBLE TALENT HIDDEN INSIDE ME, RIGHT?
RIGHT?

...

HEY! HEY!
SO WHY DID YOU CHOOSE ME?
MAYBE CUZ YOU HAVE TO GET AS GOOD AS ME IN ORDER TO BE INITIATED INTO SAGE-LEVEL SUPER-JUTSU...?
SKIP SKIP
HEH HEH HEH HEH HEH...

...

YOU KNOW... A LONG TIME AGO, THE FOURTH HOKAGE WAS MY STUDENT.
AND YOU SEE, IT'S ALMOST FUNNY HOW MUCH YOU KIND OF REMIND ME OF HIM...

WELL... I SUPPOSE THAT'S WHY.

I REMIND HIM OF THE FOURTH HOKAGE...?

MASTER KAKASHI! TEACH ME THE CHIDORI, WILL YA!

...SASUKE... THANKS.

...YOU SAVED ME FROM THE SAND GAUNTLET.

...

IT WASN'T ME...

HUH?

...

NARUTO'S THE ONE WHO RESCUED YOU.
GRR
OH, COME ON, SASUKE!♡ YOU'RE ALWAYS SO MODEST.
I KNOW NARUTO'S GOTTEN STRONGER TOO, BUT THAT SAND FELLOW...
IT'S TRUE.

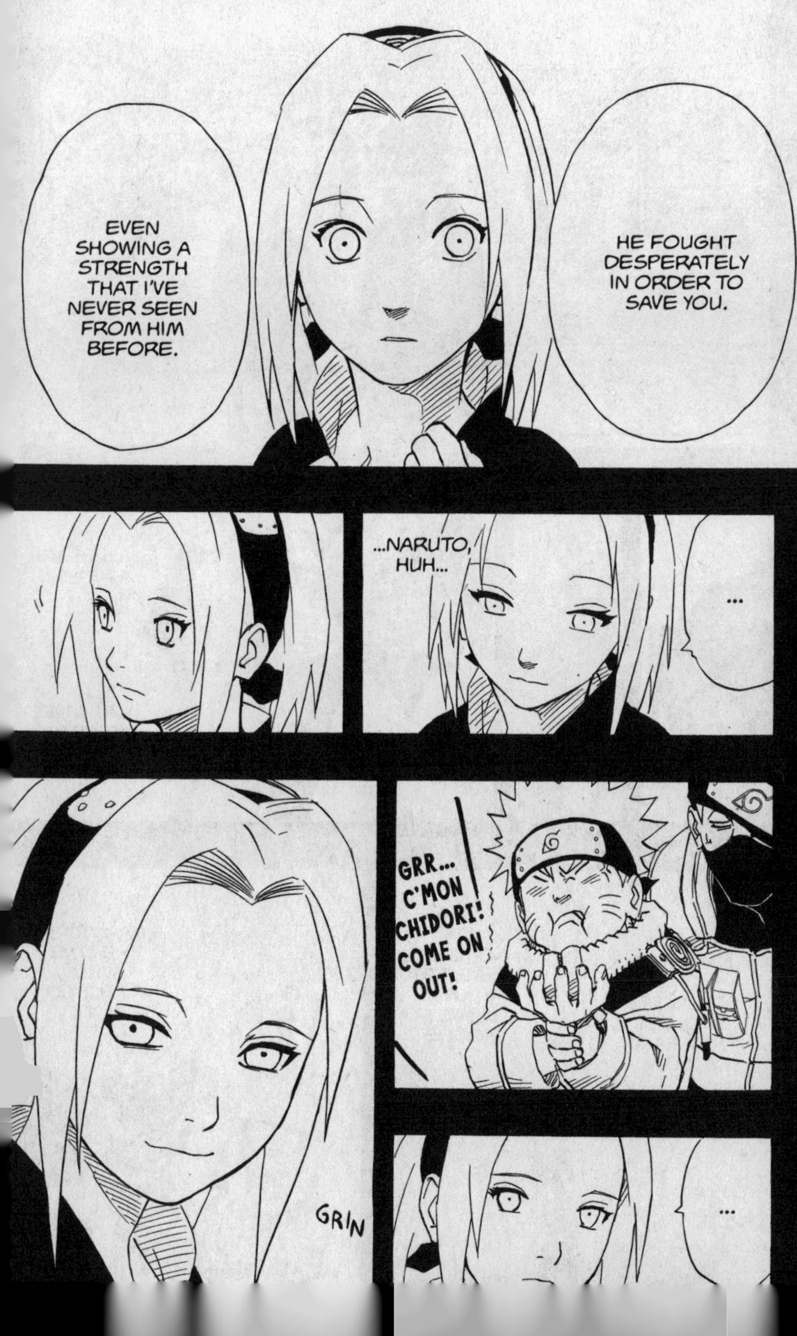
HE FOUGHT DESPERATELY IN ORDER TO SAVE YOU.
EVEN SHOWING A STRENGTH THAT I'VE NEVER SEEN FROM HIM BEFORE.
...NARUTO, HUH...
...
GRR... C'MON CHIDORI! COME ON OUT!
...
GRIN

READ
THIS
WAY

HUF
HUF

HUF
HUF

I... WAS
UTTERLY
USELESS...
HUF
HUF

NARUTO KEEPS GETTING STRONGER, ALMOST ABNORMALLY...
COMPARED TO OUR NINJA ACADEMY DAYS, WHEN HE WAS CALLED A FAILURE... IT'S VIRTUALLY UNBELIEVABLE PROGRESS...!!

WHEN I WATCH HIM UP CLOSE, I CAN TELL... HE'S... GOT SOME MASSIVE POWER HIDDEN INSIDE HIM...
SOMETIMES... I EVEN FEEL AFRAID...

...I...
...HOW CAN I GET STRONGER...

UZUMAKI NARUTO...
WHAT IN THE WORLD ARE YOU...?

HUF
HUF

EVEN IF YOU MIGHT BE ABLE TO TAKE HIM ON, I'M NOT SO SURE ABOUT ME...
HE'S IN A DIFFERENT LEAGUE.

YEAH... IF WE FACED OFF, WE MIGHT END UP KILLING EACH OTHER.
AT THE VERY LEAST, WE'D HURT EACH OTHER BADLY.
...AND EVEN IF I HAD MORE BACKUP, IT PROBABLY WOULDN'T CHANGE THE OUT-COME.

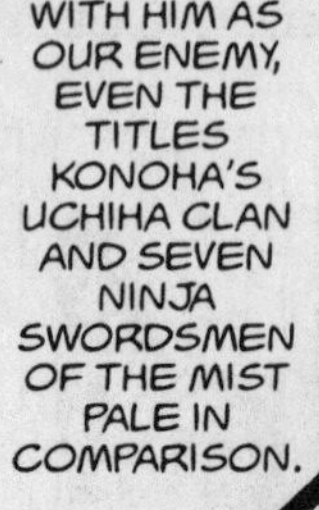
IT WAS GREAT FINALLY FINDING HIM AT THE RAMEN SHOP, BUT... HIS BABYSITTER WAS ONE OF THE THREE GREAT SHINOBI OF KONOHA LEGEND.
WITH HIM AS OUR ENEMY, EVEN THE TITLES KONOHA'S UCHIHA CLAN AND SEVEN NINJA SWORDSMEN OF THE MIST PALE IN COMPARISON.

YEAH... HOWEVER ...
...

EVEN THE STRONGEST HEROES HAVE THEIR WEAK-NESSES...

FROM THEIR BEHAVIOR, IT DOESN'T SEEM LIKE THEY'VE FOUND NARUTO YET...
...BUT DON'T YOU THINK THAT'S ODD... THEY'VE ALREADY BEEN HERE INSIDE THE VILLAGE.
IT'S EASY TO FIND NARUTO IN THE VILLAGE... AND ITACHI KNOWS NARUTO'S FACE.
SHH!

CLACK
KAKASHI...

!

READ THIS WAY

...WHY'S KAKASHI BEDRIDDEN?
AND WHAT ARE ALL YOU JÔNIN DOING HERE... WHAT THE HECK'S GOING ON?!

...OH... NOTHING REALLY...
IS IT TRUE THAT ITACHI SHOWED UP IN TOWN...?!
AND THAT HE'S AFTER NARUTO...
POP

...OH!

IDIOT...
GAH...

SHOOO
WHY DOES IT ALWAYS HAVE TO BE LIKE THIS!!

SHOOO
PAK

SPROO
SPROO
HE'S BACK, HERE, IN THIS VILLAGE?!

FAP

AND HE'S AFTER NARUTO?!
WHY, WHAT'S GOING ON?!

IN ANY CASE... IF HE GETS AHOLD OF HIM... NARUTO'S FINISHED!!
FLAP

I WON'T LET THAT HAPPEN!
!
HEY, MISTER! I KNOW NARUTO WAS HERE FOR LUNCH! DO YOU HAVE ANY IDEA WHERE HE WENT AFTER-WARDS?!

HMM, NARUTO, EH.
ER, IF I REMEMBER RIGHT... LORD JIRAIYA CAME ALONG AND ATE RAMEN WITH HIM...

THEY DID MENTION GOING SOME-WHERE...
UHH... SOMETHING ABOUT SOME NEARBY TOWN WHERE THERE IS A PLEASURE DISTRICT...
...AND HE WENT OFF TOGETHER WITH LORD JIRAIYA.

JIRAIYA?!

LORD JIRAIYA, ONE OF THE PRODIGAL SHINOBI THREE...
WELL, HE MAY LOOK LIKE AN ORDINARY WHITE-HAIRED BIG GUY AT FIRST SIGHT, BUT...

HEY!
SHOOO

...SHEESH...
IF YOU'RE GOING TO ASK SOME-THING OF SOME-ONE, YOU OUGHT TO SIT DOWN AND BUY A BOWL IN RETURN...!!

フィンフィン通り

(Street Sign: Fun Fun Avenue)

THIS PLACE SEEMS MIGHTY SUSPECT...
WAVE WAVE
NARUTO... WE'RE GOING TO STAY HERE TONIGHT!

!

READ THIS WAY

FAF
ホテル
CLICK
CLICK

WHOA!!

LOOK AT HER!!
NARUTO!
CLOP
CLOP
HUH?!

HERE, HERE'S OUR ROOM KEY!
GO UP TO THE ROOM AND PRACTICE MANIPULATING YOUR CHAKRA! EH!
PLINK
WHAT?!
SLAP
YOU CAN'T DRAG ME HERE AND THEN JUST LEAVE ME!!

THAT CITY'S NOT THAT FAR AWAY...!

SHEESH! THAT PERVY SAGE, HE'S ALWAYS LEAVING ME HANGING!!
HE BETTER BE SERIOUS ABOUT SUPERVISING MY TRAINING...?!!

FEH...!
SO MANY INNS! DO I JUST HAVE TO KNOCK ON EVERY DOOR?!
CRUNCH

フロント
!
HEY, IS THERE A FOOL-FACED BLONDIE ABOUT MY AGE...
...AND A WHITE-HAIRED BIG GUY STAYING HERE?!
...HMM.

(Forehead: Haku Hatsu Chun, or White Green Center which is a Mah Jong tile formation.)

READ THIS WAY

AAH! I WONDER IF IT COULD BE THEM... YES, I BELIEVE SO.
SHP
WHICH ROOM NUMBER ?!

!
RAP RAP

RAP RAP

WHAT, COMING HOME REJECTED ALREADY?
RAP
RAP
SHFF
SHLEP SHLEP

CLACK

DAK
NARUTO!

SHIF

...IT'S NOT THEM...

I'M COMING, I'M COMING!
SHEESH, ALL RIGHT ALREADY!
RAP RAP
CLICK

!
CLACK

NARUTO

岸本斉史

Recently, I haven't been exercising at all!! And so now, when I bike up even a slight incline, I get muscle cramps...And not just in my legs, but in my arms, too! Why?

—Masashi Kishimoto, 2003

NARUTO

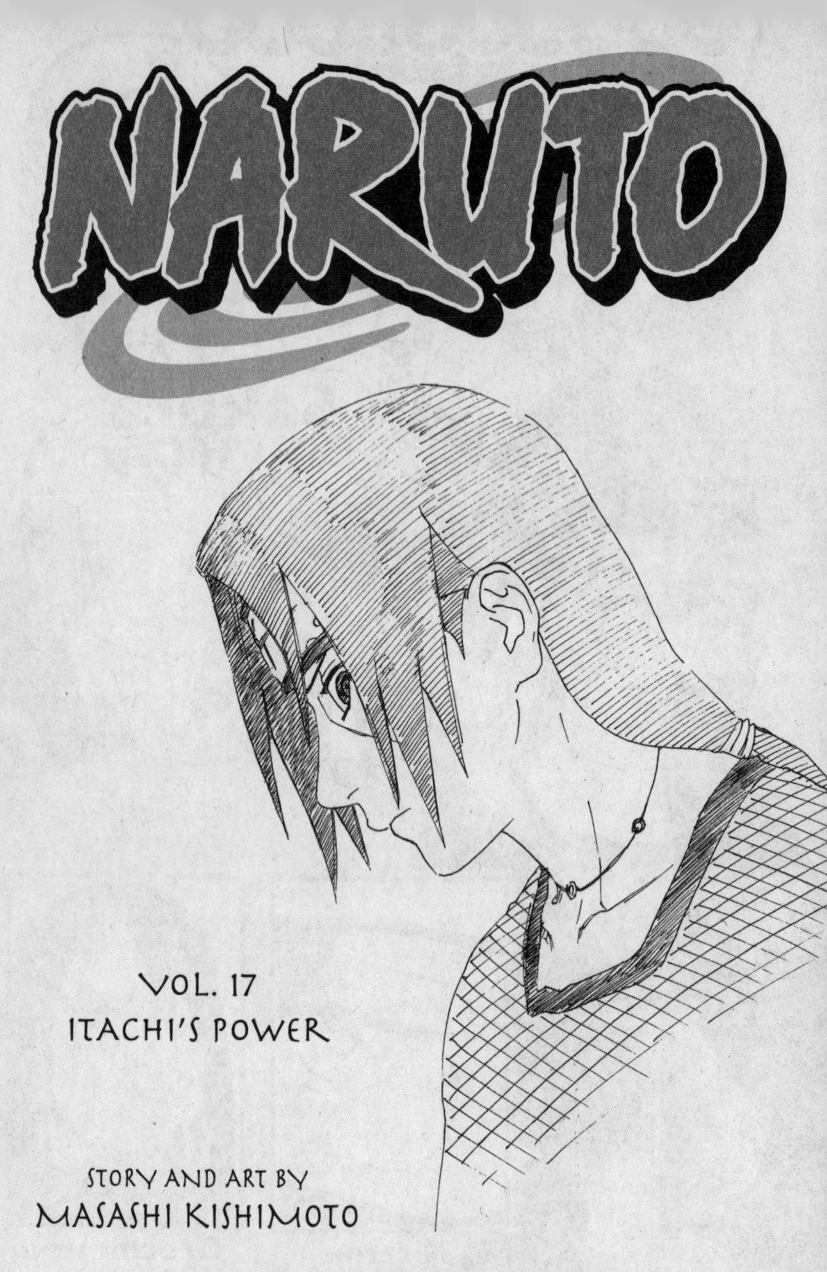
NARUTO
VOL. 17
ITACHI'S POWER
STORY AND ART BY
MASASHI KISHIMOTO

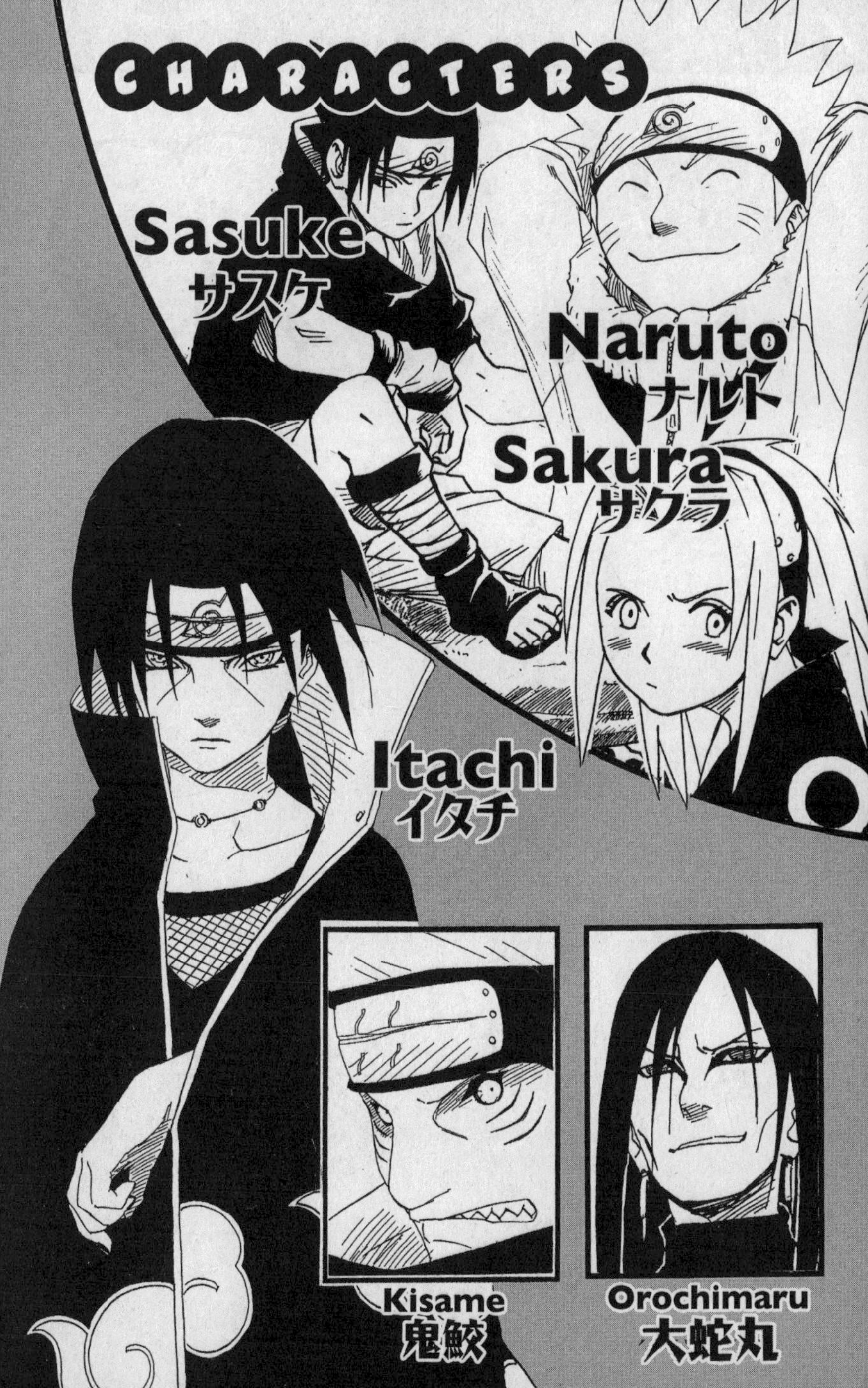
CHARACTERS
Sasuke
サスケ
Naruto
ナルト
Sakura
サクラ
Itachi
イタチ
Kisame
鬼鮫
Orochimaru
大蛇丸

マイト・ガイ

Might Guy

Kakashi

はたけカカシ

Jiraiya 自来也

Tsunade 綱手

The Story So Far...

Twelve years ago a destructive nine-tailed fox spirit attacked the ninja village of Konohagakure. The Hokage, or village champion, defeated the fox by sealing its soul into the body of a baby boy. Now that boy, Uzumaki Naruto, has grown up to be a ninja-in-training, learning the art of ninjutsu with his teammates Sakura and Sasuke.

Naruto and company take on the Chûnin Selection Exams but suffer a sudden attack from Orochimaru in the Forest of Death. Orochimaru leaves a curse mark on Sasuke's body and vanishes, only to return during the final round to launch *Operation Destroy Konoha!*

While Naruto battles Gaara, the Third Hokage sacrifices himself to defeat Orochimaru. Konohagakure is saved, and Jiraiya and Naruto set out to hunt down the elusive Tsunade to fill the position of Fifth Hokage, but they are pursued by two menacing shadows...

NARUTO

VOL. 17
ITACHI'S POWER

CONTENTS

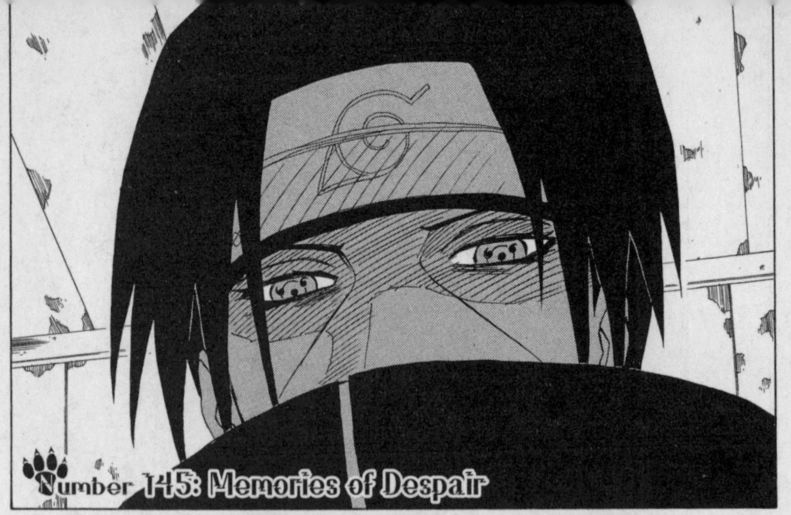
Number 145: Memories of Despair

SASUKE...!?!
!

NO, IT'S NOT... SO WHO?!
SHUDDER

HE'S GOT THE SHARINGAN, JUST LIKE SASUKE...

HARD TO BELIEVE THAT SUCH A CHILD CARRIES THE NINE-TAILED...

CHAK

Number 145: Memories of Despair

!!

READ
THIS
WAY

...HOW THE HECK DO THESE GUYS KNOW ABOUT NINE TAILS...?!

NARUTO, WHY DON'T YOU COME WITH US.

!

PSH...!

FOR SURE, IT'S A FOOL-FACED BLONDIE AND A BIG WHITE-HAIRED GUY...
BUT IT'S THE WRONG PAIR!

SHOO

HE'S CLOSE BY, I CAN FEEL IT!!

BIG BRO- THER...

HELP ME WITH MY SHURIKEN JUTSU TODAY, PLEASE...
...
I'M BUSY... WHY DON'T YOU ASK FATHER.
BUT YOU'RE BETTER AT SHURIKEN JUTSU...
EVEN I CAN TELL THAT.
...
...WHY DO YOU ALWAYS TREAT ME LIKE SUCH A PEST?
...
TROT TROT
POINK
CH CH

WHAP
SORRY, SASUKE...
...MAYBE NEXT TIME.
OWW!

PF...

...

!

I DON'T HAVE TIME FOR THIS.
SHWU

YOU ALWAYS SAY **SORRY, SASUKE** AND JAB ME IN THE FOREHEAD...
...AND YOU NEVER HAVE TIME. IT'S ALWAYS THE SAME STORY.
CHAK

CLATTER

FATHER, WHY DOESN'T BIG BROTHER EVER LOOK AFTER ME?
EVEN THOUGH I'M HIS LITTLE BROTHER ...
CLINK CLINK

...
YOUR BROTHER'S ALWAYS BEEN A LITTLE DIFFERENT, SON...
HE DOESN'T LIKE TO GET TOO CLOSE TO PEOPLE.

WHY?

WHO KNOWS...
I CAN'T EVEN READ HIM... HIS OWN FATHER...
HERE, SASUKE! YOUR LUNCH.
IF YOU WANT SHURIKEN PRACTICE, I CAN HELP YOU WITH IT WHEN YOU GET HOME TODAY.
GRP
IT'S NOT PRACTICE, IT'S TRAINING!
I'M OFF!
BIG BROTHER GRADUATED TOP SEAT FROM THE ACADEMY WHEN HE WAS ONLY SEVEN... HE WAS ABLE TO USE THE SHARINGAN BY THE TIME HE WAS EIGHT... AND THEN WHEN HE WAS TEN, HE ROSE TO CHÛNIN RANK...
I'M ALREADY THE SAME AGE AS WHEN HE GRADUATED, BUT I'M NOT EVEN CLOSE...

...BUT I'VE GOT THE SAME UCHIHA CLAN BLOOD FLOWING IN MY VEINS.
I WON'T LAG BEHIND BIG BROTHER!!
TROT TROT
I STAYED BEHIND TO THROW SHURIKEN SO LONG IT'S GOTTEN LATE...
!

...
WHAT WAS THAT...?

...I THOUGHT I SAW SOMETHING JUST NOW...

!!

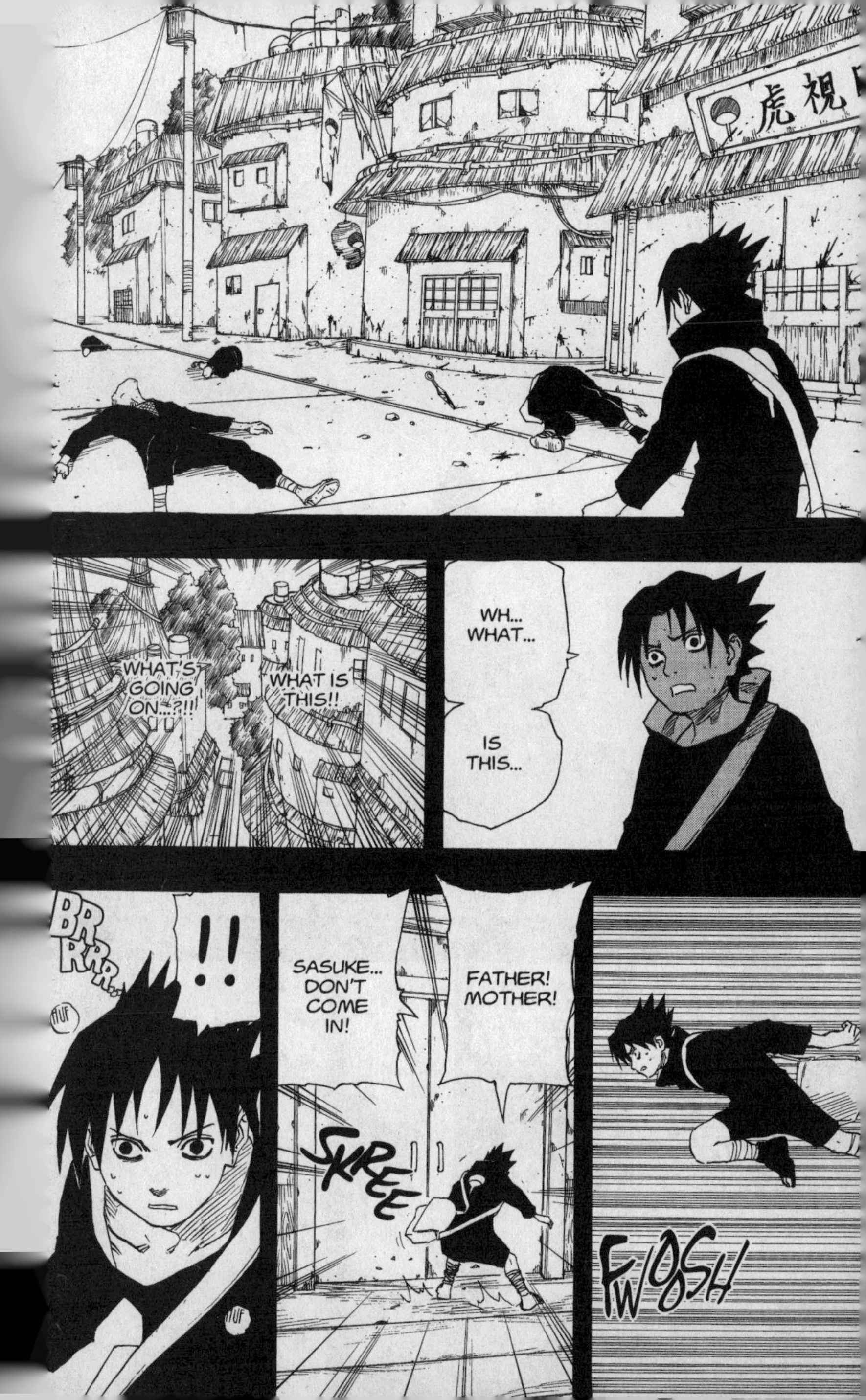

虎視
WH... WHAT...
IS THIS...
WHAT IS THIS!!
WHAT'S GOING ON...?!!!
FWOOSH
FATHER! MOTHER!
SASUKE... DON'T COME IN!
SKREE
!!
BRRRR...
HUF
HUF

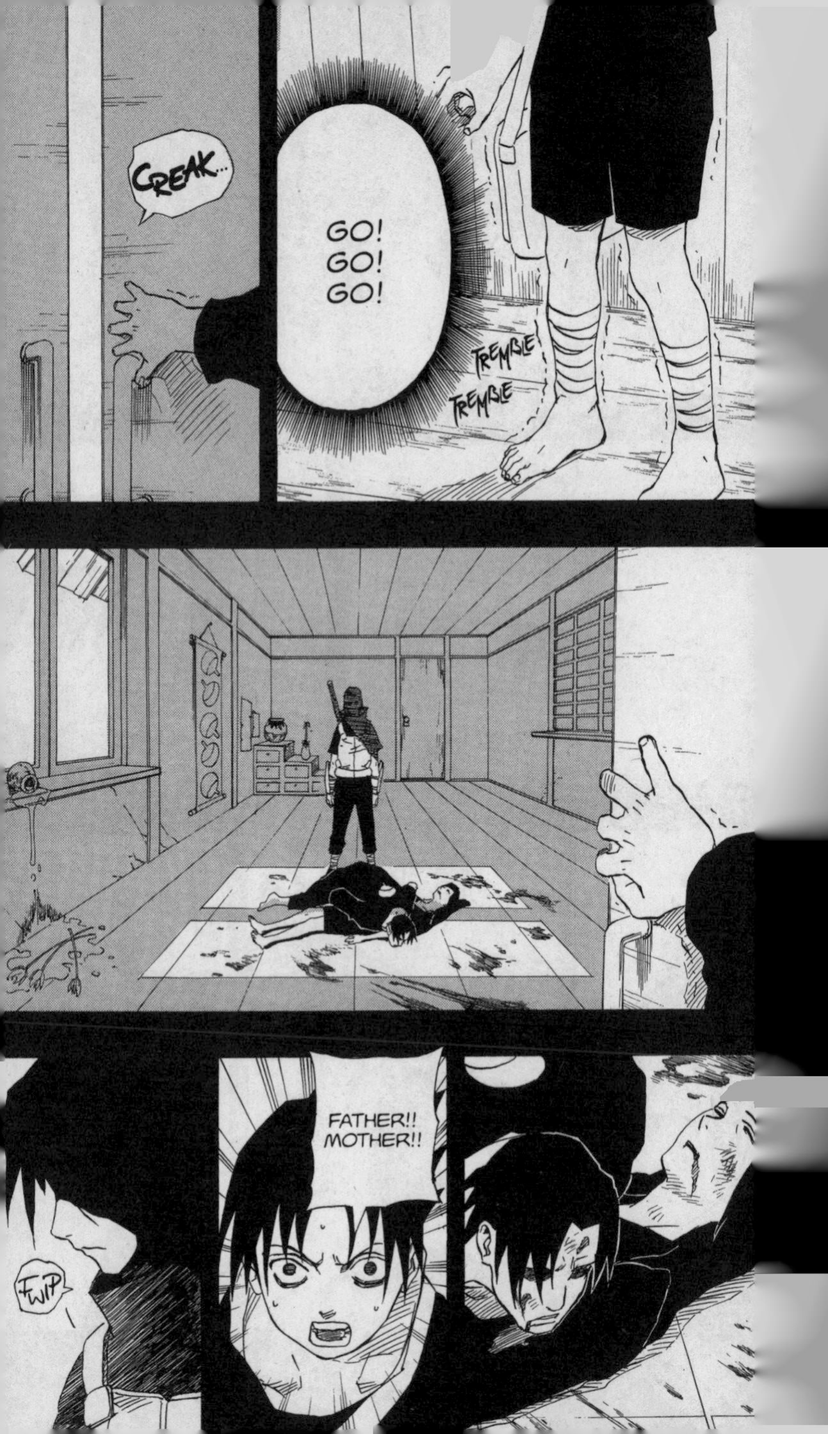
GO!
GO!
GO!
TREMBLE
TREMBLE
CREAK...
FATHER!!
MOTHER!!
FWIP

!!
BIG BRO- THER!

...BIG BROTHER!! BIG BROTHER!! FATHER AND MOTHER ARE...!!

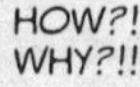
HOW?! WHY?!!
WHO WOULD DO SUCH A...

!!
THOCK

UGH...!
SLASH

...?!

FOOLISH LITTLE BROTHER ...

HUNH..
MANGEKYO SHARINGAN!!
THROB
AAAARGH!! STOP IT!!
WHY?! ...NO!! ITACHI!! AAARRRGH!!
WAAAAAH!!
DON'T SHOW ME SUCH THINGS!!!
STOP!! BIG BROTHER!!
DON'T... FATHER AND MOTHER, AAAARGH!!

GRRRR

WHY DON'T YOU STEP OUT OF THE ROOM...?

TH...THESE GUYS, THEY'RE NOT ORDINARY...

TMP

...HMM...
ITACHI...
IT WOULD BE BOTHER-SOME TO HAVE HIM WANDER-ING OFF...

PERHAPS WE SHOULD CUT OFF ONE OF HIS LEGS OR SOME-THING...
CLENCH...

!!
WH... WHAT?!

...

WELL THEN...

TMP
TMP

...!

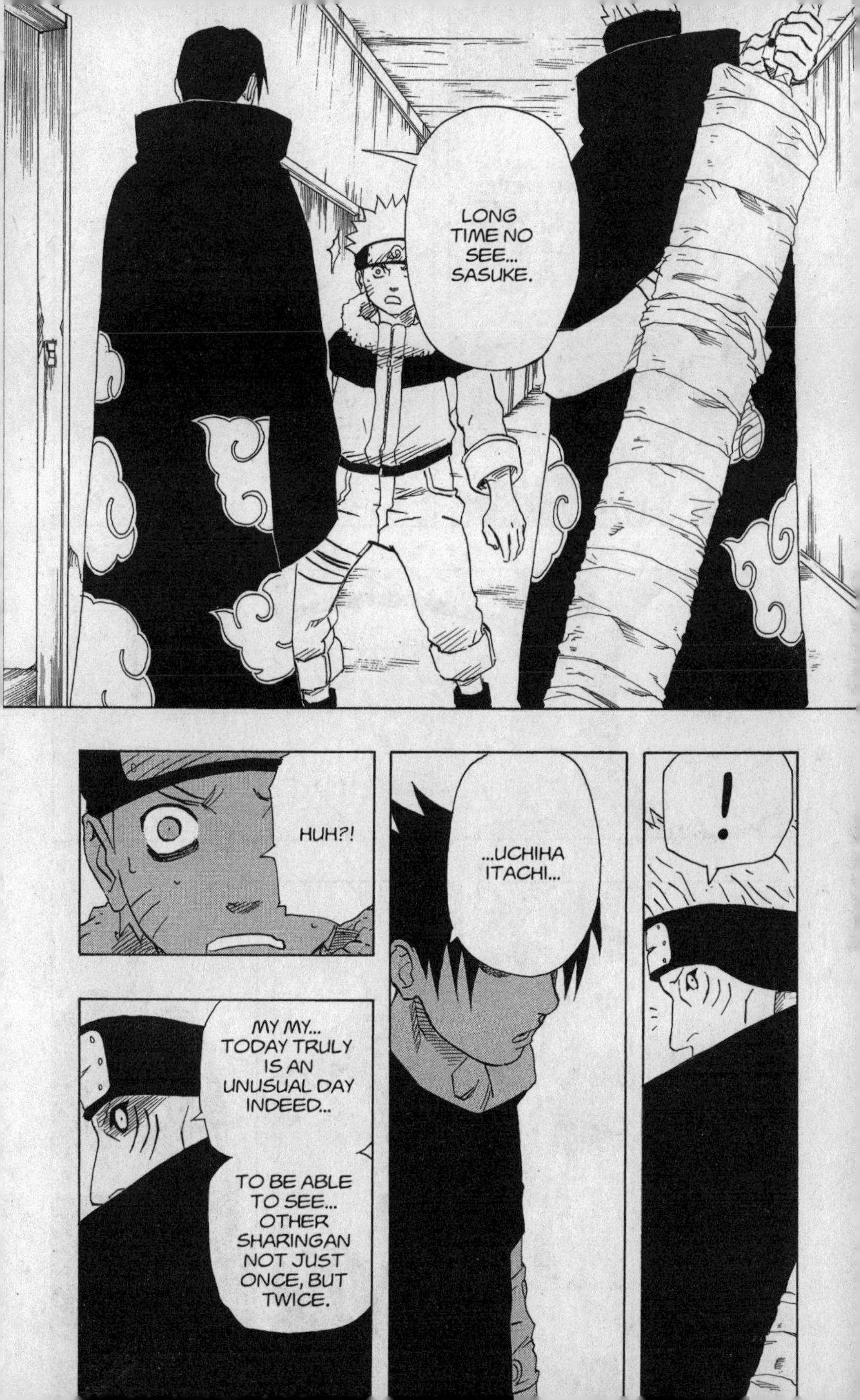

LONG TIME NO SEE... SASUKE.

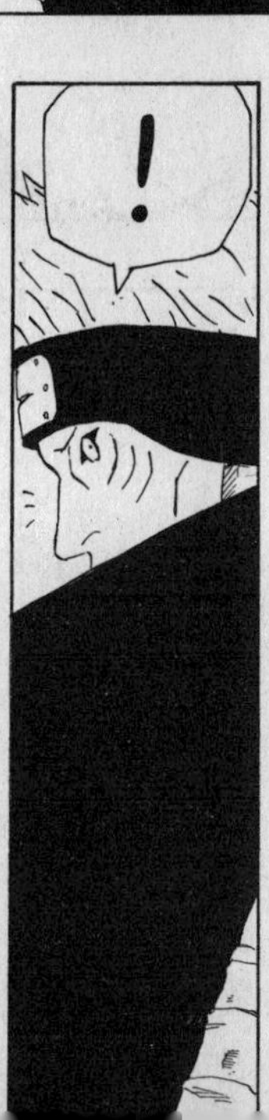
!

...UCHIHA ITACHI...

HUH?!

MY MY... TODAY TRULY IS AN UNUSUAL DAY INDEED...
TO BE ABLE TO SEE... OTHER SHARINGAN NOT JUST ONCE, BUT TWICE.

I WILL...
... KILL YOU!!

CONGRATULATONS!! 祝・3周年。
THE 3RD ANNIVERSARY OF THE SERIALIZATION!!

KISHIMOTO-SAN, WHO ALMOST EVERY DAY IS LIKE A STUDENT THE NIGHT BEFORE AN EXAMNATION.
PLEASE KEEP PUSHING THROUGH ENERGETICALLY.

NOVEMBER. 8. 田坂亮
RYO TASAKA

Number 146: Along with Hatred...!!

?!
UCHIHA... ITACHI...?

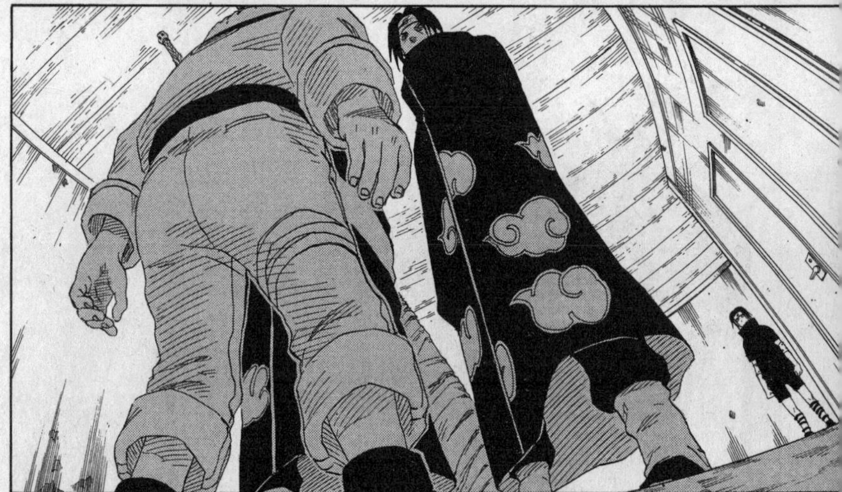

...THE SAME UCHIHA... AS SASUKE...?

...

READ THIS WAY

WHO ARE THESE PEOPLE...?!
WHAT ARE THEY?!

WELL... SHARIN-GAN.
AND HE LOOKS AN AWFUL LOT LIKE YOU...
WHO IS THAT KID, ITACHI?

...

HE'S... MY BROTHER.

!!

...THAT'S FUNNY, CUZ THE WHOLE UCHIHA CLAN WAS WIPED OUT THE WAY I HEARD IT...

...BY YOU!

THERE'S SOMEONE I HAVE SWORN... TO KILL.
...I SWORE I WOULDN'T DIE UNTIL I KILLED HIM, MY OWN BROTHER.

GRRRR
SO THIS IS THE GUY SASUKE WAS TALKING ABOUT!

THE ONE HE WANTS TO KILL...

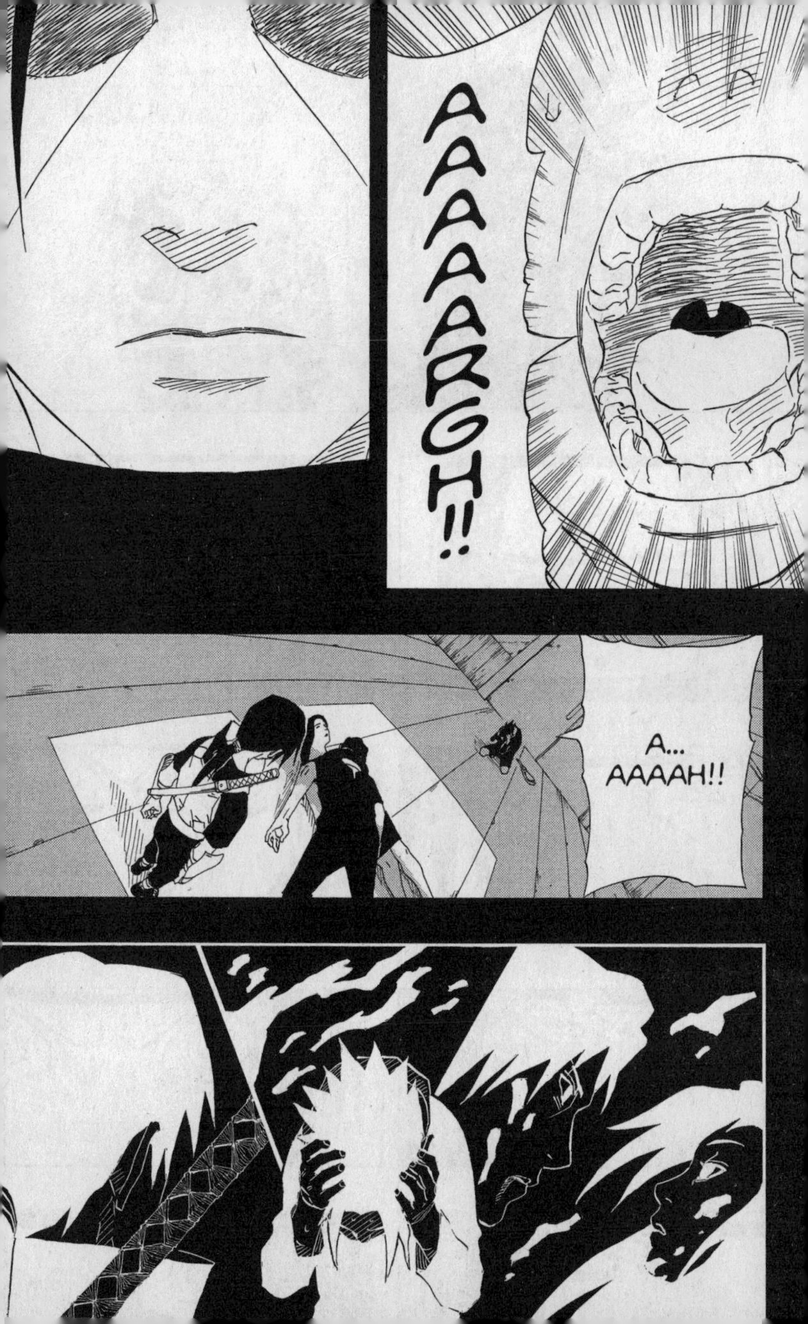

AAAAARGH!!

A...
AAAAH!!

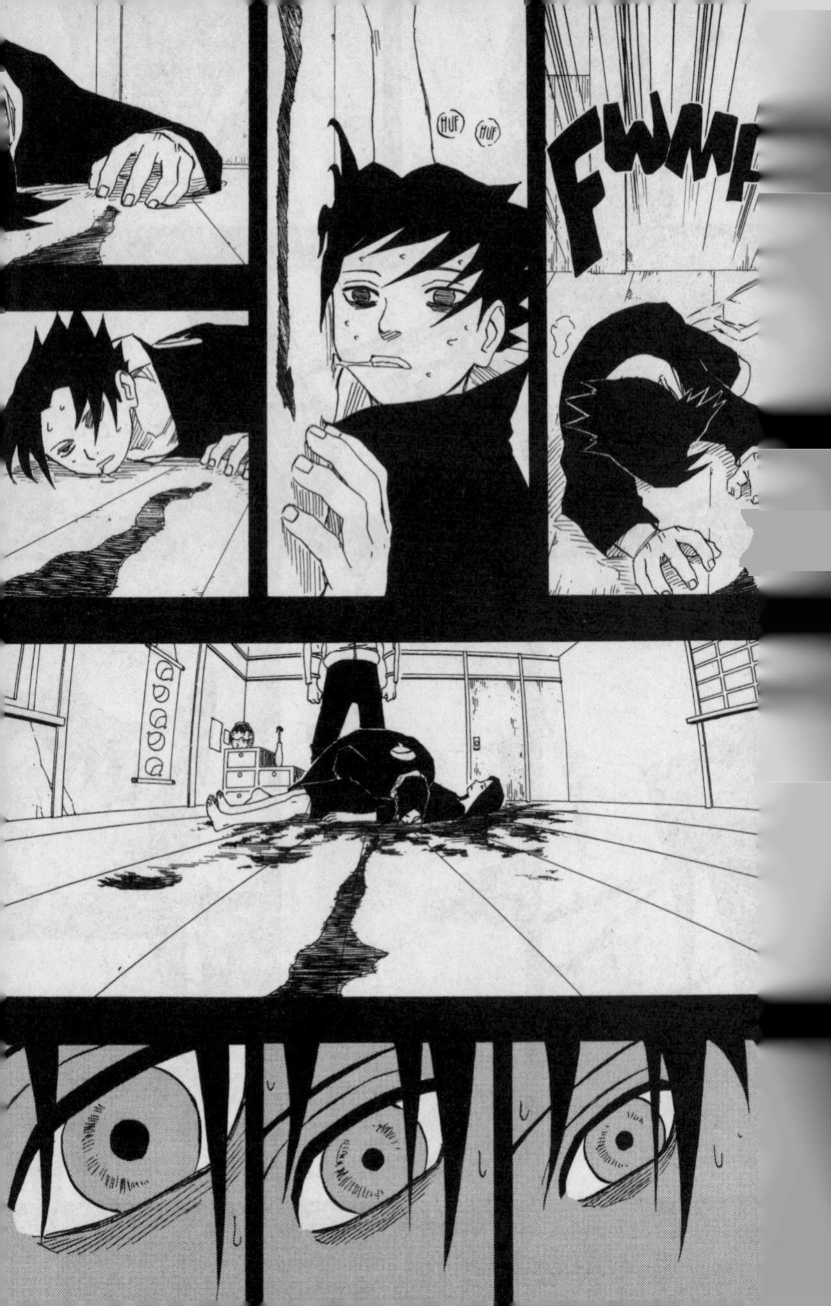

HUF
HUF
FWMP

WHY
...DID YOU...?
TO MEASURE MY CAPACITY.
...
MEASURE YOUR CAPACITY...?
THAT'S IT...?
...
THAT'S... THE ONLY REASON... FOR KILLING... EVERYBODY...?
...
I HAD TO.

READ THIS WAY
...
WHAT KIND... OF EXCUSE IS THAT...
FWEEE
WHAT'S WRONG WITH YOU?!
CLOD
THUMP

'FRAID...
CHAK
SHUMP
AFRAID!!
SHOO
WAAAH! DON'T KILL ME!!
SLAM
WHEEE
SKREE
YOU... ARE NOT EVEN WORTH KILLING.
BABY BROTHER, YOU'RE PATHETIC.

IF YOU WANT TO KILL ME...
... SETTLE FOR...
... HATING ME...
HATE ME AND LIVE LIKE THE COWARD YOU ARE!
CLINGING TO LIFE WITHOUT HONOR!
...JUST AS YOU TOLD ME TO... I'VE RESENTED AND HATED YOU...
AND LIVED SOLELY...
SH
FF
CRACKLE
CRACKLE
CHIRP
CHIRP

...TO KILL YOU!!

CHIRP-CHIRP-CHIRP

SHZZZ

SHZZZ

CHIRP-CHIRP-CHIRP

!!

...CHIDORI: 1000 BIRDS ...?

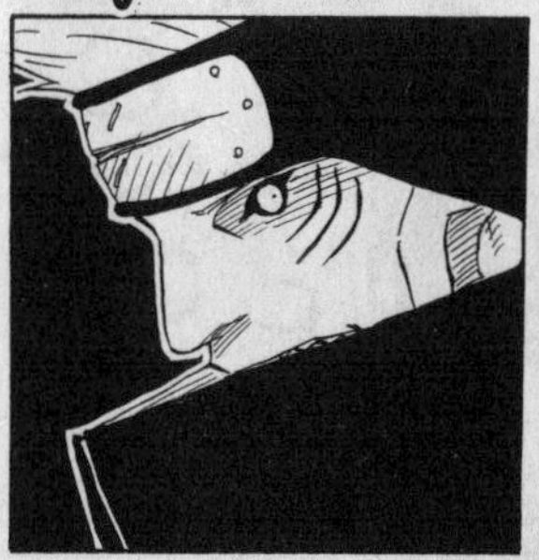

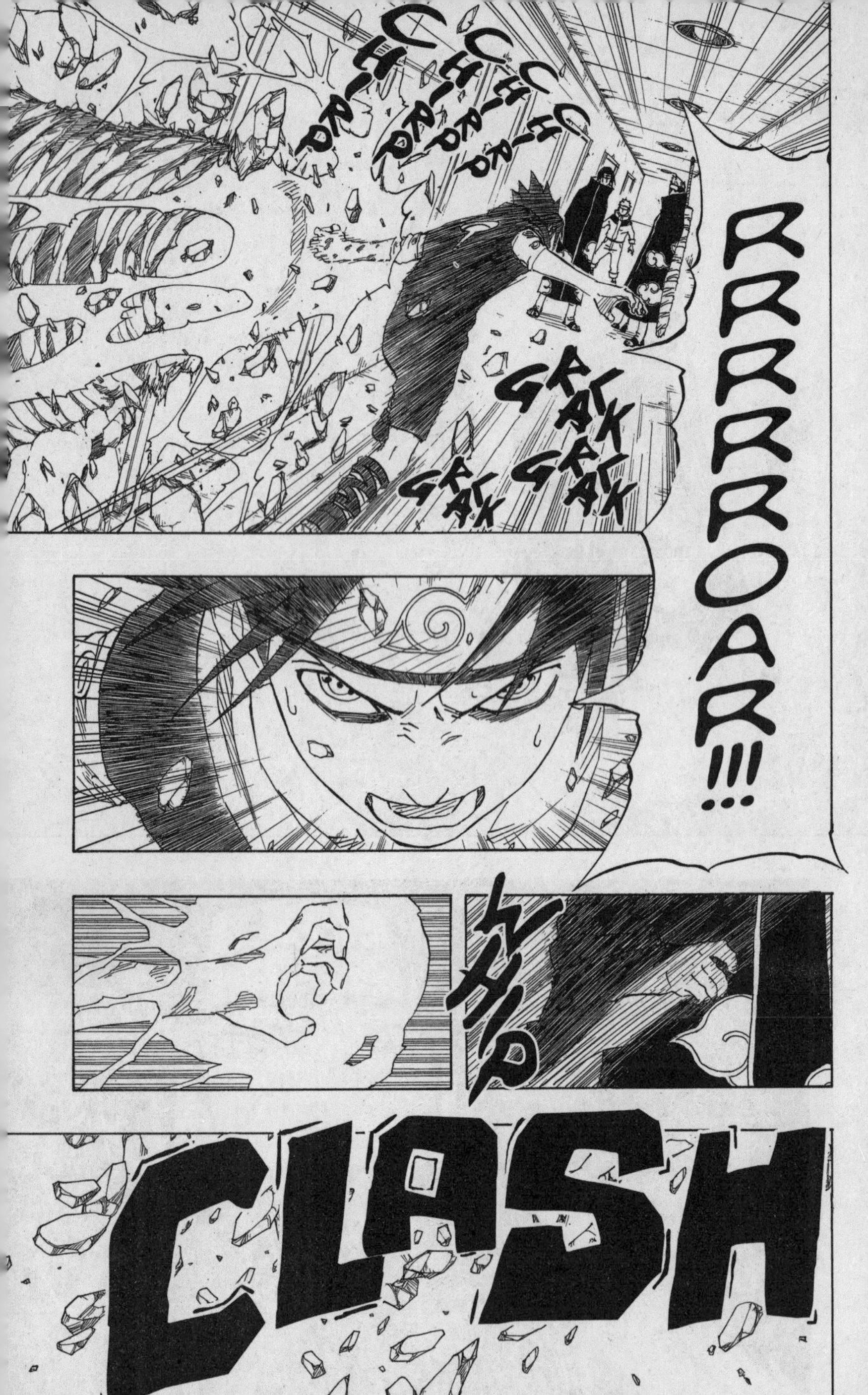

CCCC
CHIRRP
CHIRRP
CHIRRP
RRRRROAR!!!
GRACK
GRACK
GRACK
WHIP
CLASH

CRACKLE
CRACKLE

SHOOT!!

UNNNH!!
I GOTTA DO SOMETHING...!!

!

THE AIR IS RIPE WITH CHAKRA... THERE'S NO MISTAKE...
...THE POWER OF THE NINE-TAILED FOX...!!

!!

READ THIS WAY

YOU...!!

YOU'RE IN THE WAY...
SNAP

AAAARGH!!
SHMP
SASUKE!!

ARGH!!
KUCHI-YOSE! SUMMON-ING...
FWIP

TOO SLOW!
SHOOOM

?!
OH!

REEEEEE
ARGH! ARGH!
WHAT'S GOING ON?!

I CAN'T FEEL... MY CHAKRA?!
HUH...?!

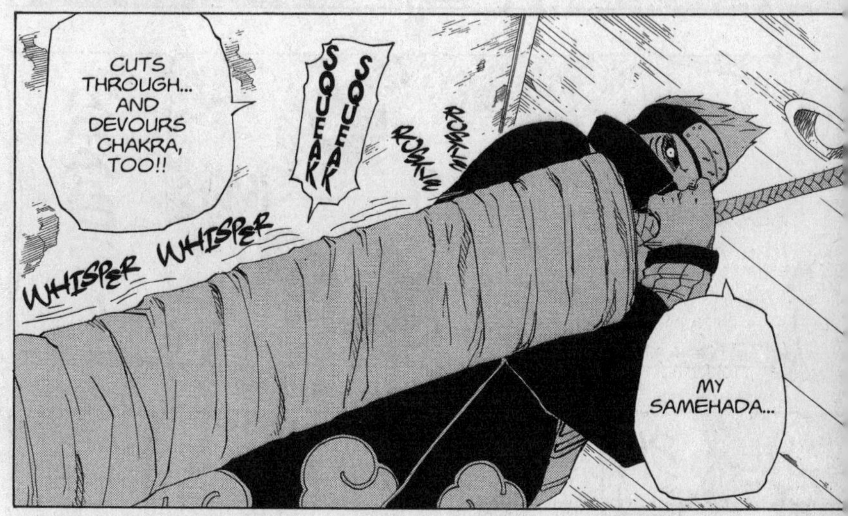
CUTS THROUGH... AND DEVOURS CHAKRA, TOO!!
SQUEAK SQUEAK
ROSKLE ROSKLE
WHISPER WHISPER
MY SAMEHADA...

...FORGET THE LEGS. MAYBE I SHOULD START WITH THOSE ARMS.
SWIP

WE DON'T NEED THIS KID WHIPPING OUT ANY MORE JUTSU...
!

READ THIS WAY

URRRRR!
!!
VACHINK
POP
!
YOU DON'T KNOW ME AT ALL. YOU SHOULD HAVE DONE YOUR HOMEWORK...
THE TOAD SAGE JIRAIYA FALLS VICTIM TO NO WOMAN'S CHARM.
BEAUTIES DROP FOR ME LIKE BLOSSOMS IN A STORM!

THE! EXCITING NINJA MANGA
NARUTO
3rd. ANNIVERSARY
池本幹雄
MIKIO IKEMOTO

A MAN LIKE ME ISN'T WIRED TO JUST BLINDLY FOLLOW A WOMAN LIKE A DOG!!
WHEN YOU GET TO MY LEVEL, THE WOMEN ARE THE ONES WHO WRITHE AT MY CHARM!!
油
Number 147: It's My Fight!!

THIS IS NO TIME TO BE ACTING SO HIGH AND MIGHTY! PERVY SAGE!!
YEAH, RIGHT! YOU'RE THE ONE WHO GOT EXCITED WHEN A WOMAN WINKED AT YOU!

UGH...

WE'VE GOT WORSE THINGS TO WORRY ABOUT THAN WHAT THESE GUYS THINK OF YOU!
ARGH!! I REALLY WISH YOU WOULDN'T CALL ME THAT IN FRONT OF OTHER PEOPLE!
GET ON WITH IT, PERVY SAGE!!

READ THIS WAY

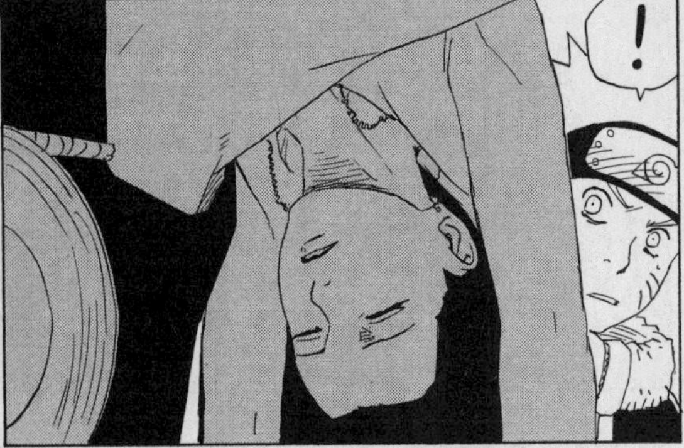
!

...

CACKLE CACKLE...
AAH, LORD JIRAIYA, TOUTED AS ONE OF THE LEGENDARY THREE GREAT SHINOBI.
NO MATTER HOW MUCH OF AN UNRIVALED WOMAN-CHASER YOU ARE, I DIDN'T THINK OUR DELAYING TACTIC WOULD SUCCEED THAT EASILY, BUT...

WHAT, YOU EVEN KNOW PERVY SAGE'S TRUE IDENTITY?!
...ER, THAT'S NOT REALLY MY TRUE IDENTITY...

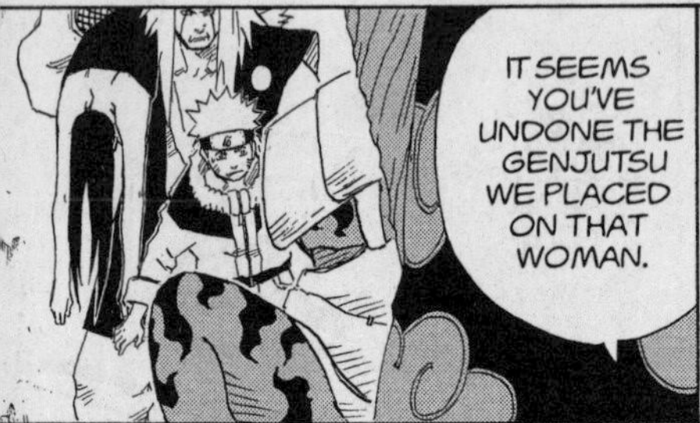
IT SEEMS YOU'VE UNDONE THE GENJUTSU WE PLACED ON THAT WOMAN.

...

PLACING A SAIMINGAN GENJUTSU ON A WOMAN TO SEPARATE ME FROM NARUTO...
WHAT KIND OF COWARD WOULD DO SOMETHING LIKE THAT?
SHP
BMP

...
SEPARATE US... BUT WHY...?

I KNOW HE'S THE ONE YOU'RE REALLY AFTER.

...!!

READ THIS WAY

...?!

...

...NOW I KNOW HOW KAKASHI KNEW.
I SEE... SO YOU WERE HIS INFORMATION SOURCE ...

...

TO TAKE NARUTO WITH US...

...IS THE SUPREME ORDER GIVEN UNTO US BY THE AKATSUKI.

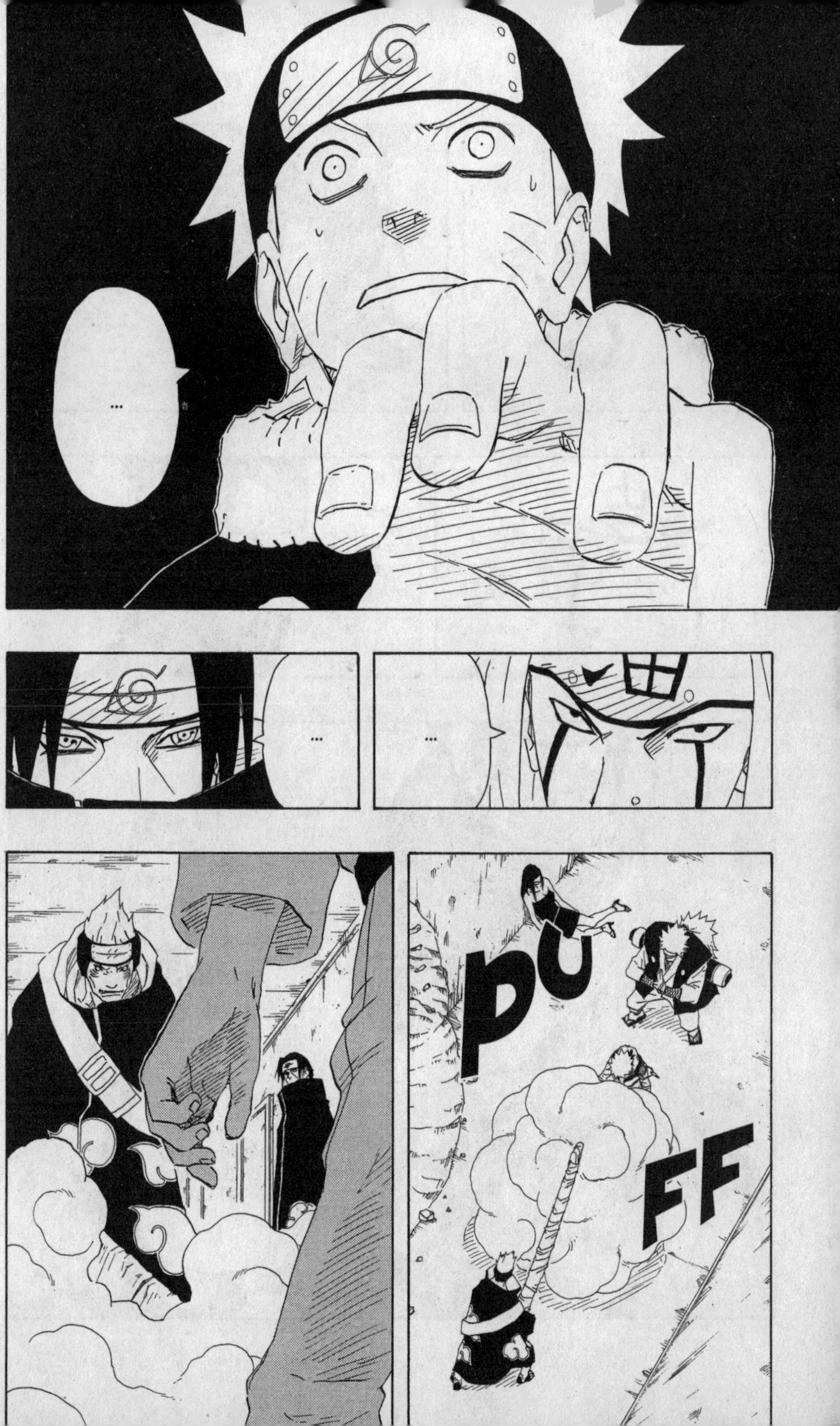

...

...

...

PUFF

READ THIS WAY

SORRY, CAN'T GIVE YOU NARUTO...

REALLY...

FINE, JUST AS WELL...
I'LL JUST TAKE CARE OF THE TWO OF YOU RIGHT HERE!

...STAY OUT OF THIS...

!
DOINK

...

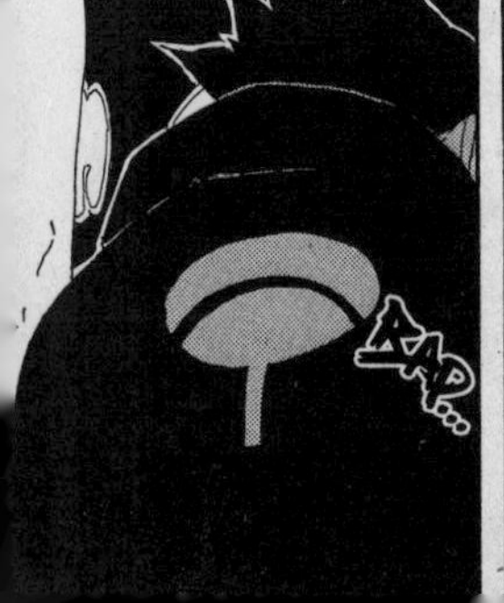

...THE ONLY ONE WHO'LL DO ANY ELIMINATING...
IS ME...!!
HUF
URRR
SHF

!!
SASUKE...!

!

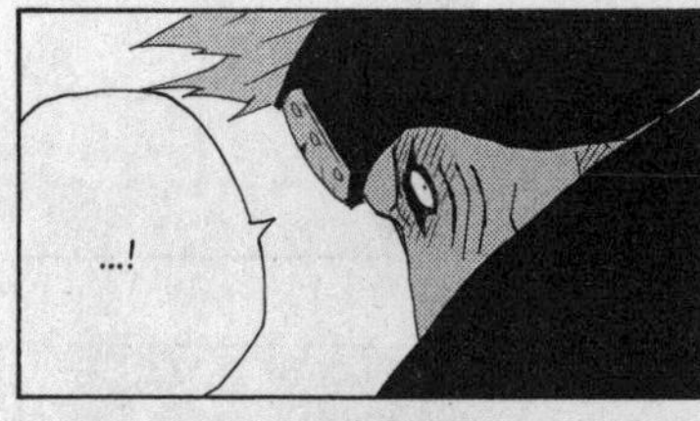
...!

...
GO AWAY... I HAVE ABSOLUTELY NO INTEREST IN YOU!

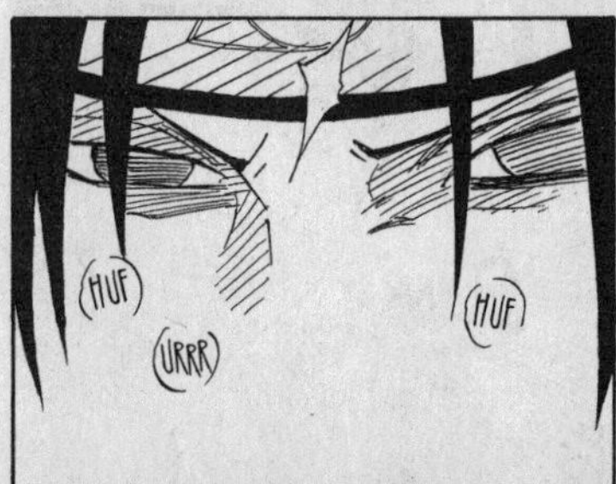
HUF
HUF
URRR

!!

SLAM

ARGH!
BAM

SASUKE!!

SKRRRR

YEA-
GGH!!
WHEEE

HUF
URRR
NARUTO!!!
...DON'T BUTT IN! MIND YOUR OWN BUSINESS!!!

!
DOINK
FREEZE

QUIVER QUIVER

...
AT THIS POINT, HE SHOULD NO LONGER BE ABLE TO WEAVE SIGNS...

THIS IS MY FIGHT!!!

READ THIS WAY

...
...REVENGE, HUH...

!
TMP
TMP

TMP
HUF
HUF

WHEEE

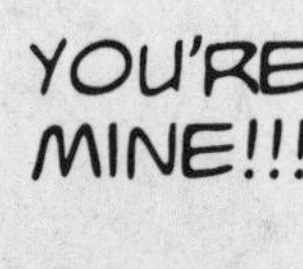
YOU'RE MINE!!!

THUD

UGH!!

...
HUF
HUF
HUF
WH... WHY...?

ARGH!!
THWACK

THWACK
GAH!!

...
GNASH GNASH

HACK!!
THUD

WHAT IS THIS GAP...
THAT DOESN'T SEEM TO HAVE SHRUNK AT ALL...
SINCE THAT DAY...?

NO MERCY, EH...

UGH...

...

WHAT HAVE I BEEN DOING...

...ALL THIS TIME?!

CHOK...

THOK

HUNH...

...WHAT...
...IN THE WORLD..

...YOU ARE WEAK...
?!

...

FOR THE NEXT 24 HOURS... RELIVE THAT DAY.

SLASH

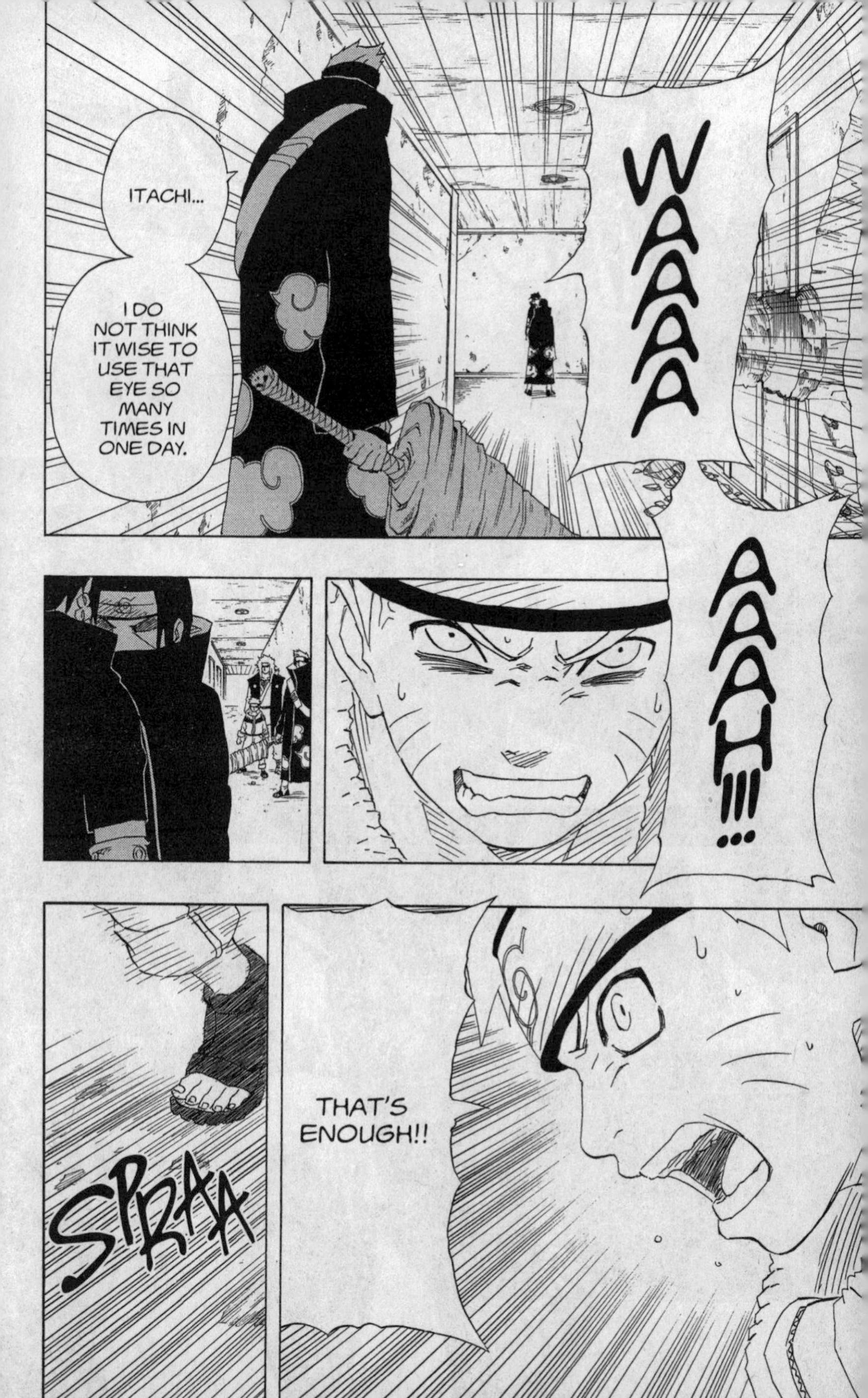
WAAAAAAAAH!!!
ITACHI...
I DO NOT THINK IT WISE TO USE THAT EYE SO MANY TIMES IN ONE DAY.
THAT'S ENOUGH!!
SPRAA

READ THIS WAY

SHF
SHF

!

SHOO

!

!!

NINJA ART! GAMA-GUCHI SHIBARI! TOAD MOUTH TRAP.

SSSSHUF
SHA

!
SSHUF

VOOO

!

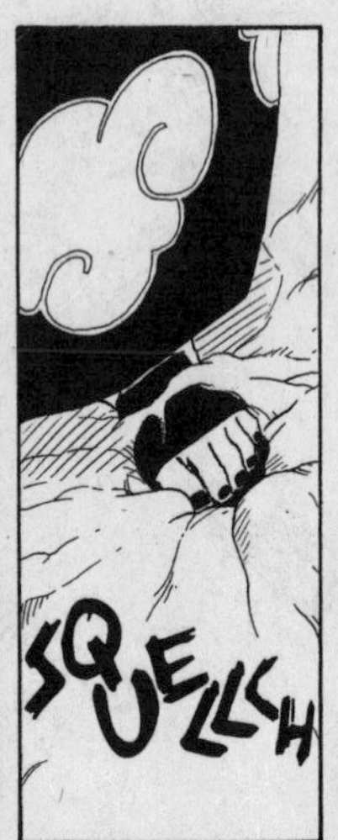
SQUELLCH

TOO BAD, ITACHI... AND KISAME.
YOU TRULY CAN'T ESCAPE ME NOW. YOU ARE IN ME!

CONGRATULATIONS ON THE
3RD ANNIVERSARY OF THE
SERIALIZATION
*
THE TV ANIMATION
CONTRACT
Finally, with little threat of missing deadlines,
things are looking more and more favorable, aren't they.
Please keep churning
it out
'02
Nishiya

Number 148: Itachi's Power!!

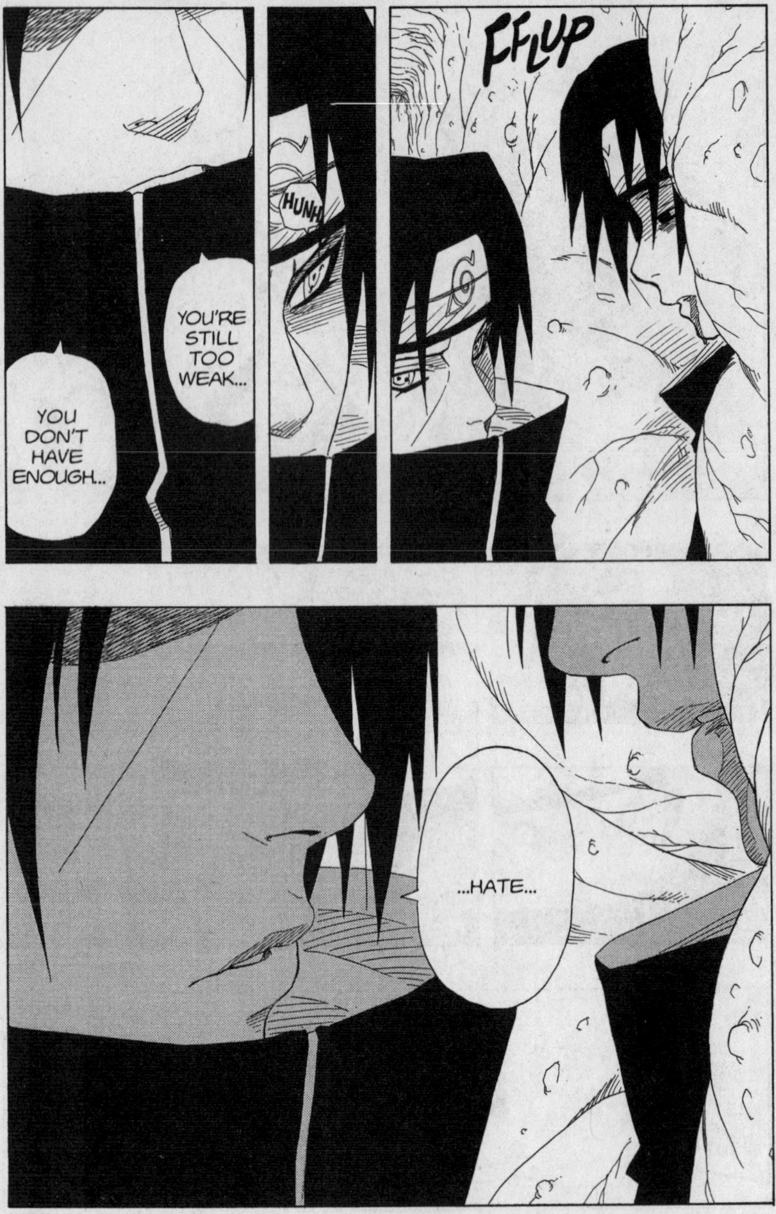

FFLUP

HUNH
YOU'RE STILL TOO WEAK...
YOU DON'T HAVE ENOUGH...

...HATE...

Number 148: Itachi's Power!!

I'VE JUST PERFORMED THE NINJA ART OF GAMAGUCHI SHIBARI! TOAD MOUTH TRAP!
YOU'VE JUST BEEN SWALLOWED BY THE ROCK-DWELLING GIANT TOAD OF MOUNT MYOBOKU. WELCOME, MY FRIENDS, TO THE BELLY OF THE BEAST.

WH... WHAT'S GOING ON?
NARUTO, YOU STAY PUT!
DON'T WORRY, THIS ALL IS PART OF MY JUTSU!

READ THIS WAY

WHOOO
KISAME, LET'S GO!

HMPH!
URRR

SPLECH SPLECH

!
OH!
DSSH

NO ONE'S EVER SUCCESS-FULLY ESCAPED FROM THIS!

SMOOSH

RRRR RM
RR
RR RRBL
SHOOM

LOOOOOM

THE WALLS ARE CLOSING IN ON US...!!

SSSS

READ THIS WAY

DON'T LOOK NOW BUT THERE'S A WALL OF FLESH COMING AFTER US....

THACK
!

GRRR...
...

DSSSH
!!

HUNH
!!

WHAT'S THE MATTER?!
SHOO

!

SCREEEECH

SPUTTER

HEY!!
THEY'RE GONE!!

...THEY'RE POWERFUL ENOUGH TO BURST THROUGH THIS WALL...

READ THIS WAY

SPLASH
SPLASH

WHY DID WE HAVE TO RE-TREAT...?
...WITH YOUR POWER...

...THERE'S NO NEED TO BE IMPATIENT... NONE.
...BESIDES WHICH, I MUST ALSO... REST MY BODY IN ONE PLACE FOR THE FORESEEABLE FUTURE.
FOR NOT ONLY TSUKUYOMI, THE NIGHT-MARE REALM...
HUF
HUF

BUT I WAS FORCED TO USE THE **AMA-TERASU** AS WELL...
WHIR

酒
FLICKER
FLICKER
FLICKER

GRRR
WHAT'S UP WITH THESE FLAMES? THEY'RE BLACK...

HOW DID THEY GET OUT? ...AND WHAT ARE THESE BLACK FLAMES?
THE ROCK TOAD NORMALLY SPEWS FIRE HIMSELF, SO FOR HIS NATURALLY FLAMEPROOF INNARDS TO GET CHARRED...

DON'T GO NEAR THEM WITHOUT CAUTION!
EH?!

SLMP

scribble
scribble
scribble scribble
?

ALL RIGHT!

STAMP
FIRE SEAL!!

SEALING JUTSU!
FWIP
FWIP

WHOA!!
SLURRRRRRP

YANK!

...!

ALL RIGHT! NOW WE'RE GOOD TO GO.
STOW
ALL THAT'S LEFT IS SASUKE.
!

SHWUP...

SASUKE!
TROT
TROT

STOMP

KOOSH...

BUMP

READ THIS WAY

TMP

THOCK

!
!!

SHAROOM
DYNAMIC ENTRY!!

GUY...?!

?!!

SLAM

...HUH?

PF

OH MY... I'M SO SORRY... I WAS IN SUCH A RUSH I FORGOT MY HAND MIRROR... *HA HA...*

SO I USED MY HEADBAND INSTEAD, BUT IT DIDN'T GIVE ME THE CLEAREST IMAGE AND I THOUGHT YOU WERE THE ENEMY...

TIP

HEY... IS THAT SUPPOSED TO BE AN APOLOGY?

WELL, NEVER MIND...
WHAT'S IMPORTANT IS GETTING SASUKE TO THE MEDICAL CORPS ASAP...

HIS ARM AND SOME RIBS ARE FRAC-TURED...
AND HE'S BLACKED OUT FROM WHATEVER JUTSU THAT WAS THAT ITACHI USED ON HIM.

...
COULD IT BE THE SAME THING HE USED ON KAKASHI?

HEY PERVY SAGE! IS SASUKE... ALL RIGHT?

...PHYSICALLY YES, BUT I'M WORRIED ABOUT WHAT MAY HAVE BEEN DONE TO HIS MIND...

GAH...!
WHAT... WHAT DID SASUKE DO TO DESERVE THIS?!

CLENCH...

HEY PERVY SAGE!
CHANGE OF PLANS...!

I WAS FREAKED EARLIER, BUT THIS TIME...
I SWEAR I'LL HUNT THOSE BLACK-CAPED CROOKS DOWN AND BEAT THEM UP!!

THEY'VE GOT SOME BUSINESS WITH ME, RIGHT?!
WELL I'LL GO SEE THEM THEN!!

HUMPH. IF YOU GO NOW, YOU'LL JUST BE KILLED...
THERE'S TOO MUCH OF A GAP BETWEEN YOU AND THEM.
I MEAN, IT EVEN TOOK ME A HUGE EFFORT JUST NOW ...
... JUST TO DISTANCE THEM FROM YOU...
ARE YOU SAYING THAT I HAVE TO KEEP RUNNING AND HIDING FROM THEM FOR THE REST OF MY LIFE?!
LIVE EACH DAY SHIVERING IN FEAR?!!
GRRR
SHUT YOUR MOUTH.
SLAP
!

READ THIS WAY

...YOU ARE STILL WEAK.

...

FORGIVE ME, GUY... I WAS TRYING TO HONOR THIS BOY'S FEELINGS, BUT...
I SHOULD HAVE STEPPED IN SOONER...

...RIGHT NOW... KAKASHI'S ALSO BEDRIDDEN FROM THIS SAME JUTSU... AND WE DON'T KNOW WHEN HE'LL WAKE UP...

MASTER KAKASHI?!

...

WHEN MY PUPIL WAS INJURED... AND SUCH TIMES AS THESE, I TRULY WISH...
THAT THAT MEDICAL SPECIALIST WERE STILL HERE WITH US...

...

博打場
すろっと

SNORT SNORT

CLICK

...AH, AIEE!
STUTTER STUTTER
WH... WHERE'D THAT MONEY COME FROM?!
I BOR-ROWED IT!

...THAT'S WHY... I'M ABOUT TO GO SEARCH FOR **HER.**

YOU MEAN... YOU'RE REALLY...
?

THE THIRD OF THE SHINOBI THREE.
THE QUEEN OF SLUGS AND ELIXIRS...

ALRIGHTY!

THE ONE WHO WEARS "BETTING" ON HER BACK, PRINCESS TSUNADE.

WITH THIS, I'M NOT JUST GOING TO WIN BACK MY LOSSES, BUT FLIP MY FORTUNES AS WELL!!

CONGRATULATIONS ON
THE 3RD ANNIVERSARY!!!
WE DID IT ♡
河原
KAWAHARA
02. 11. 8

Number 149: The Legendary...!!

...

LORD JIRAIYA ...
!

PLEASE DO...
FIND AND BRING BACK LADY TSUNADE.

I PROMISE WE'LL FIND HER AND BRING HER BACK RIGHT AWAY!

SO TAKE GOOD CARE OF SASUKE UNTIL THEN! MASTER ÜBER-BROWS!!

...
!
PAT

WELL THEN, GUY.
I'M LEAVING SASUKE IN YOUR HANDS.
SPARKLE

NOTHING INTRIGUES ME MORE THAN GUTS, KID!
LET ME GIVE YOU THIS!
SHFFLE SHFFLE

?
THIS HELPED LEE GET STRONGER...
OH! WHAT IS IT?! WHAT IS IT?!

THIS!!!

!
...

IT'S BREATHABLE, RETAINS MOISTURE, AND OFFERS COMPLETE FREEDOM OF MOVEMENT ALL IN ONE SWEET PACKAGE!!

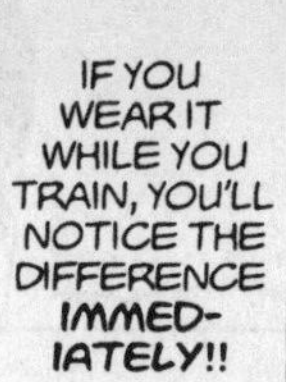
IF YOU WEAR IT WHILE YOU TRAIN, YOU'LL NOTICE THE DIFFERENCE **IMMED-IATELY!!**

SOON, YOU'LL START WANTING TO WEAR IT ALL THE TIME, JUST LIKE LEE!! I'VE GOT A BIT OF A THING FOR IT M'SELF!!
WOW!!

IF YOU CANWALK AROUND CARRYING **THAT** THING, YOU OUGHT TO PACK A HAND MIRROR OR TWO, YOU IDIOT.
SPARKLE

READ
THIS
WAY

DON'T... TELL ME YOU'RE PLANNING TO WEAR THAT THING?
WHADDYA THINK...?
JUST DON'T.
MAN, THAT IS GOOFY.
BYE-YA!

大入
丁半ばくち

AIEE!

Y...YOU HAD TO CHOOSE THE ESTABLISHMENT WITH THE HIGHEST ANTE...!!

WILL YOU STOP FREAKING OUT. C'MON, I'M GOING IN...
FALIP

イカサマ禁止!!

... HMM?!
...

!
SH... SHE'S THE...!

READ THIS WAY

...

I KNOW HE'S THE ONE YOU'RE REALLY AFTER.

TO TAKE NARUTO WITH US...
...IS THE SUPREME ORDER GIVEN UNTO US BY OUR ORGANIZATION AKATSUKI.

!
WHAT'S THE MATTER?

...PERVY SAGE...
WHY... DO THEY WANT ME...?

...

...YOU KNOW TOO, DON'T YOU?!
WHAT'S GOING ON...

...
IT'S NOT YOU THEY WANT...
...IT'S WHAT'S INSIDE YOU.

...WHAT IS THIS *THING*...?
PAT

...

READ THIS WAY

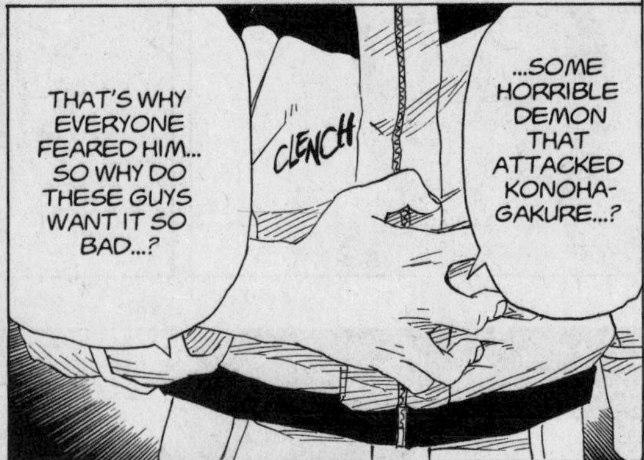
...SOME HORRIBLE DEMON THAT ATTACKED KONOHA-GAKURE...?
CLENCH
THAT'S WHY EVERYONE FEARED HIM... SO WHY DO THESE GUYS WANT IT SO BAD...?

...

INDEED... THE NINE-TAILED FOX HAS APPEARED IN TIMES OF CONSEQUENCE ALL THROUGH THE AGES. IT'S A GHASTLY SPIRIT...
...DESTROYING EVERYTHING IN ITS PATH.

THAT'S WHY PEOPLE IN ANCIENT TIMES FEARED IT AS ONE OF THE DIVINE RETRIBUTIONS.

...

...

AND WHY THEY WANT SUCH A THING...
...I HONESTLY DON'T HAVE A CLUE YET...

...

THEY MIGHT BE THINKING OF PLACING ITS POWER UNDER THEIR CONTROL.
WHILE THE NINE-TAILED FOX SPIRIT IS STILL SEALED INSIDE OF YOU...

...

THEY'LL NEVER STOP COMING FOR YOU. IT IS YOUR DESTINY.
油
BUT, I'LL BE AROUND TO PROTECT YOU, SO DON'T WORRY...
THEN I'VE GOT TO HURRY UP ...
... AND GET STRONGER!

ALL RIGHT! SO LET'S FIND THIS TSUNADE LADY...
HAVE HER SAVE SASUKE, AND START TRAINING AGAIN!!

... WHAT?

HMM?!

HEH HEH...
THAT'S SO LIKE HIM... ONE TRACK MIND!

READ
THIS
WAY

THAT BEAUTY YOU SAID YOU WANTED TO LOOK FOR...
YOU MEANT THIS TSUNADE?

HO! THAT'S PRETTY SHARP, FOR YOU.
AND SO, WHAT OF IT?
YOU AND SHE WERE BOTH PART OF THE THREE GREAT SHINOBI, WEREN'T YOU?!

YEAH, SO?

...HOW OLD IS SHE?

SAME AS ME.
SHE'S ANCIENT!!

SO WHAT'S SHE LIKE?
SHAKE
SHAKE
HUH? YOU INTERESTED IN HER?

HMM, LET'S SEE...
IN ONE SENTENCE, SHE'S KINDA UNPLEASANT...

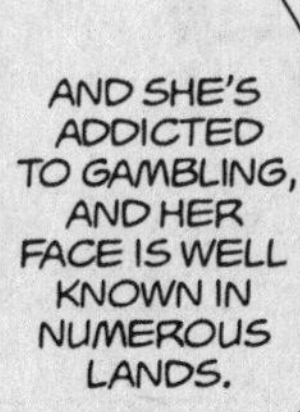
AND SHE'S ADDICTED TO GAMBLING, AND HER FACE IS WELL KNOWN IN NUMEROUS LANDS.

THEN SHE'LL BE EASY TO FIND! IF SHE'S SO FAMOUS...

SHE'S QUITE INFAMOUS...
SHE'S THE LEGENDARY...

LOOM

CAN YOU CHANGE ALL OF THIS CASH INTO CHIPS?
THUMP

禁止!!
留
乱素
賭

SH... SHE'S...

WHO OR WHAT THE HECK IS SHE? THIS LADY...

YOU... DON'T KNOW OF HER...?
...SHE'S... THE ONE WITH THAT NICKNAME...
NICK-NAME?

THE LEG-END-ARY...

THE LEGEND-ARY...?

THE LEGENDARY LOSER!!

AIEE! THEY'RE ALL GLOATING ALREADY!!

HMM! ...BUT NO MATTER HOW FAMOUS OR INFAMOUS SHE IS, SHE PROBABLY WON'T BE FOUND SO EASILY.
SHE'S NOT THE TYPE TO GROW OLD GRACEFULLY, SO SHE'S PROBABLY USING JUTSU TO MASK HER APPEARANCE.

EVEN THOUGH SHE'S ACTUALLY FIFTY, SHE PROBABLY LOOKS LIKE SHE'S STILL IN HER TWENTIES...
SHHFL
SHHFL

AND THAT'S NOT ALL. THE WORD I HEAR ON THE WIND OF LATE IS SHE'S STARTED TRANSFORMING ON THE FLY...
GOING FROM HER TEENS TO HER THIRTIES OR FORTIES, ALL SO SHE CAN CUT OUT ON ANY MONEYLENDERS SHE'S IN TOO DEEP WITH...

...
THAT'S TERRIBLE... YEESH.
SHHFL
SHHFL

TSUNADE'S LOVED GAMBLING SINCE SHE WAS A KID.
BUT BOTH HER LUCK AND HER SKILL ARE TOTALLY ABYSMAL...

BECAUSE SHE KEPT GETTING MARKED BY EVERYONE AROUND HER, THAT NICKNAME STUCK.
AND SO SHE'S ALWAYS IN DEBT AND ON THE RUN... WOW.
THIS IS NO TIME FOR TRIPS DOWN MEMORY LANE, OLD MAN!

SO, HOW DO WE HUNT HER DOWN?!

WHO KNOWS ...
OUR ONLY CHOICE IS TO DO IT BY THE BOOK. BUT THERE ARE PLENTY OF WAYS...

WHAT?!
ARE YOU SAYING YOU DON'T EVEN KNOW HOW LONG THIS IS GOING TO TAKE?!

THE TIME SPENT WON'T BE A COMPLETE WASTE.

'CUZ THE WHOLE TIME WE'RE ON THE ROAD, I'M GOING TO FOCUS ON YOU!

ME?

IT'LL BE TIME SPENT ON MAKING YOU STRONGER ...

TRAINING TIME!

!!

ALL RIGHT!!
FASH
NO, NO... I TOLD YOU, NOT THAT THING...
I DON'T WANT TO WALK NEXT TO SOMEONE WEARING **THAT**...

THIRD ANNIVERSARY CELEBRATION!

祝三周年

KISHIMOTO-SAN, PLEASE STAY HEALTHY
AND KEEP WORKING HARD

大久保 章

AKIRA OKUBO

Number 150: Training Begins...?!

SO, HEY! HEY! PERVY SAGE!
AMBLE
AMBLE
HURRY UP AND TEACH ME SOMETHING!!

NOW, NOW, STOP BEING SO IMPATIENT...
IT WOULD BE POINTLESS TO JUST TRAIN WITHOUT COLLECTING INTELLIGENCE ON TSUNADE AT THE SAME TIME.
COLLECT INTELLIGENCE?

Number 150: Training Begins...?!

IN THIS CITY.

SCREEECH

WHF

WHOA!!

MUR MUR

MMBL

CHATTR

MUR MUR

CHATTR

CHATTR

MUR MUR

READ THIS WAY

わたあめ
たこ焼
CHATR
MTR MTR
JABBR

HEY!
LOOK!
CHATTER
CHATTER
祭

WOW! THIS IS COOL!
I'VE NEVER BEEN IN A PLACE LIKE THIS!
HUNH HUNH
CHATTER
CHATTER
PLAY IS JUST AS IMPORTANT AS WORK! REST FIRST, AND THEN WE'LL START TRAINING AGAIN.

THIS FESTIVAL WILL PROBABLY GO FOR A WHILE, SO...
WE'LL STAY HERE WHILE IT'S GOING ON.
WE'LL TRAIN HERE TOO.
YES!!
SHUUUUF
SCRREEP

SHAKE SHAKE
TA
DA
なるとさいふ

HO! YOU GOT QUITE A FORTUNE THERE!
YOU MILLION-AIRE!!
I DO HAVE QUITE A BIT! I'VE BEEN SAVING UP FROM EACH MISSION HEH HEH HEH HEH.

SEE YA!!
HOLD UP! NARUTO!

!

(*300 RYO IS APPROXIMATELY 3000 YEN, OR 30 DOLLARS.)

I'LL BE IN CHARGE OF YOUR WALLET!
THIS IS ALL YOU'RE ALLOWED TO SPEND TODAY...
WHAT?! JUST 300 RYO*?!

WHAT'S WITH THE "WHAT?!"
DON'T YOU KNOW THE THREE PROHIBITIONS OF THE SHINOBI?!

READ THIS WAY

THE THREE PROHIBITIONS? WHAT'S THAT?!
WHAT! YOU DON'T KNOW THEM?!
THE THREE PROHIBITIONS ARE THE THREE VICES THAT CAN DESTROY A SHINOBI!

AND THOSE THREE VICES ARE: DRINK, PRETTY GIRLS, AND COLD HARD CASH.

THEN IT DOESN'T REALLY AFFECT ME!
I CAN'T DRINK!
OR DATE!

AND I WORKED SO HARD TO SAVE THIS MUCH, I'M NOT REAL EAGER TO SPEND IT.
GAH!
FOOL! DO NOT MOCK BEING FRUGAL.
ONCE YOU START SPENDING MONEY, YOU WON'T BE ABLE TO STOP!!

THE MAGICAL POWER OF MONEY IS A FEARSOME THING!
EVEN TSUNADE, WHOM WE ARE SEARCHING FOR, IS ON THE VERGE OF SELF-DESTRUCTING FROM IT!
YEAH, LIKE YOU'RE IMMUNE TO VICES, PERVY SAGE!
AND TAKE MY PACK INSTEAD! YOU CAN RELY ON MY TRACKER TOAD TO SNIFF OUT MY SCENT.
I'M GOING TO GO START COLLECT-ING INTELLI-GENCE.

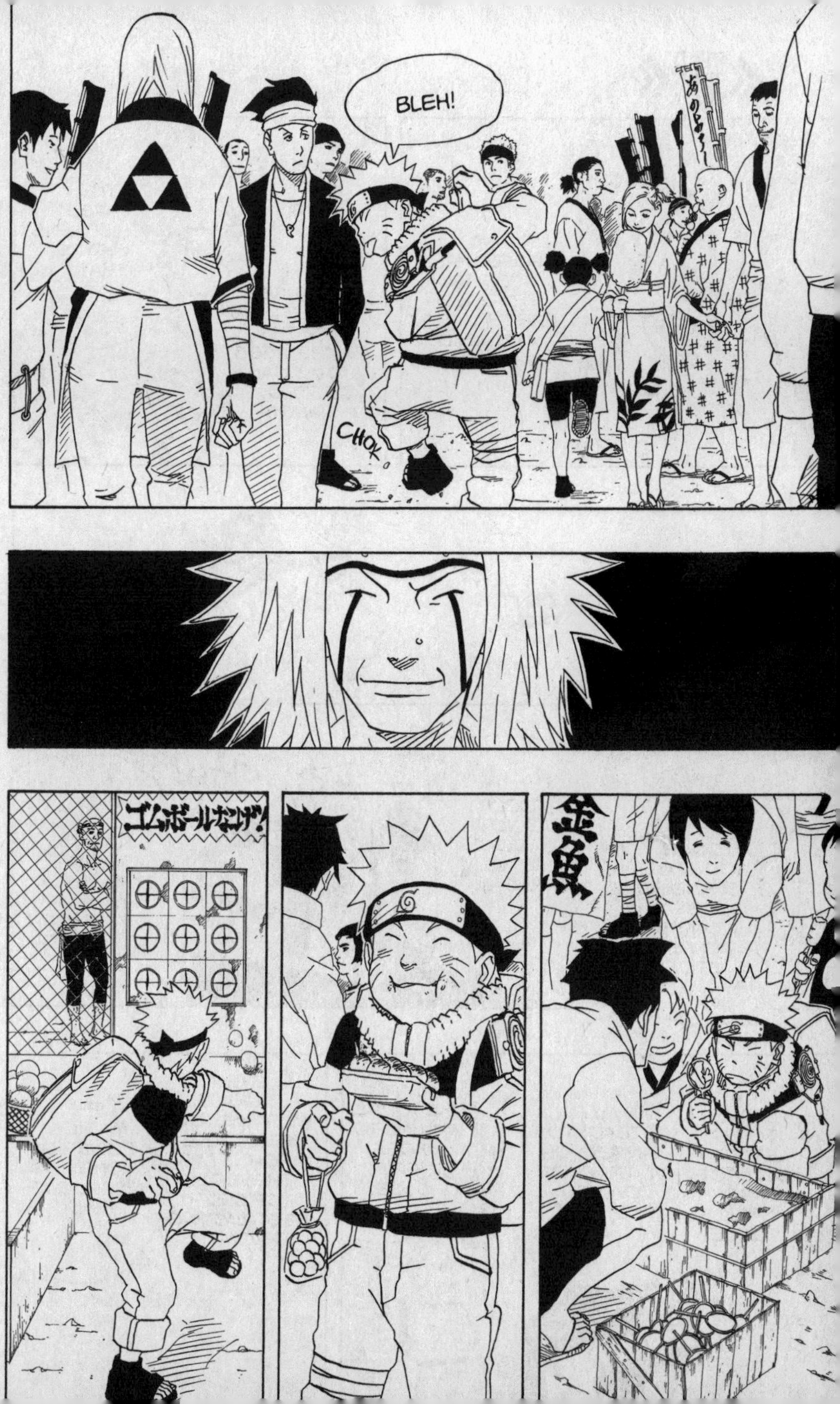

BLEH!
CHOK
ゴムボールなげ!

金魚

READ THIS WAY

串だんご
そば
たこ焼
おでん

FMP
!

YOU KNOW, IF YOU WALK AROUND WITH THAT MASK ON, YOU CAN'T REALLY SEE WHERE YOU'RE GOING!
OWW!

HMM?!

預金通帳
D-1237
自来也

IT'S PERVY SAGE'S SAVINGS PASSBOOK...
RIFLE

IT'S FULL OF ZEROS!

IF HE HAD THAT MUCH, HE COULD HAVE BOUGHT ME SOME-THING!
THAT CHEAP-SKATE!!

THERE'S ONLY A LITTLE BIT LEFT... I GUESS I'M DONE AFTER THE NEXT SHOP...

...

IT'LL BE TIME SPENT ON MAKING YOU STRONGER.
TRAINING TIME!

GRIN

SIZZLE
SIZZLE
SIZZLE
HEY, MISTER! CAN I GET TWO OF THESE SKEWERED SQUIDS?!
SHOO
MAKE ONE A BIG ADULT-SIZED ONE!
SURE! RUNNING ERRANDS EH, LAD!
HERE, YOU CAN HAVE THE KID-SIZED ONE ON THE HOUSE! TAKE IT!!

WOW, YOU'RE THE MAN, MISTER!
HA! YOU GOT THAT RIGHT!
ALL RIGHT, YOU CAN HAVE THE ADULT-SIZED ONE FOR HALF PRICE TOO!!

BUSTLE
BUSTLE
いか焼

HUNH
HUNH
HUH, HOW FAR DID HE GET?!

GYA-HA HA HA HA HA HA!
OH! THAT'S PERVY SAGE'S VOICE!

!
SHUP

GYA-HA HA HA, GOTTA LOVE 'EM!

...

!
HEY... NARUTO! HAVE YOU HAD YOUR FILL OF THE FESTIVAL ALREADY?
!

Reeeeee
...

TELL ME
THOSE
THREE
PROHIBITIONS
AGAIN!!
I THINK
YOU GOT
YOURSELF
AN INSTANT
TRIFECTA!!

SLIP

SPENDING
MY HARD-
EARNED
MONEY
LIKE WATER!
IF YOU'RE
GOING TO
DO SUCH A
THING, YOU
BETTER
START
TRAINING
ME ASAP!!

SPLAT

BONK
BONK
N...
NARUTO,
STOP!
I'M SORRY,
OK, H...HEY!!

YO!!
LOOKIE
WHATCHA
DONE,
BRAT!

!

YOU'VE MUSSED UP MY BRO'S TOP-SHELF COAT!
DO YA KNOW HOW MUCH THIS HERE COAT COSTS?! PAY UP!
100,000 RYO !!
WHAT?!! THAT CHEAP-LOOKING COAT COSTS 100,000 RYO?!
100,000 RYO FOR SUCH AN **UGLY** COAT IS A BIT MUCH, DONCHA THINK...

WHAT, YOU WANNA FIGHT?! EH?!
THAT AIN'T A WISE DECISION, I TELL YA!
BRO'S A FORMER IWAGAKURE CHÛNIN AND A SUPER-NINJA WHO WAS FEARED AS THE LEGENDARY NINJA OF THE DARK!
EH? LEGENDARY... WHAT?

IT SEEMS YOU'RE ITCHING TO GET HURT!!
GRAHH
NAR-UTO...
FWOOSH
!

GREAT TIMING... I CAN SHOW YOU THE JUTSU THAT I'M GOING TO BE TEACHING YOU.
SO WATCH CLOSELY!
ZZWIRRRRRRRRR
!
THUD
!!

SHHHK
BLAST
WAA
AA
AH!!

READ
THIS
WAY

A... AWESOME!

BOING

SHAF
SQUISH

...

HMM...

TMP
TMP
HERE, TAKE THIS FOR REPAIRS. SORRY ABOUT THAT... DIDN'T MEAN TO DESTROY YOUR STAND...
...

...WH... WHO ARE YOU...
YOU KNOW, I HELD BACK QUITE A BIT ON THAT...
YOU ALL ARE WEAK.

HEY MISTER! CAN I BUY ALL OF YOUR WATER BALLOONS AND REGULAR BALLOONS WHILE I'M AT IT?
SURE, I GUESS...
...

...
THAT WAS NO ORDINARY PALM PRESS...> WHAT THE HECK WAS THAT, THAT JUTSU JUST NOW...?!!

NARUTO! COME ON!
LET'S GO TRAIN!

YEAH!!

I'M STARTING TO FEEL IT!

HERE! TAKE THIS WATER BALLOON!
TOSS
!
BOING

BOING
BOING
HUH?! WHAT'S THIS FOR?!

YOU WERE WATCH-ING JUST NOW, WEREN'T YOU?
YUP!
WHAT DID THE JUTSU LOOK LIKE TO YOU?

HIS LINE OF SIGHT'S A BIT OFF, BUT... I GUESS THAT'S GOOD ENOUGH...
...
GRIN

IT SEEMED LIKE THE ENEMY WAS SPUN AROUND A LOT...
MMM ...

SPLISH SPLASH
THAT'S RIGHT... ROTATION'S PROBABLY THE BEST WORD.
PAK

WITH THE **WALK ON WATER** TECHNIQUE, YOU LEARNED TO CONTINUOUSLY EMIT A TINY AMOUNT OF CHAKRA... YOU'VE ALREADY GOT THOSE TWO UNDER YOUR BELT...
WITH THE **TREE-CLIMBING** TECHNIQUE, YOU LEARNED TO FOCUS AND MAINTAIN A SET AMOUNT OF CHAKRA EMISSION FROM SPECIFIC AREAS OF YOUR BODY.

HE'S SWIRLING THE WATER INSIDE THE BALLOON...
...WITHOUT MOVING HIS HAND?!
POP
WHOA!!

CREATE A STREAM OF CHAKRA...

SO! NOW, WITH THIS WATER BALLOON EXERCISE YOU'LL LEARN TO CREATE A STREAM OF CHAKRA.
IN OTHER WORDS, ROTATION!

WELL, I'LL EXPLAIN THE JUTSU MORE FULLY AFTER YOU'VE ACCOMPLISHED THIS FIRST STEP.

FIRST, YOU'LL USE THE GIST OF THE TREE-CLIMBING TECHNIQUE TO FOCUS AND MAINTAIN CHAKRA EMISSION FROM YOUR PALM.
AND THEN YOU'LL USE THE GIST OF THE WALK ON WATER TECHNIQUE TO CONTINUOUSLY EMIT CHAKRA OUT OF YOUR PALM.
THE POINT OF THIS EXERCISE IS TO USE THAT CHAKRA TO AGITATE AND SPIN THE WATER INSIDE THE BALLOON!!

GOT IT!
SO I NEED TO ROTATE THE WATER FAST ENOUGH SO THAT THE BALLOON POPS, RIGHT!!

YOUR PERCEPTION'S GETTING SHARPER AND SHARPER!
ALL RIGHT, LET'S GO AT IT UNTIL DARK!
YES, SIR!!

Number 151: The Hook...!!

Chirp

Chirp

Snore
UGH...
THUNK

MM ...?
SHF

TWITCH TWITCH

Number 151: The Hook...!!

NARUTO
-ナルト-

READ THIS WAY

KLAK

MEEOW
!

SHOO, TIME TO GO DOWNSTAIRS.
MEW

HEY, WHERE'S THE BATH-ROOM?

THIS IS BAD, EVEN IF I DON'T HAVE TO WEAVE SIGNS...
TWITCH TWITCH

...

SSSSHOO...

GLUG GLUG
GLUG GLUG

SPLISH SPLISH
YES!
THE WATER'S SWIRLING AROUND!!
SPLISH
SPLISH
I THINK IT'S GONNA BE EASIER TO POP THIS THING THAN I THOUGHT!
WELL, I'M GOING TO GO CATCH SOME Z'S UNTIL YOU'RE DONE.
WHOOO
AT THIS RATE, YOU'RE NOT EVEN GONNA GET A NAP!
GRIN

CAW
CAW
NGA-HHH NGA-HHH...
...
Splich Splich
ARGH! SHEESH! WHY WON'T YOU BURST, EH!
SQUEEZE
SPLASH
...!
HUNHH ...?

HO... DID YOU GET IT...?
UNF
DOINK!
...
SSHOO SSHOO
OY! THAT WASN'T JUST A NAP...
THAT WAS A GOOD SNOOZE...
PF...
...SO HEY...
HOW DO I GET IT TO POP?
Oomph!
I TOLD YOU, I'M NOT GOING TO EXPLAIN FURTHER UNTIL YOU CAN BURST IT!
...
...

AW, ALL RIGHT...
SIGH
YOU'RE REALLY SUPPOSED TO MASTER JUTSU ...
...ON YOUR OWN, THROUGH TRIAL AND ERROR, BUT...
JUST THIS ONE TIME, I'LL GIVE YOU A FEW HINTS...
NOW MAKE THE WATER SWIRL AROUND!
!!
O-OK!
CHOK
ZPLASH
ZPLASH

READ THIS WAY
IN WHICH DIRECTION ARE YOU IMAGINING THE WATER SWIRLING AROUND... CLOCKWISE OR COUNTER-CLOCKWISE?
UH... COUNTER-CLOCKWISE...
OK, COME OVER HERE.
COME, COME
TAP
?
SHK
HEH.
JUST AS I THOUGHT...
?!
WH... WHAT...?

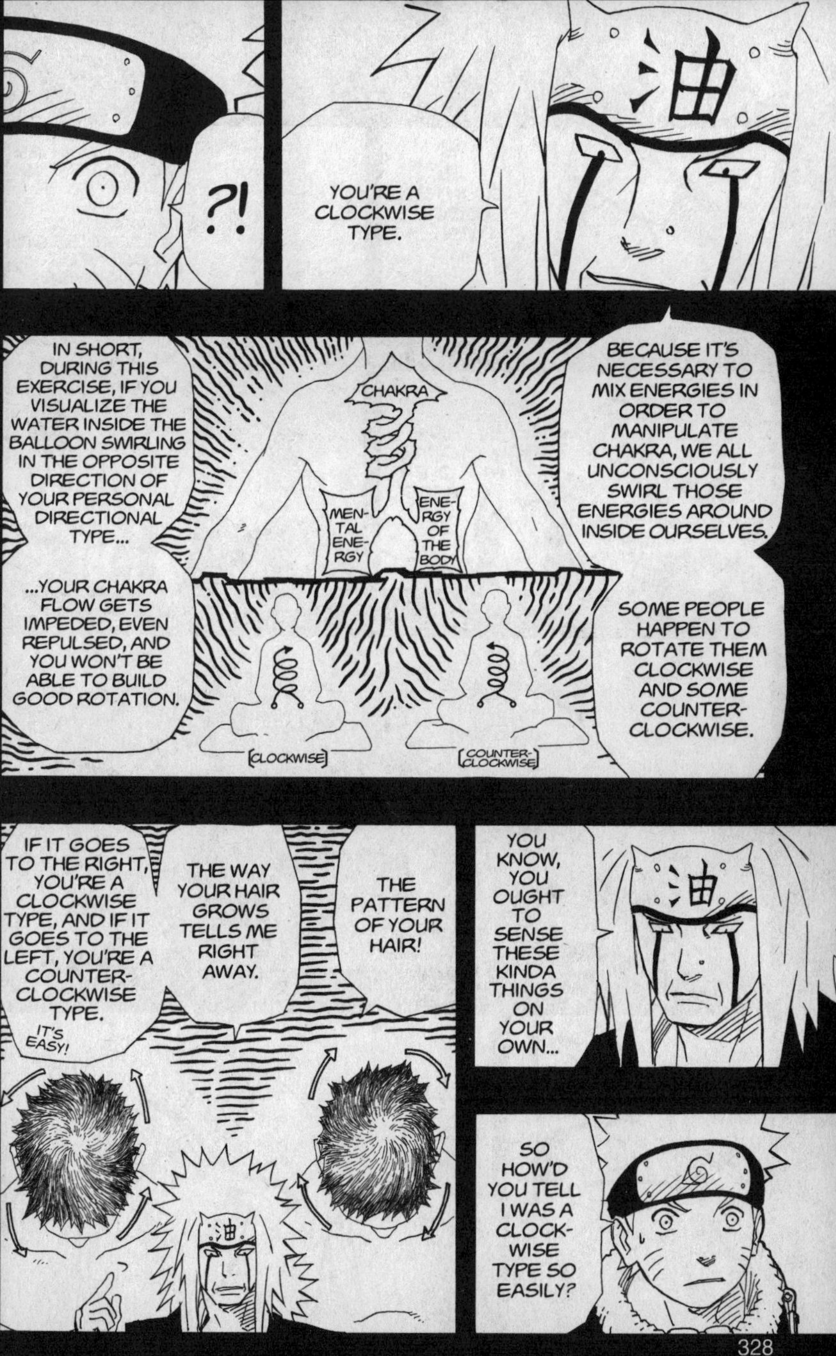
?!
YOU'RE A CLOCKWISE TYPE.
BECAUSE IT'S NECESSARY TO MIX ENERGIES IN ORDER TO MANIPULATE CHAKRA, WE ALL UNCONSCIOUSLY SWIRL THOSE ENERGIES AROUND INSIDE OURSELVES.
SOME PEOPLE HAPPEN TO ROTATE THEM CLOCKWISE AND SOME COUNTER-CLOCKWISE.
CHAKRA
MEN-TAL ENE-RGY
ENE-RGY OF THE BODY
CLOCKWISE
COUNTER-CLOCKWISE
IN SHORT, DURING THIS EXERCISE, IF YOU VISUALIZE THE WATER INSIDE THE BALLOON SWIRLING IN THE OPPOSITE DIRECTION OF YOUR PERSONAL DIRECTIONAL TYPE...
...YOUR CHAKRA FLOW GETS IMPEDED, EVEN REPULSED, AND YOU WON'T BE ABLE TO BUILD GOOD ROTATION.
YOU KNOW, YOU OUGHT TO SENSE THESE KINDA THINGS ON YOUR OWN...
SO HOW'D YOU TELL I WAS A CLOCK-WISE TYPE SO EASILY?
THE PATTERN OF YOUR HAIR!
THE WAY YOUR HAIR GROWS TELLS ME RIGHT AWAY.
IF IT GOES TO THE RIGHT, YOU'RE A CLOCKWISE TYPE, AND IF IT GOES TO THE LEFT, YOU'RE A COUNTER-CLOCKWISE TYPE.
IT'S EASY!

HUH!
SO I'M A CLOCK-WISE TYPE, HUH!
YUP. THAT'S WHY YOU NEED TO IMAGE THAT WATER SWIRLING CLOCK-WISE.
I NEVER THOUGHT ABOUT THESE THINGS BEFORE...
BUT YOU KNOW, THIS JUTSU IS IDEAL FOR YOU.
YOU DON'T NEED TO WEAVE ANY SIGNS. ALL YOU NEED IS CHAKRA.
NO COMPLICATED SEQUENCES TO MEMOR-IZE!
EVEN A DUNCE CAN DO IT!
JAB
ALL RIGHT! NOW THAT I KNOW, THIS JUTSU WILL BE A PIECE OF CAKE...
I'LL MASTER IT IN THREE DAYS!!
...

THIS JUTSU IS ONE OF THE LEGACIES OF THE FOURTH HOKAGE!
IT TOOK LORD FOURTH A FULL THREE **YEARS** TO PERFECT THIS JUTSU...
A LEVEL FIVE OUT OF SIX. SECOND FROM THE TOP!
AN A-RANK SUPER-ADVANCED NINJUTSU.
...

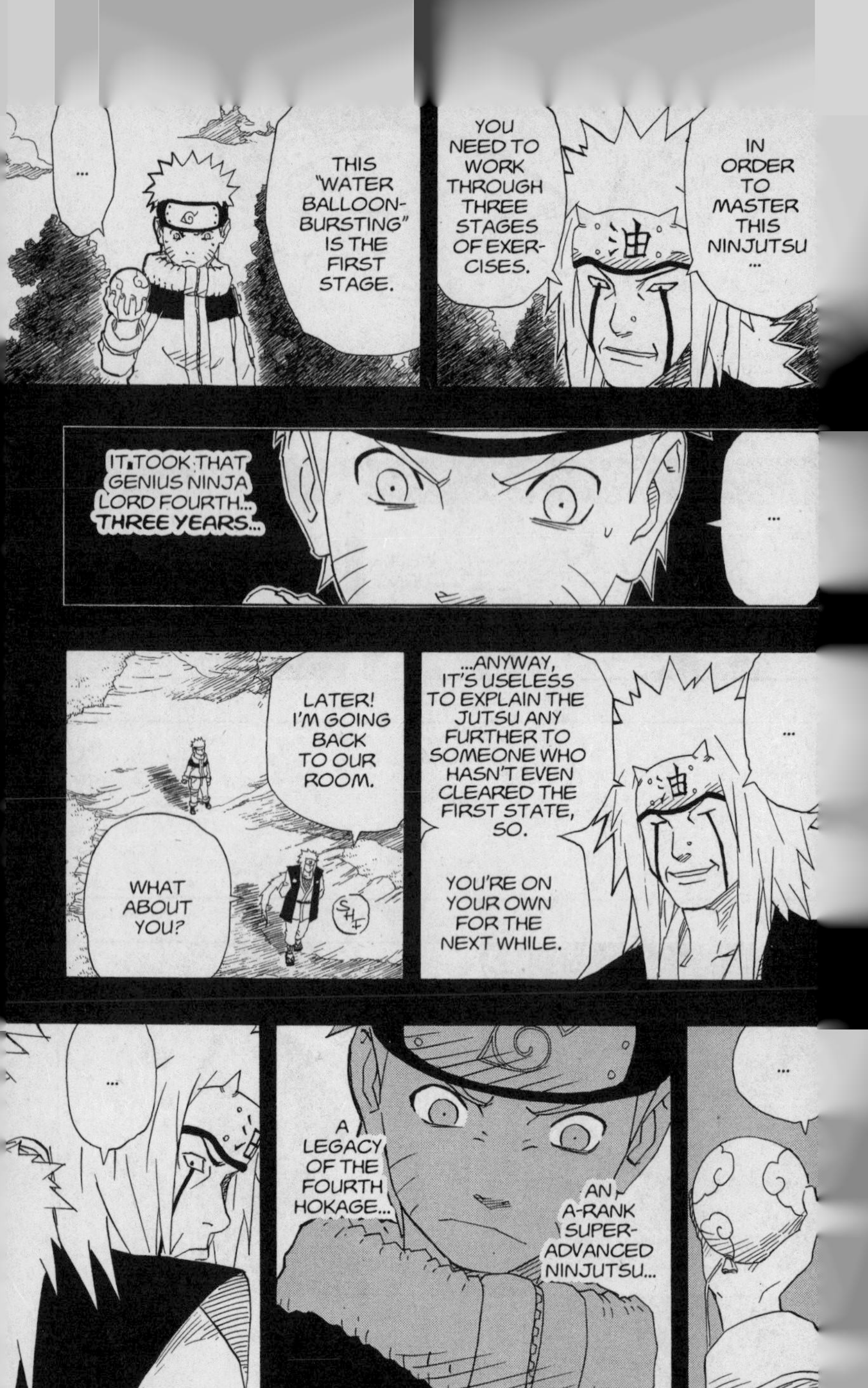
IN ORDER TO MASTER THIS NINJUTSU...
YOU NEED TO WORK THROUGH THREE STAGES OF EXER-CISES.
THIS "WATER BALLOON-BURSTING" IS THE FIRST STAGE.
...
...
IT TOOK THAT GENIUS NINJA LORD FOURTH... THREE YEARS...
...
...ANYWAY, IT'S USELESS TO EXPLAIN THE JUTSU ANY FURTHER TO SOMEONE WHO HASN'T EVEN CLEARED THE FIRST STATE, SO.
YOU'RE ON YOUR OWN FOR THE NEXT WHILE.
WHAT ABOUT YOU?
LATER! I'M GOING BACK TO OUR ROOM.
...
AN A-RANK SUPER-ADVANCED NINJUTSU...
A LEGACY OF THE FOURTH HOKAGE...
...

NAH, I'M GONNA STAY HERE A LITTLE LONGER!
GRIN
WELL THEN...
DON'T OVERDO IT!

ZWIRL ZWIRL

GAH!

IT'S BEEN THREE DAYS ALREADY SINCE PERVY SAGE GAVE ME THAT HINT...

HUF HUF

AND I CAN NOW STRETCH THE RUBBER THIS MUCH, SO WHY WON'T IT BURST?!

HUF HUF

HUF HUF HUF

WHY...?!

I MUST STILL BE DOING SOMETHING DIFFERENT THAN PERVY SAGE...

PURRR PURRR

!

PURRRR
Boing
Boin

HEY!
SHOO
THAT'S NOT A TOY...

THWAP
THWAP
BOING BOING

THWAP

POP!
WHEEE
THACK
MEW!!

...THAT'S IT...!

WAKE UP ALREADY!
HEY! PERVY SAGE!!

READ THIS WAY

WHOOSH

HEH
HEH
HEH.

MM
HH...?!

POP!
SPLATTER
WHA?!

FIRST
STATE
CLEARED!

THE WORLD OF KISHIMOTO MASASHI
MY PERSONAL HISTORY, PART 25

ACCEPTED FOR THE HOP☆STEP AWARD! I HAD WON! THE WINNING WORK FOR THAT MONTH'S HOP☆STEP AWARD WAS PROMISED PRINTING IN *AKAMURU JUMP*. "FINALLY, MY MANGA WILL BE SEEN BY THE WORLD!" I RECALL BEING SO OVERJOYED THAT I PRANCED AROUND, TALKING TO MYSELF IN A HIGH-PITCHED VOICE AND LAUGHING AT HOME. I WANTED TO TELL SOMEONE HOW HAPPY I WAS! SO I IMMEDIATELY CALLED MY PARENTS' HOUSE. MY MOTHER ANSWERED.

MASASHI: "MOM! I WON JUMP'S HOP☆STEP AWARD! I'VE BEEN ACCEPTED! ACCEPTED!"
MA: "WHAT? ACCEPTED FOR WHAT?"
MASASHI: "...UH...! UM... JUMP CHOOSES FROM AMONG SUBMITTED ENTRIES OF NEWCOMER ARTISTS AND GIVES THEM AN AWARD. I GOT PICKED FOR AN AWARD FOR PEOPLE WHO WILL ONE DAY BECOME MANGA ARTISTS!"
MA: "WHO?"
MASASHI: "ME, I DID!"
MA: "AHH, I SEE! GOOD FOR YOU..."
MASASHI: "SO NOW I'M ONE STEP CLOSER TO BECOMING A MANGA ARTIST! I'M GOING TO START DRAWING MORE AND MORE MANGA... AND..."
MA: "SO, ARE YOU EATING PROPERLY?"
MASASHI: "...💧"
MA: "DON'T YOU BE EATING THOSE GROCERY STORE RAMEN! YOU HAVE TO EAT YOUR VEGGIES!"
MASASHI: "..."
MA: "AND EAT STEWED THINGS! IT'S GOOD FOR YOU!"
MASASHI: "...ALL RIGHT... HEY, I GOTTA GO... MY CALLING CARD'S ALMOST EMPTY..."
MA: "SURE! WELL THEN... TAKE CARE OF YOURSELF!"
MASASHI: "YEAH..."

SHE DIDN'T REALLY GET MY HAPPINESS... IT SEEMS MY MA WAS MORE CONCERNED ABOUT MY HEALTH THAN ABOUT A MANGA AWARD. SO I THOUGHT I WOULD START CHURNING OUT MANGA WHILE WATCHING MY HEALTH. THAT HELPED COOL ME OFF FROM MY HIGH.

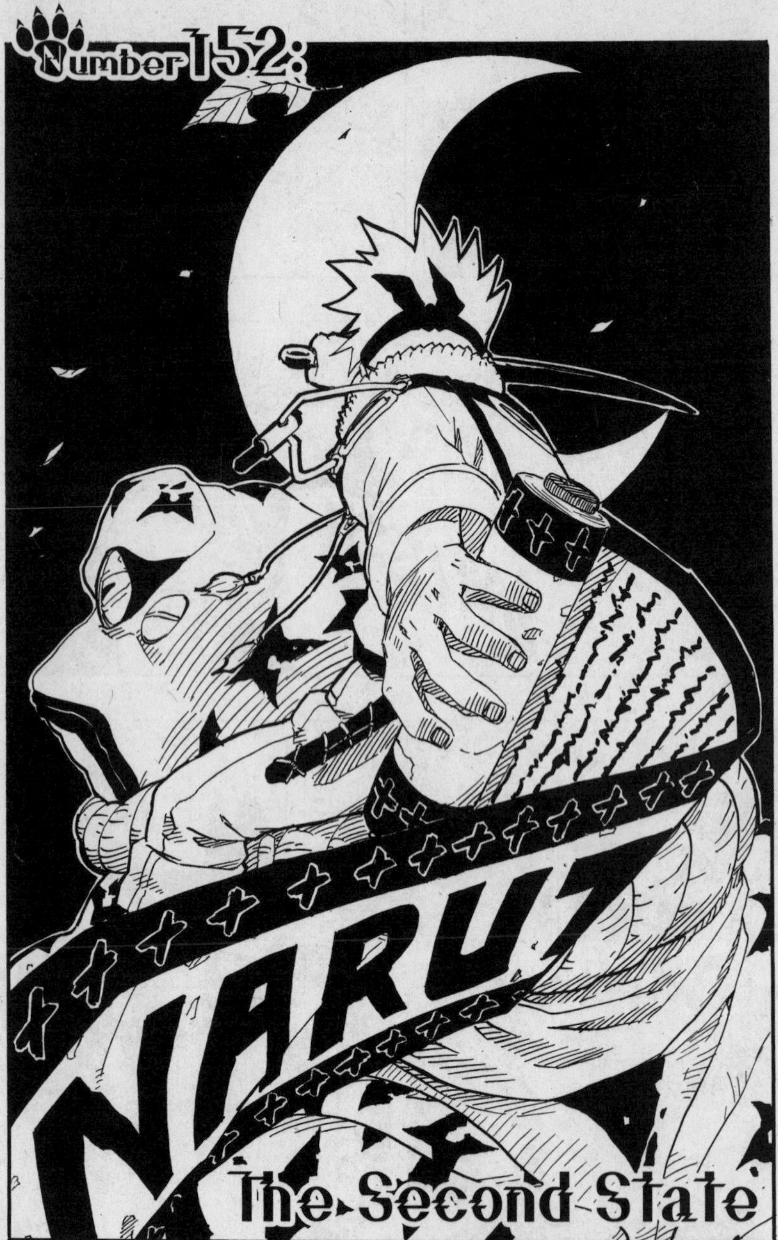
Number 152:
NARUTO
The Second State

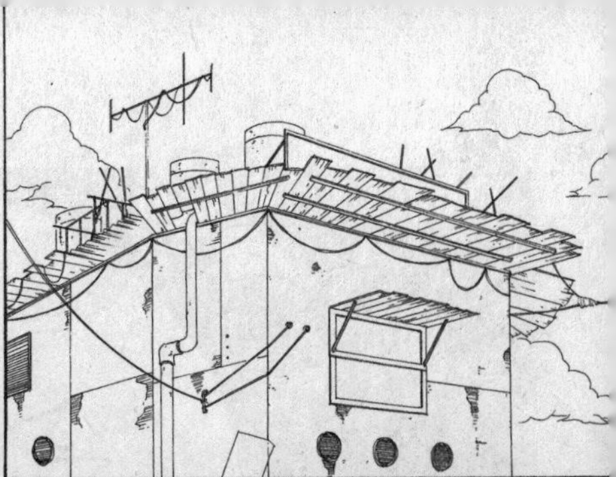

WELL THEN...
WHY DON'T YOU SHOW ME...
Rub Rub

HERE WE GO! WATCH CLOSELY!!
WHSSH

...
HIS LEFT HAND...?

SHUUF

GRRRR
HAAAH!!

SWWWWWWWWIRL

GLU GLU GLUG
GLU GLUG
SLURG
SLURG SLURG
VWOOH
POP!
YEAH!!
SEE! I DID IT!

ZZZ SSS...
FMP
HEYYY! YOU FELL ASLEEP!

CHIRP
CHIRP
...

AWW, SORRY, MY BAD...
I'VE BEEN OUT SO LATE COL-LECTING INTELLI-GENCE, I'M BEAT.
...YEAH, RIGHT, I BET YOU ARE!!

...HOWEVER...
ZRISH
ZRISH
ZRISH
YAH!
TO MAKE THE WATER SWIRL AROUND BY HOLDING THE WATER BALLOON IN HIS LEFT HAND AND BRINGING HIS RIGHT HAND TO IT... IT'S A BIT UNORTHODOX, BUT... HE'S SUCH A FUNNY FELLOW.

WELL... I DO HAVE TO SAY, I'M QUITE IMPRESSED YOU WERE ABLE TO GRASP THE TECHNIQUE IN SUCH A SHORT TIME...
IT'S ALL THANKS TO HIM!

HIS NAME IS SHOO!
SWAY
SWAY
MEW

?

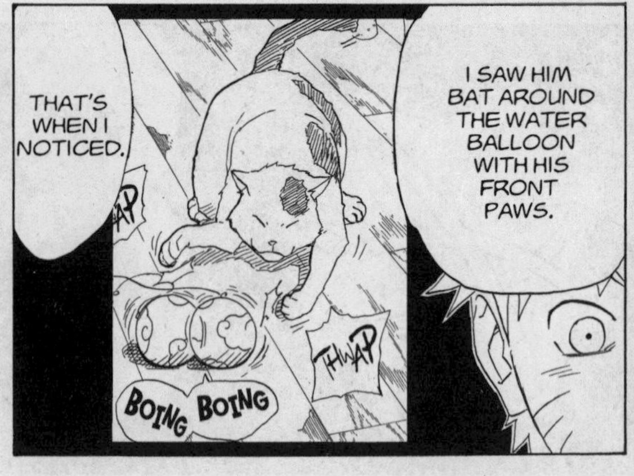
I SAW HIM BAT AROUND THE WATER BALLOON WITH HIS FRONT PAWS.
THWAP
THAT'S WHEN I NOTICED.
BOING BOING

BECAUSE HE KEPT BATTING AT IT OVER AND OVER...
BOING BOING
THE WATER INSIDE WAS SWIRLING AROUND IN ALL DIFFERENT DIRECTIONS...
SPLISH SPLISH
AND THEN IT CAME TO ME!

WHAT CAME TO YOU?

I REMEM-
BERED
THAT THE
WATER
BALLOON
GOT ALL
LUMPY...
THE FIRST
TIME YOU
SHOWED
ME THIS
EXERCISE.
SPLURG
SPLURG
SPLURG
SPLURG
SPLURG

UNTIL NOW,
I HAD BEEN
FOCUSING ON
SWIRLING THE
WATER IN
ONLY ONE
DIRECTION...
ZWIRL

I
REALIZED
THAT...
...YOUR
WATER
BALLOON
WAS
ALL
LUMPY...
... BECAUSE
YOU WERE
SWIRLING THE
WATER
AROUND IN
MANY
DIFFERENT
DIRECTIONS.

...

SO,
I KINDA
IMPROVISED,
AND WHEN
I TRIED IT
OUT...
...IT
BURST!

READ THIS WAY

...
IT SEEMS IT'S STILL BEYOND HIM TO AGITATE HIS CHAKRA WITH ONE HAND, BUT...
HE DID DO PRETTY WELL, CONSIDERING... I GUESS.

HEH HEH HEH HEH

ALL RIGHT, YOU'VE CLEARED THE FIRST STATE.
POMP
POMP
YESSSSS!!
MEOW!
THUMP

OWW!!
SZZZ

...
THE TOLL ON HIS KEIRAKUKEI* IS STARTING TO SHOW.

(*CHAKRA NETWORK)

...AND THE SECOND STATE DEFINITELY WON'T BE AS EASY.

OK! SO LET'S START WORKING THE SECOND STATE.
YAY!
FINALLY, I'M GOING TO GET SOME-WHERE!

HERE.
TOSS
?!

WHA!
NOT THIS AGAIN!

...!
...A RUBBER BALL...?
SHAP
SQUSH

THIS TIME, YOU'RE GOING TO TRY BURSTING ONE OF THESE!
WOMP

POP!

WHOA!

IT'S A HUNDRED TIMES STIFFER THAN A WATER BALLOON.

...

...
WHSSSH

WHUP
WHUP
WHUP
WHUP
WHUP WHUP

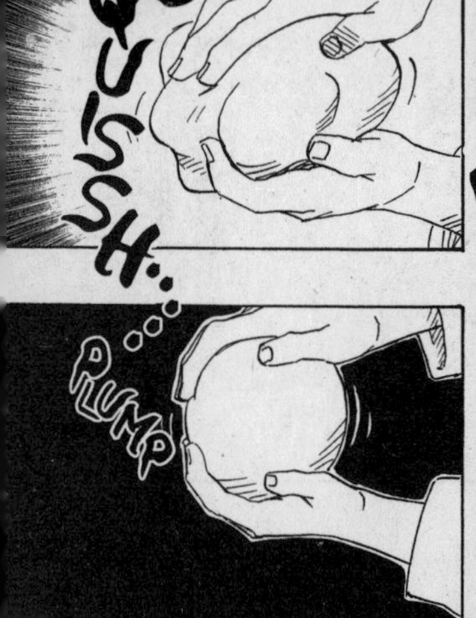
SQUISSH...
...PLUMP

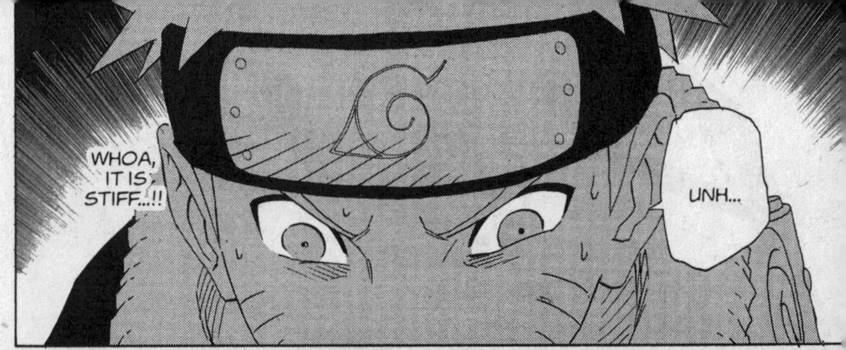
UNH...
WHOA, IT IS STIFF...!!

THE FIRST STATE IS ABOUT ROTATION, THE SECOND ABOUT POWER.
BECAUSE THERE'S NO WATER INSIDE...
...IT'S HARDER TO VISUALIZE AND THUS SWIRL YOUR CHAKRA AROUND.
!
SO GOOD LUCK...
...
...I WONDER IF THERE'S A KNACK TO THIS TOO...

WELL THEN, I'M OFF TO COLLECT MORE INFO...
OH! HEY! WAIT!
LET'S TRAIN TOGETHER TODAY!
DON'T BE SUCH A BABY! I THINK YOU'VE MISUNDER-STOOD SOMETHING...
I DID PROMISE TO TEACH YOU JUTSU, BUT I NEVER SAID I WOULD HOLD YOUR HAND AND WALK YOU THROUGH IT.
IF YOU CAN'T MASTER IT ON YOUR OWN, THAT'S IT.
STOP BEING SO JUVENILE... AND START ACTING LIKE A PROPER SHINOBI!
ALL RIGHT, ALL RIGHT...
SO WHAT ABOUT... GIVING ME SOME SORT OF HINT AGAIN, AT LEAST, EH...

YOU'RE NOT PROPER, EITHER!!
AND YOU'RE A DIRTY GROWN-UP!!
GRRRR

PAY UP.
GIMME

...

HUF
HUF
URRR
URRR
SIGH. UNH-UH, IT'S NOT EVEN CLOSE TO BURST-ING!

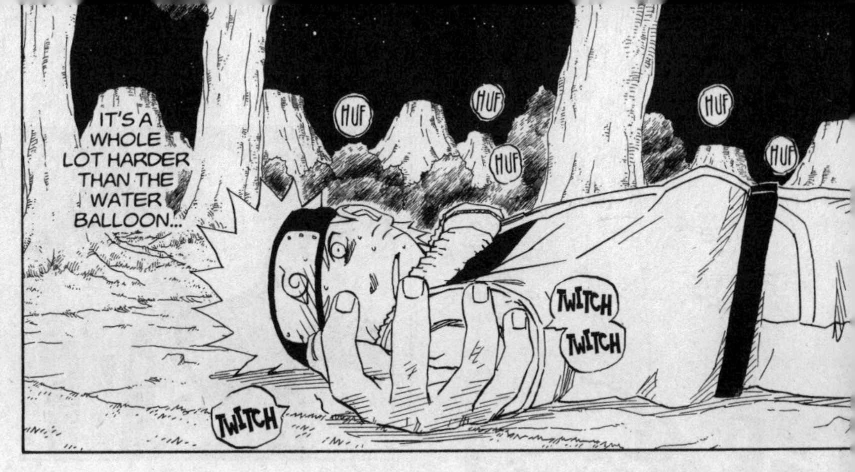

HUF
HUF
HUF
HUF
HUF
IT'S A WHOLE LOT HARDER THAN THE WATER BALLOON...
TWITCH
TWITCH
TWITCH

AND... BOTH OF MY HANDS AND ARMS HURT THIS TIME...
TWITCH
TWITCH
HUF
THROB
THROB
URRR
THROB
TWITCH TWITCH
HUF

HUF
HUF
HUF
HUF
HUF

THAT'S WHY THIS JUTSU IS CONSIDERED A LEVEL FIVE OUT OF SIX. SECOND FROM THE TOP!
DON'T BE SUCH A BABY! I THINK YOU'VE MISUNDERSTOOD SOMETHING...

DARN IT!
URRR
HUF
HUF
HOW MANY DAYS HAVE I BEEN AT IT ALREADY!!

HEY, NARUTO!
HUF
HUF
HUF

...WHAT IS IT...?
HUF
HUF
HUF

GO DOWN INTO THE CITY
AND BUY US BOTH LUNCHES, WILL YA.
WHO, ME!?!

YOU KNOW... YOU ARE MY DISCIPLE, AFTER ALL. ♡
HUMPH
...

CHATTER
BUSTLE
CHATTER

HEY, DADDY! CAN YOU BUY ME A POPSICLE?
ALL RIGHT, LET'S GET THIS ONE, THEN... ONE THAT WE CAN SPLIT.
!

HE WON'T TEACH ME ANYTHING...
AND YET HE'LL PULL MASTER RANK ON ME.

AWW, BUT I CAN FINISH IT ALL BY MYSELF!
NO, NO!
MOMMY'S WAITING AT HOME WITH LUNCH ALL COOKED.

NNG

SNAP

READ THIS WAY

BUSTLE
BUSTLE
たいやき

...

...HEY... I WAS WONDERING...

...IF JUST FOR A BIT...
YOU COULD WATCH ME TRAIN... TODAY...?
I DON'T HAVE THE TIME... I'M NOT EVEN GOING TO SIT AND EAT HERE.
I'M GOING TO SCARF IT DOWN ON MY WAY INTO THE CITY.

...

...

IF YOU CAN'T THINK IT THROUGH AND FIGURE OUT THE KNACKS ON YOUR OWN...
...YOU'LL NEVER GET BETTER.

I ALREADY TOLD YOU THREE WEEKS AGO, STOP BEING SUCH A BABY... DIDN'T I?
YOU'RE A NINJA!

...
HEH HEH!
OF COURSE, YOU DON'T HAVE TO TELL ME THAT!!

HUF
HUF
HUF
URRR
DARN IT... NO MATTER HOW HARD I TRY, I CAN'T BURST IT...
ALL I'M DOING IS JUST DRAINING MY CHAKRA.

AND EVERY TIME I LET MY CHAKRA FLOW, IT'S LIKE MY NERVES ARE GETTING STABBED, AND PAIN SHOOTS DOWN MY ARMS AND HANDS...
THE MORE I INCREASE THE VOLUME OF CHAKRA FLOW, THE WORSE THE PAIN...
THROB
THROB
THROB

READ THIS WAY

BUT... SOME-HOW...
I GET THIS FEELING THAT... UNLESS I MAKE MY CHAKRA EXPLODE...
HUF
LIKE IN A SINGLE BLAST, IT WON'T BURST...
HUF

...

!

THAT'S IT!!
URK

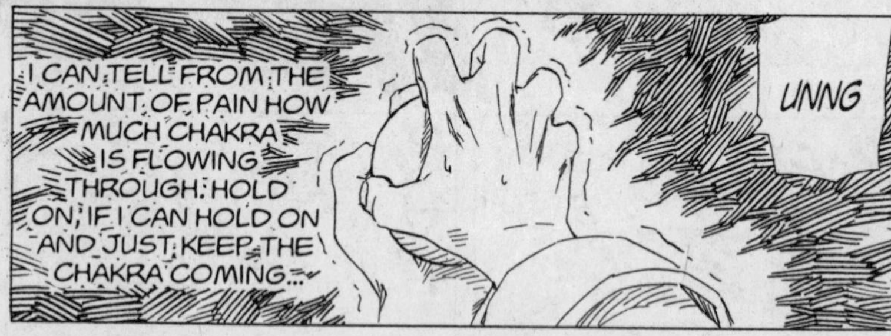
UNNG
I CAN TELL FROM THE AMOUNT OF PAIN HOW MUCH CHAKRA IS FLOWING THROUGH. HOLD ON, IF I CAN HOLD ON AND JUST KEEP THE CHAKRA COMING...

THROB
THROB
UGGH!
NOT YET... NO, NOT YET. J-JUST A... LITTLE BIT MORE...
THROB

NOW!!
WHUP
WHUP
WHUP
WHUP
WHUP

THROB

OWW!!

ARGH!

BOP

BOP

THROB

PSHHH

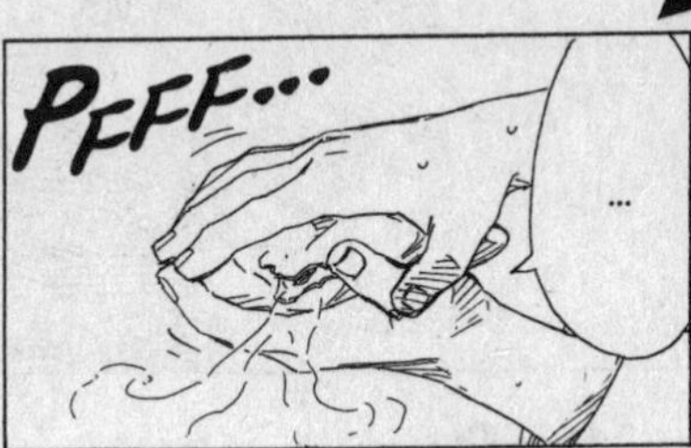
PFFF...
...

HO... IT LOOKS LIKE YOU'VE MADE SOME PRO-GRESS...
TAP
!

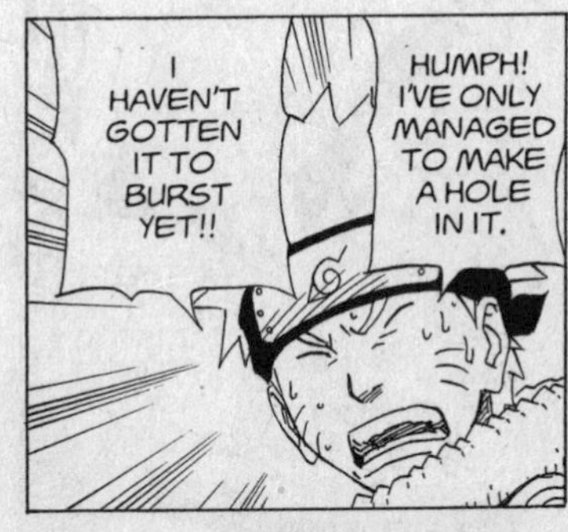
HUMPH! I'VE ONLY MANAGED TO MAKE A HOLE IN IT.
I HAVEN'T GOTTEN IT TO BURST YET!!

AW, COME ON. DON'T BE SO HUFFY.
HERE!
!

HERE
CONGRAT-ULATIONS FOR GETTING THIS FAR ON YOUR OWN!

...

HEH HEH...
NOW THAT YOU'VE MADE IT TO THIS POINT, THE REST IS JUST KNACK...
SHALL WE TRY SOMETHING OUT...?

HUH?! WHAT?! WHAT IS IT?!
GIVE ME YOUR RIGHT HAND.

HMM?
WHAT IS IT?

THE WORLD OF KISHIMOTO MASASHI
MY PERSONAL HISTORY, PART 26

BACK THEN, I DIDN'T HAVE A PHONE IN MY ROOM, SO I WAS MAKING AND RECEIVING CALLS FROM MY BOARDINGHOUSE LANDLORD'S PHONE. THE NIGHT THE AWARDS ANNOUNCEMENT WAS PRINTED IN *JUMP*, I RECEIVED A CALL FROM SHUEISHA'S *JUMP* EDITING DEPARTMENT.

"KISHIMOTO-KUN! I THINK YOU'VE GOT A CALL FROM A *JUMP* EDITOR," MY LANDLORD SAID WHILE STANDING OUTSIDE MY ROOM CLUTCHING THE EXTRA HANDSET OF THE HOME PHONE. (WH...WHAT?!) "UH, OK! I'LL BE RIGHT THERE!" I KICKED OUT OF MY ROOM AND TOOK THE RECEIVER AWAY.

THE HOLD BUTTON OF THE HANDSET WAS BLINKING.

(SH-SHOOT! ARE YOU SAYING THAT I'M CONNECTED TO A J...*JUMP* EDITOR RIGHT NOW?! THIS RECEIVER'S CONNECTED TO *JUMP!*)

I WAS SO NERVOUS THAT I THOUGHT MY HEART WOULD BURST, AND I EVEN FORGOT TO BREATHE.

(...UM, WHAT SHOULD I SAY? HOW AM I SUPPOSED TO TALK TO HIM... U...UH... I-I'VE GOT TO PICK UP THE LINE... I SHOULDN'T KEEP HIM WAITING!) (...BUT I HAVE TO MAKE SURE NOT TO BE DISCOURTEOUS!...)

(OH, MAN, I'M SO NERVOUS! 'CUZ IT'S *JUMP!*)

(AARGH! IT'S NO USE DAWDLING! ONE GIANT NEW STEP FOR MEEE!)

AND WITH THAT, THE YOUNG KISHIMOTO PRESSED THE BUTTON...

BZZZZZZZZ...

I HAD MISTAKENLY PRESSED THE END BUTTON INSTEAD OF THE HOLD BUTTON, AND HUNG UP ON THE *JUMP* EDITOR THAT HAD TAKEN THE TIME TO CALL ME. BUT THE KIND AND GENTLE YAHAGI-SAN GENEROUSLY CHOSE TO CALL THIS INCREDIBLY DISCOURTEOUS FOOL BACK...

"HELLO? THIS IS YAHAGI OF *JUMP*. SORRY WE WERE DISCONNECTED. IS THE RECEPTION BAD WHERE YOU ARE...?"

Number 153: The Searchers!!

THERE YOU GO...
?

...WHAT IS THIS?

TUG

LOOK.
?!

TA-DA

READ THIS WAY

YOU GOT ONE TOO...
BUT WHAT'S IT FOR...?!
CLENCH CLENCH

I'M ABOUT TO TELL YOU.
RUSTLE
?

ALL RIGHT, NARUTO, LOOK AT THIS PIECE OF PAPER.

DA DUM

...

I LOOKED!
GOOD!
NOW LOOK AT IT AGAIN!

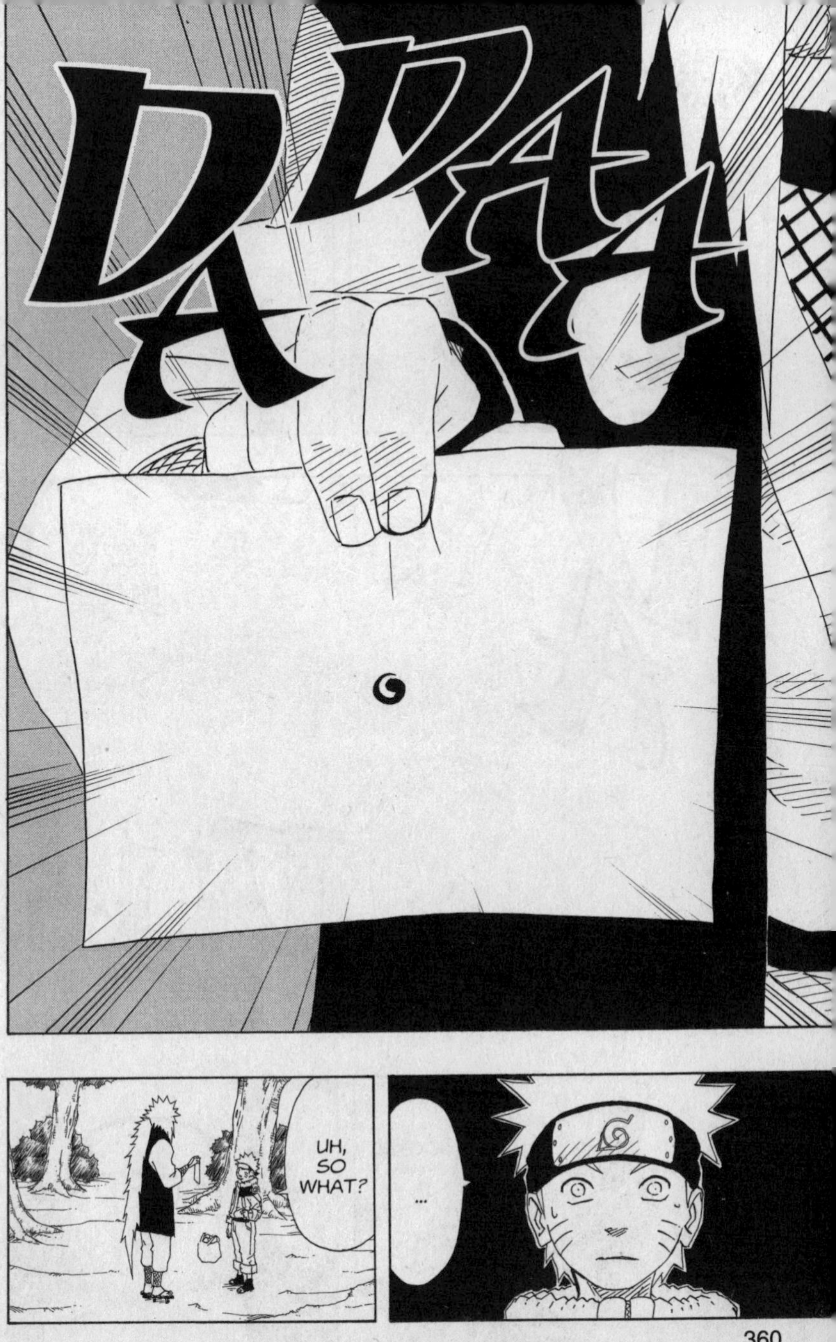

DADAA

...

UH, SO WHAT?

READ
THIS
WAY

HO HO... IT'S NOTHING TOO COMPLI-CATED...
THE FIRST TIME, WHEN YOU WERE LOOKING AT THE BLANK SHEET...
YOU WERE KIND OF LOOKING ALL OVER AT THE ENTIRE THING RIGHT?
油

MMM...
I GUESS.

WELL THEN, WHERE WERE YOU LOOKING ON THE SHEET WITH THE DOT?
PROBABLY AT THE DOT, RIGHT?

YEAH!
THAT'S RIGHT!
NOD

SO? WHAT'S THAT GOT TO DO WITH ANYTHING?

HE REALLY IS SLOW...
THAT'S WHAT'S CALLED FOCUS! CONCEN-TRATION!

...
FOCUS?

NARUTO'S LINE OF SIGHT: THE BLANK SHEET
NARUTO'S LINE OF SIGHT: THE SHEET WITH THE DOT
WHEN YOU LOOK AT A BLANK SHEET OF PAPER, YOUR EYES DON'T KNOW WHAT TO FOCUS ON, SO THEY WANDER AROUND...
BUT IF YOU DRAW EVEN A SINGLE DOT ON IT...
IT BECOMES A FOCAL POINT FOR YOUR EYES, AND THEY INSTANTLY ZOOM IN ON IT.

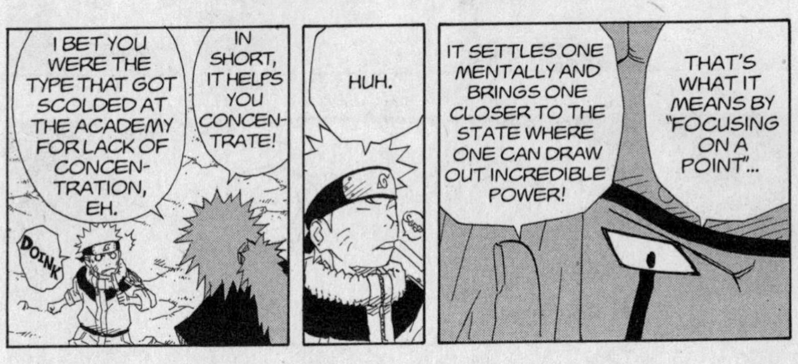
THAT'S WHAT IT MEANS BY "FOCUSING ON A POINT"...
IT SETTLES ONE MENTALLY AND BRINGS ONE CLOSER TO THE STATE WHERE ONE CAN DRAW OUT INCREDIBLE POWER!
HUH.
IN SHORT, IT HELPS YOU CONCEN-TRATE!
I BET YOU WERE THE TYPE THAT GOT SCOLDED AT THE ACADEMY FOR LACK OF CONCEN-TRATION, EH.
DOINK

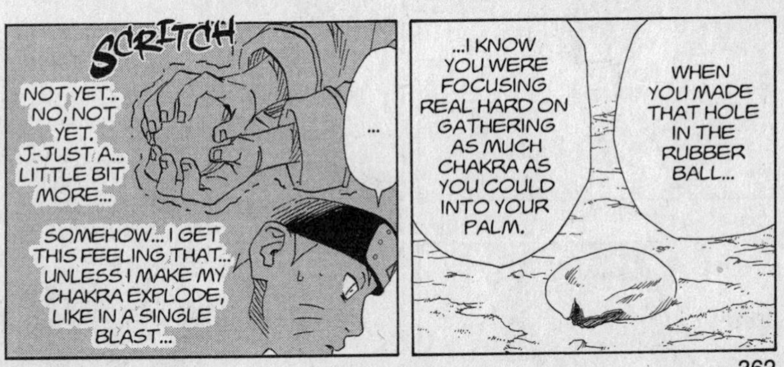
WHEN YOU MADE THAT HOLE IN THE RUBBER BALL...
...I KNOW YOU WERE FOCUSING REAL HARD ON GATHERING AS MUCH CHAKRA AS YOU COULD INTO YOUR PALM.
...
SCRITCH
NOT YET... NO, NOT YET. J-JUST A... LITTLE BIT MORE...
SOMEHOW... I GET THIS FEELING THAT... UNLESS I MAKE MY CHAKRA EXPLODE, LIKE IN A SINGLE BLAST...

READ THIS WAY

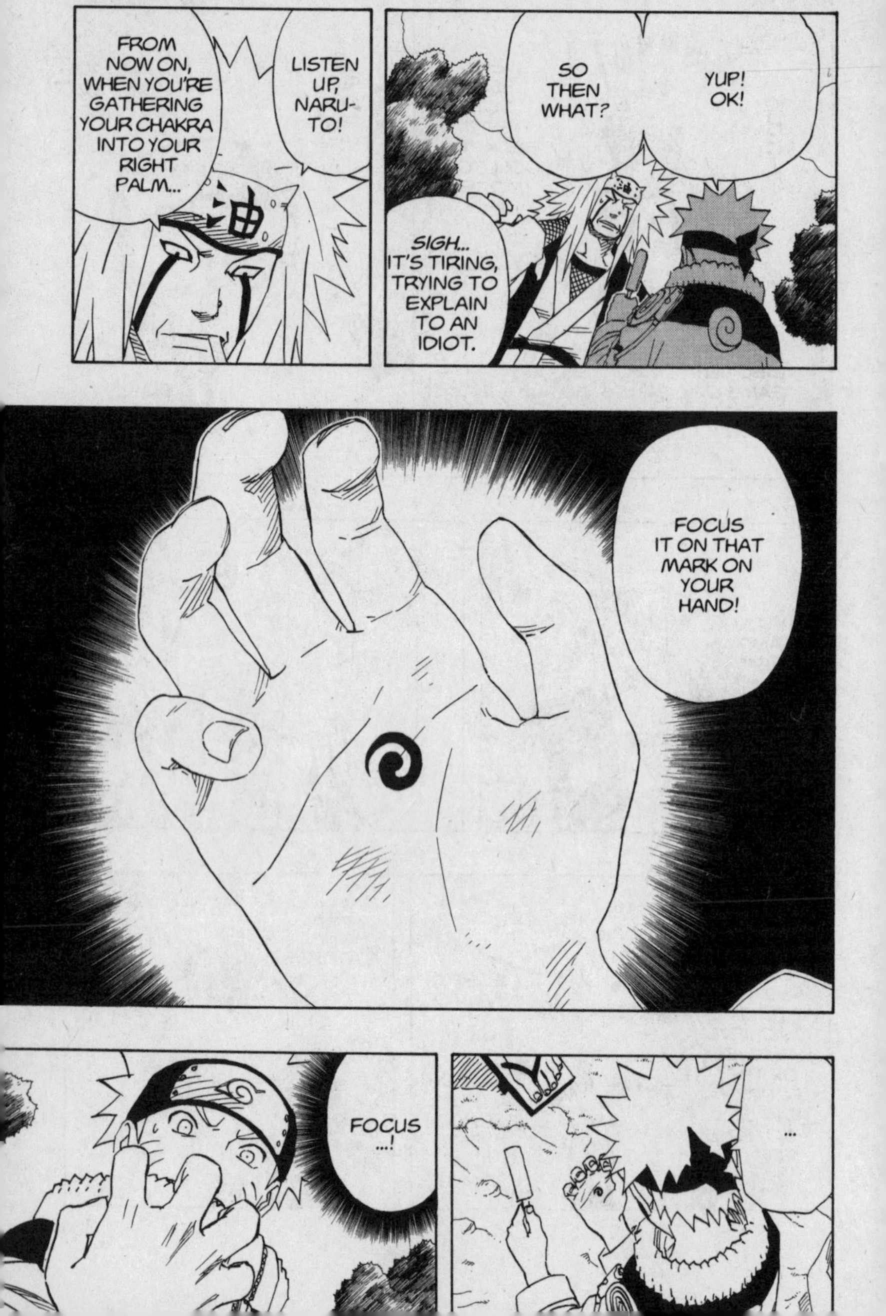

YUP! OK!
SO THEN WHAT?
SIGH... IT'S TIRING, TRYING TO EXPLAIN TO AN IDIOT.

LISTEN UP, NARUTO!
FROM NOW ON, WHEN YOU'RE GATHERING YOUR CHAKRA INTO YOUR RIGHT PALM...

FOCUS IT ON THAT MARK ON YOUR HAND!

...

FOCUS ...!

ALL RIGHT!

I'M GONNA GO FOR IT!!

CLENCH

WELL THEN... I'M GONNA HEAD BACK TO COLLECT MORE INFO.

GRAB

Hurl

GAH HA HA HA

WHAT?!

NO FRIENDLY MASTER-DISCIPLE GAME OF CATCH?!

STRI-I-I-I-IKE!!
CLAMP

THERE! GAME OVER.
Peh
...

GAH-HA HA, LATER!

...

SORRY, NARUTO... YOU HAVE TO MASTER THIS EXERCISE ON YOUR OWN...
YOU HAVE THE POTENTIAL TO ACHIEVE THE LEVEL OF THE FOURTH HOKAGE... SO GO FOR IT.
I don't need no Pervy Sage... I can do it, I can dooooo it!
PUMP

READ
THIS
WAY

木ノ葉病院
木ノ葉病院

(SIGN: KONOHA HOSPITAL)

SASUKE
...

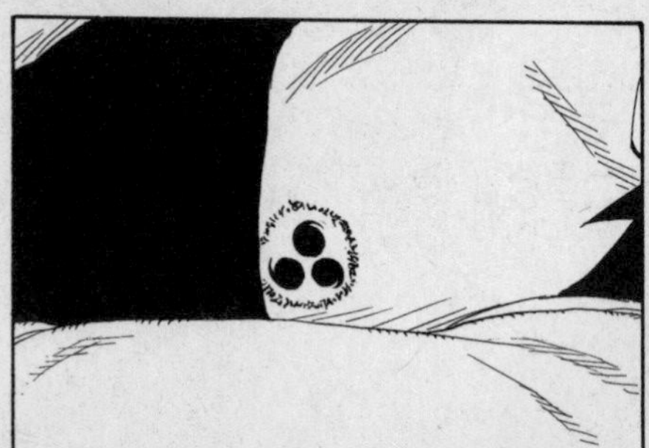

AAAARGH!!
UNNNH, UGH...
SPASM
SPASM
M... MY ARMS...
SPASM
HUF HUF
LORD OROCHI-MARU... PLEASE TAKE YOUR MEDICINE!!
GRRRR

SPLAT

HUF
HUF
HUF

HUF
HUF
HUF
HUF

DO PLEASE TAKE YOUR MEDICINE.
...OH DEAR, I GET BACK AND HAVE TO CLEAN THE ROOM RIGHT AWAY, EH.

...I DON'T NEED YOUR USELESS MEDS...
BUT I MADE THEM FOR YOU ALONE!
THEY SHOULD RELIEVE AT LEAST A LITTLE OF THE PAIN...

...UGH.

HUF
HUF
HUF
...I FEEL LIKE MY ARMS ARE BURNING UP...
...I DIDN'T THINK IT WOULD BE THIS PAINFUL...
TAP
WELL, THEY ARE THE CURSED WOUNDS OF SARUTOBI...
IT'S THE THIRD HOKAGE'S FINAL ACT...

...CAN THE TEDIOUS SPEECH...
HUF
HUF
HUF
UGH... MORE TO THE POINT...

HAVE... YOU LOCATED HER?

...YES.
IT SEEMS SHE IS HANGING AROUND A TOWN CALLED TANZAKU.

HUF
HUF
...TAN-ZAKU, EH...
HUF

...
...I SEE...
SNEER
HUF
HUF

...
HOW-EVER... I DON'T BELIEVE IT WILL BE THAT SIMPLE TO...
...UGH...

...HUMPH...

THE BEST MEDICINE ALWAYS TASTES BITTER, YOU KNOW...

HUF
HUF
HUF
HUF
HUF

SHF
IT'S USELESS...
I'VE GOT TO FOCUS HARDER!

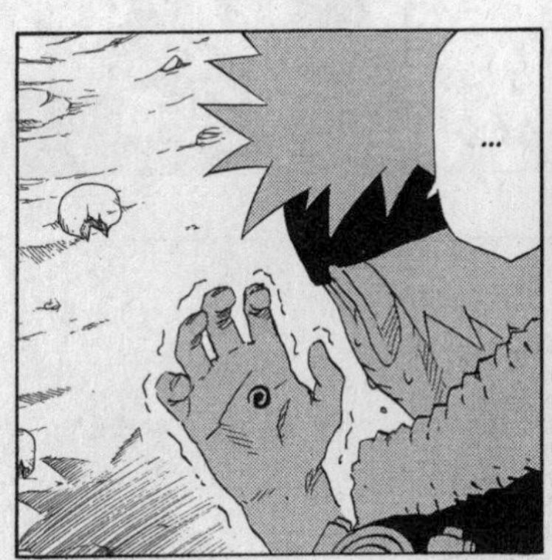
...

SHUUUH
FOCUS... FOCUS!

...

HAA...
FOCUS ...!

READ THIS WAY

FOCUS ON ONE POINT...

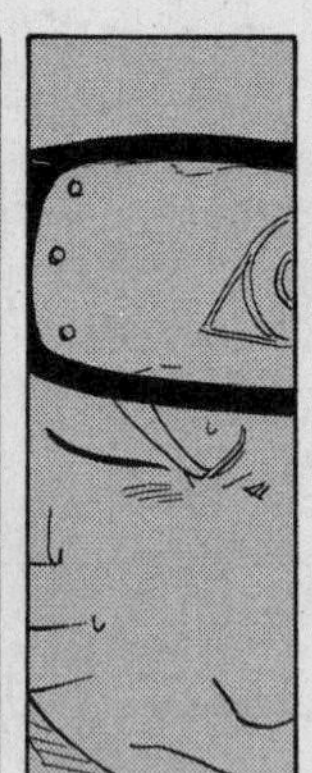

SHWOOM

STRI-I-I-I-IKE!

TWITCH
TWITCH
...
A-HAHAHAHA!!
HOW THE HECK AM I SUPPOSED TO FOCUS...
WHEN ALL I CAN SEE IS THAT PERVY FOOL'S FACE!!
NARUTO'S TRAINING IS STILL GOING ROUGHLY.

HM, DOESN'T LOOK FAMILIAR...
I SEE...

...I KNOW HER.
!

READ THIS WAY

AND WHERE SHE'S AT, TOO.

I'LL BUY YOU A ROUND.

HMPH... SURE!
AIEE!
'CUZ THAT LADY EARNED ME A PRETTY SUM.

AGAIN? HUNH...

THAT LEGENDARY LOSER'S AT IT AGAIN...

...WHERE?

TANZAKU.

油
HUH, NOT TOO FAR FROM HERE.

FINALLY... MY ARMS... WILL BE HEALED.

READ
THIS
WAY

EVEN IF IT'S ABOUT GOOD MEDICINE...
I DON'T THINK SHE'LL BE SIMPLY BITTER...
HUMPH... YOU COMING TO TANZAKU WITH ME OR NOT?

短冊街
(SIGN:TANZAKU)

FINALLY!
KACHINK

YAY!!
I CAN'T BELIEVE I GOT A LINE OF SEVENS.
THIS JUST DOESN;T FEEL RIGHT...

NARUTO

岸本斉史

Recently, my shoulder pain has been getting worse...And it seems to always be my left shoulder. Why does my left shoulder get stiff when I'm right-handed? It's one of the Seven Great Mysteries of Kishimoto.

—Masashi Kishimoto, 2003

NARUTO

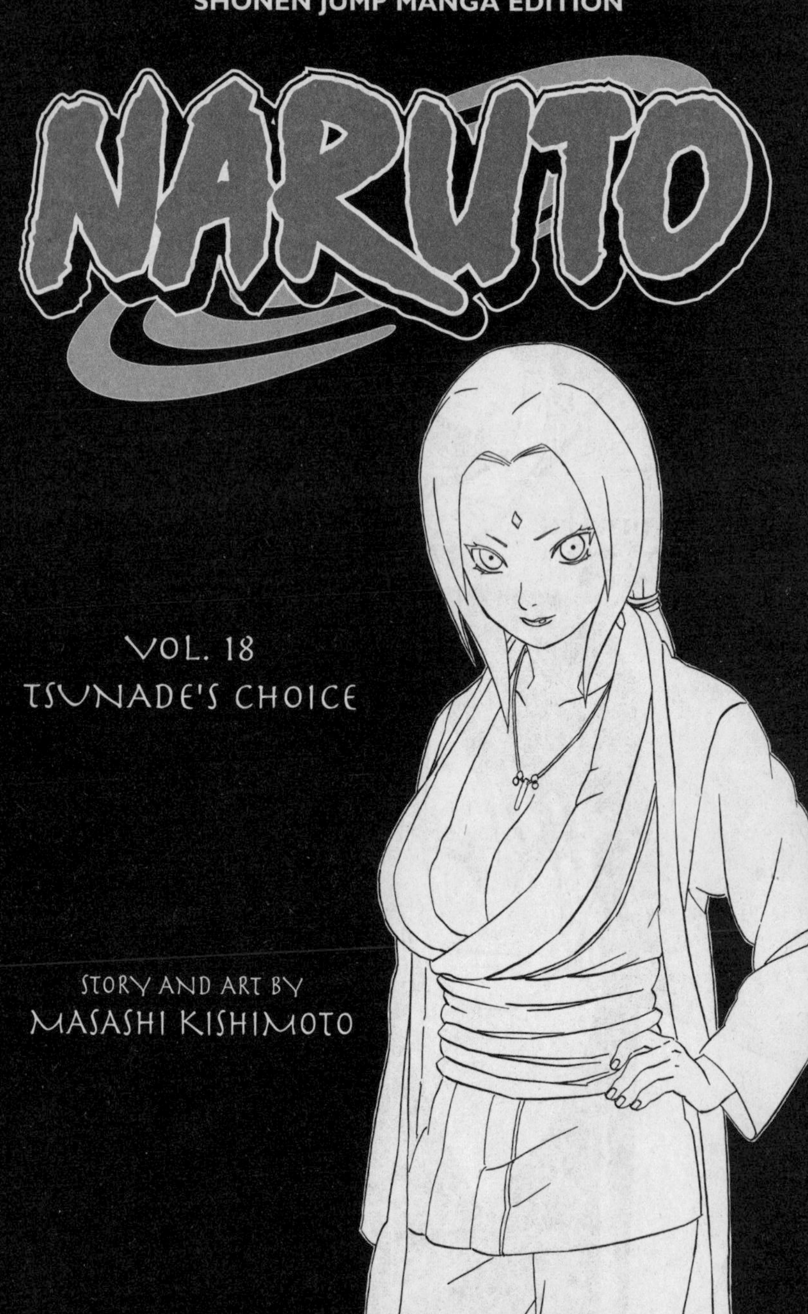

SHONEN JUMP MANGA EDITION

NARUTO

VOL. 18

TSUNADE'S CHOICE

STORY AND ART BY

MASASHI KISHIMOTO

CHARACTERS
Sasuke
サスケ
Naruto
ナルト
Sakura
サクラ
Orochimaru
大蛇丸
Kabuto
カブト

油
Shizune
シズネ
Jiraiya
自来也
Tsunade
ツナデ
綱手

The Story So Far...

Twelve years ago a destructive nine-tailed fox spirit attacked the ninja village of Konohagakure. The Hokage, or village champion, defeated the fox by sealing its soul into the body of a baby boy. Now that boy, Uzumaki Naruto, has grown up to be a ninja-in-training, learning the art of ninjutsu with his team-mates Sakura and Sasuke.

Naruto and company take on the Chûnin Selection Exams but suffer a sudden attack from Orochimaru in the Forest of Death. Orochimaru leaves a curse mark on Sasuke's body and vanishes, only to return *during* the final rounds to launch *Operation Destroy Konoha!*

While Naruto battles Gaara, the Third Hokage falls to Orochimaru. But Konohagakure is saved and Jiraiya and Naruto set out to hunt down the future Fifth Hokage, Tsunade. On the way, they encounter Itachi, Sasuke's demented older brother...

NARUTO

VOL. 18
TSUNADE'S CHOICE

CONTENTS

Number 154: Convergence...!!

(Sign: Pachinko)

WHAT'S WRONG?
YOU SHOULD BE PLEASED YOU ACTUALLY WON , LADY TSUNADE...
WHY THE LONG FACE...?

THIS TOWN...
I'VE GOT A BAD FEELING...
LET'S HURRY UP AND GET OUT OF HERE.

WHAT...?! BUT IT'S SUCH A TOURIST ATTRACTION!
I WANT TO SEE THE CASTLE AND ALL...
THEN LET'S GET IT OVER WITH!
CLOP
CLOP

I KNOW A LITTLE BIT ABOUT LADY TSUNADE TOO, YOU KNOW.
SINCE...I *WAS* PART OF THE MEDICAL CORPS AT ONE POINT.

...HUMPH...

SHE WAS THE FIRST TO PROPOSE...
...HAVING A MEDIC SPECIALIST IN THE BASIC FOUR MAN CELL.
SOMETHING WE TAKE FOR GRANTED THESE DAYS...

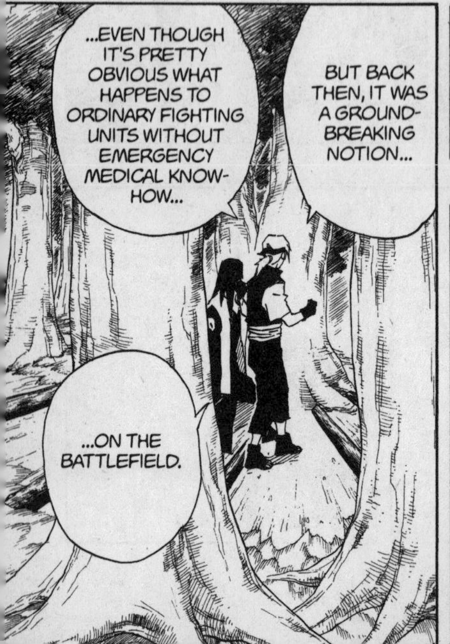
BUT BACK THEN, IT WAS A GROUND-BREAKING NOTION...
...EVEN THOUGH IT'S PRETTY OBVIOUS WHAT HAPPENS TO ORDINARY FIGHTING UNITS WITHOUT EMERGENCY MEDICAL KNOW-HOW...
...ON THE BATTLEFIELD.

HUMPH...

IT WAS PURE AND SIMPLE WAR EXPERIENCE THAT LAID THE GROUNDWORK FOR THAT IDEA...

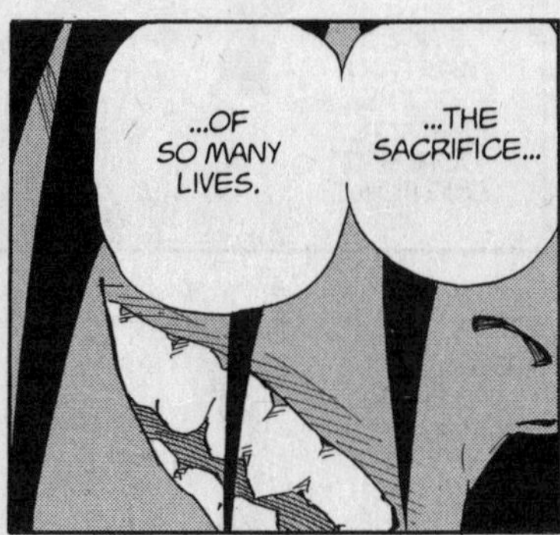
...THE SACRIFICE...
...OF SO MANY LIVES.

...

FLIT
FLIT
PEOPLE ONLY REALIZE THE TRUE VALUE OF SOMETHING AFTER THEY HAVE LOST IT.

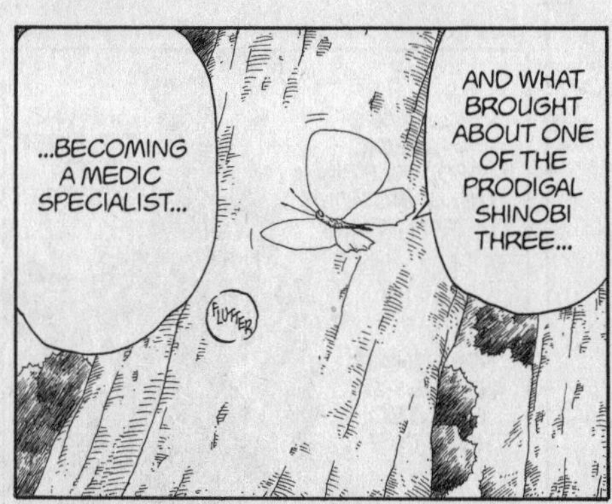
AND WHAT BROUGHT ABOUT ONE OF THE PRODIGAL SHINOBI THREE...
...BECOMING A MEDIC SPECIALIST...
FLUTTER

...WAS SIMPLY THE DESIRE TO AVOID MORE LOSS OF LIFE...

FLIT

FLIT

FLIT

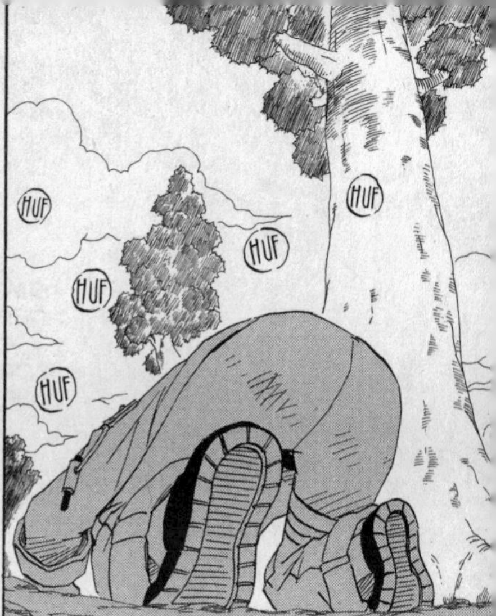
HUF
HUF
HUF
HUF

...UNH... UGH...
OWW...

...I'M AT MY LIMIT... IT HURTS SO MUCH I CAN'T EVEN BUILD UP ANY CHAKRA!
THUDD

I GOTTA TAKE A BREAK...
ROLL...
TUMP

FWHEEE

READ THIS WAY

!
HUF
FWP
HUF
HUF

HUF
HUF
TIP

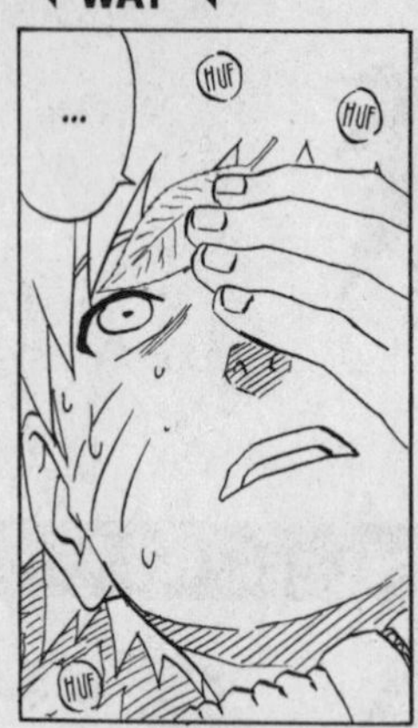
...
HUF
HUF
HUF

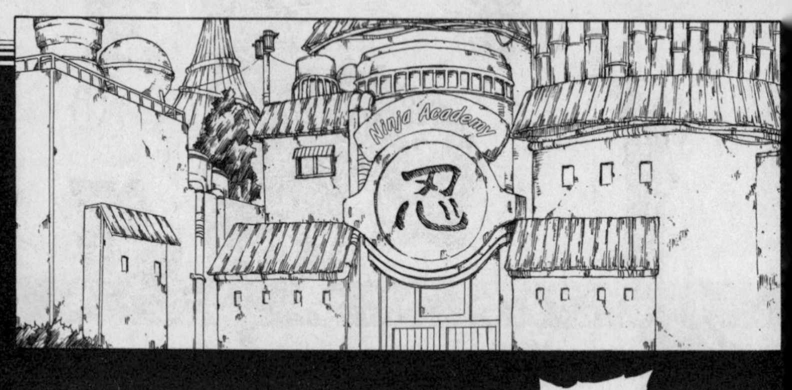
Ninja Academy
忍

HEY! CLASS IS STILL IN SESSION!!
DASH

MNCH
MNCH
KRNCH
KRNCH

ZZZ
ZZZ

YOU ALL HAVE ABSOLUTE ZERO CONCEN-TRATION!!
AT THIS RATE, YOU'LL NEVER BECOME UPSTANDING NINJA!
BUT IT'S HARD SITTING STILL AT A DESK. RIGHT, AKAMARU?
YIP !!
YAAAW...!
MASTER, DO YOU MIND SHORTEN-ING THE LECTURE ...?

FINE, BUT THAT MEANS AFTER CLASS, I'M GOING TO TEACH YOU A LESSON IN CONCEN-TRATION YOU WON'T SOON FORGET!
WHAT ...?!!
WHAT'S THIS?
WHAT YOU ARE ABOUT TO LEARN...
...IS A FOCUSING EXERCISE THAT OUR KONOHA PREDECESSORS PRACTICED EVERY DAY.
?
YOU MUST FOCUS ALL OF YOUR ENERGY INTO THE TREE LEAF ON YOUR FOREHEAD.
IT SHOULD PREVENT YOUR MIND FROM WANDERING BY FOCUSING ON A SINGLE POINT, IN THIS CASE, THE TREE LEAF, WHILE YOU BUILD YOUR CHAKRA.
HUH.

ONLY HE WHO CAN CONCENTRATE WILL BECOME A SPLENDID SHINOBI!

THIS IS WHY WE WEAR THE MARK OF THE LEAF ON OUR HEADBANDS.

YEAH, RIGHT! YOU'RE MAKING THAT UP!

IT'S STRONG NINJA THAT MAKE SPLENDID SHINOBI!

YEAH! HE'S RIGHT!

SIGH...

UNH

...

SIGH... I SHOULDA LISTENED MORE CLOSELY TO MASTER IRUKA...
WHUMP
I'M...SO STUPID SOME-TIMES...

...

THIS...IS ACTUALLY A LOT LIKE...

READ THIS WAY

...BUT FEELING SORRY FOR MYSELF WON'T GET ME ANYWHERE!
SLRP

SCRITCH
SCRITCH

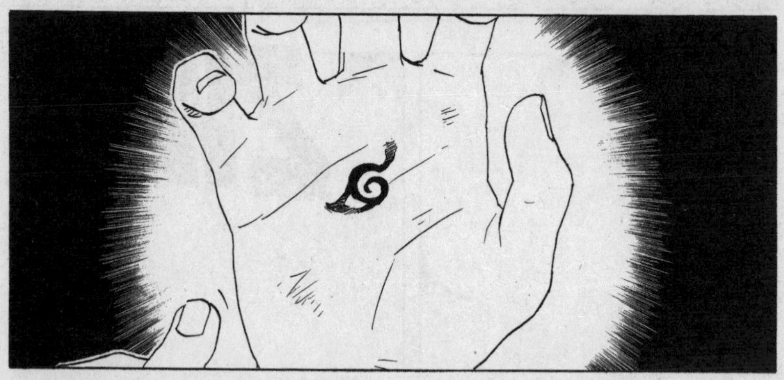

ALL RIGHT!
I'M GONNA DO IT!!
FOCUS.
FOCUS...

FOCUS...!!

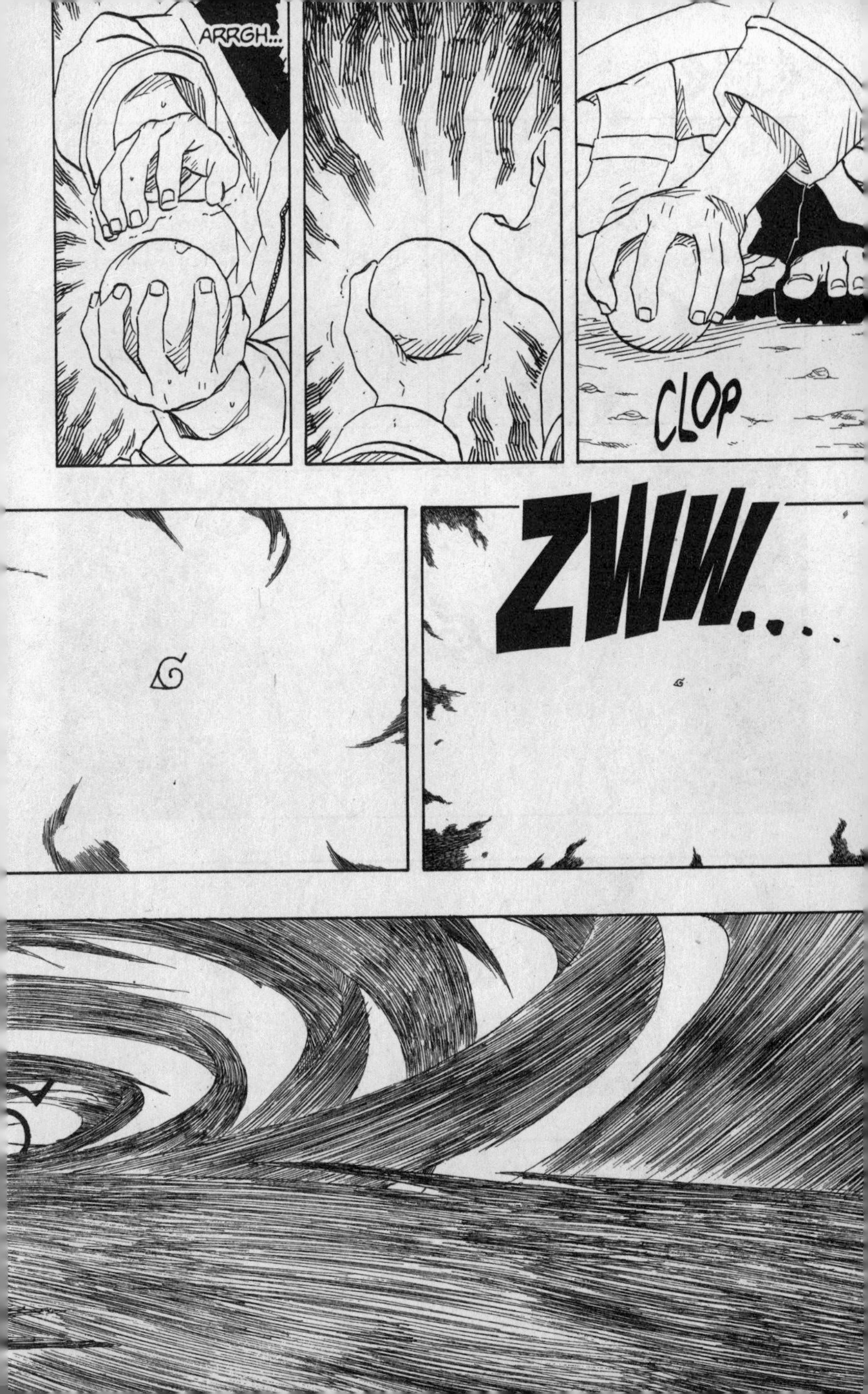
ARRGH...
CLOP
ZWW....

NOW!!

OOOOOOAR!!

WHAP

BOOF
WAAH!!

WHOMP WHOMP WHOMP

ROOOOOOOOO

Z Z Z Z Z Z Z
AAA!

CLAP!

UNH...I BROKE IT...!
HUH, IT SURE LOOKS LIKE YOU CLEARED THE SECOND STATE.

FIZZ
SIZZ
VOOSH...

...
IMPRESSIVE... HE RAISED HIS CHAKRA SO HIGH HE BURNED HIS PALM...
THIS KID MIGHT REALLY HAVE IT...

UNNH...
HURRY UP...AND SHOW ME THE THIRD STATE...
HUF
HUF
HUF

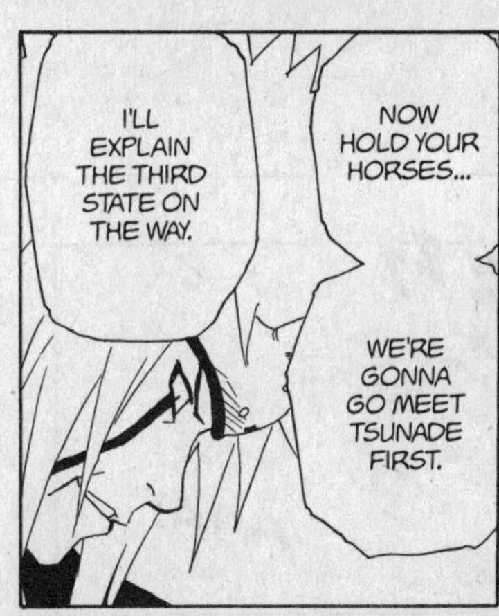
NOW HOLD YOUR HORSES...
I'LL EXPLAIN THE THIRD STATE ON THE WAY.
WE'RE GONNA GO MEET TSUNADE FIRST.

READ THIS WAY

WOW. TANZAKU CASTLE LOOKS SPLENDID WHEN VIEWED FROM BELOW. .
NO WONDER IT'S SO FAMOUS!

CALM DOWN, SHIZUNE.
LET'S GET OUT OF THIS PLACE.
AWW, WHAT'S THE HURRY? LOOKING IS FREE.

KA BOOM

!

!

KLAT KLATTER
KLAT KLATTER

SST

THAT'S...!

OROCHI-
MARU!

FOUND
YOU!

THE WORLD OF KISHIMOTO MASASHI
MY PERSONAL HISTORY, PART 27-A

SO I HAD FINALLY WON *WEEKLY SHONEN JUMP'S* NEWCOMER'S AWARD, WHICH HAD BEEN MY DEAREST DESIRE, AND TOOK ONE GIANT LEAP FORWARD TOWARD BECOMING A PROFESSIONAL MANGA ARTIST. I WAS ASSIGNED A PERSONAL EDITOR AND I RECEIVED 200,000 YEN [ABOUT $2,000] IN PRIZE MONEY, SO I WAS FLOATING ON AIR. FIRST, I DECIDED TO PUT ASIDE AND SAVE THE ENTIRE AMOUNT OF THE PRIZE PURSE. AT THE TIME, I WAS THE PROVERBIAL STARVING STUDENT ARTIST WHO HAD SO LITTLE MONEY THAT I WOULD SQUEEZE OUT AND USE EVERY LAST DROP OF PAINT IN THE TUBE.

IN PARTICULAR, MY FAVORITE COBALT BLUE OIL PAINT... THAT SURE WAS EXPENSIVE! IF I REMEMBER CORRECTLY, EACH TUBE COST ABOUT 2,000 YEN [ABOUT $20]...

BECAUSE THE SUPER-FRUGAL ME WOULD MAKE THE COBALT BLUE GO FURTHER BY THINNING IT WITH ADDITIONAL OIL, THERE STARTED TO BE A REAL DIFFERENCE IN COLOR DENSITY BETWEEN MY PAINTINGS AND THOSE OF MY BOURGEOIS CLASSMATES WHO JUST SLATHERED IT ON. IT GOT TO A POINT WHERE MY ART INSTRUCTOR WOULD REGULARLY SCOLD ME, *"TOO LIGHT!"* OR *"YOU NEED TO GIVE IT A HEAVIER, MORE OPPRESSIVE FEELING, YATTA YATTA."* ON TOP OF IT ALL, HE'D SAY, *"ARE YOU SLACKING?"* OR *"YOU OUGHT TO TAKE MORE TIME WITH IT, AND USE MANY MORE COLORS. YOU DON'T HAVE ENOUGH COLORS!"* THAT INSTRUCTOR DEFINITELY DIDN'T TAKE HIS STUDENTS' WALLET CONTENTS INTO CONSIDERATION...

I WANTED TO SHOUT BACK, I CAN'T HELP IT IF I CAN'T AFFORD MORE PAINT TUBES! BUT ACTUALLY, AT THAT POINT I DIDN'T REALLY CARE ANYMORE...THAT'S BECAUSE THE CONSTANTLY MONEY-GOBBLING OIL PAINTING BUSINESS HAD LOST ITS APPEAL, AND I WAS ALSO TIRED OF THE WHINING, HIGH-NOSED ART WORLD. I'D RATHER SPEND WHAT PRECIOUS MONEY I HAD ON THE MOVIES, WHICH MIGHT HELP ME DRAW MANGA... AND THUS, I DECIDED TO SPEND ALL MY MONEY ON MOVIES AND VIDEOS.

(TO BE CONTINUED)

Number 155: The Third State

ALL RIGHT, LET'S GO!

...

...QUIT ACTING LIKE A LITTLE KID. LET'S GO, PULEEZ.
HUH...?
YOU'RE IN A FOUL MOOD...

READ
THIS
WAY

WELL! WHY NOT?
I'M IN THE MIDDLE OF TRAIN-ING!!

HO HO HO...
YOU CAN PRACTICE THE THIRD STATE EVEN WHILE WALKING.
SRCH SRCH
HUH?!
REALLY?!

YOU SAID THERE WERE THREE STATES TO THIS DRILL, RIGHT?!
JAB
I'VE ONLY GOTTEN THROUGH TWO OF THEM SO FAR!

PWUUU

?!
A BAL-LOON?

HERE.
PONK
!

CLAP
HUH?
WHAT'S THIS...AN ORDINARY BALLOON...?
BOINN

THE FIRST STATE WAS ROTATION...
...AND THE SECOND STATE, POWER.

MMM

AND NOW *THIS* IS THE THIRD STATE!
PFFT

READ THIS WAY

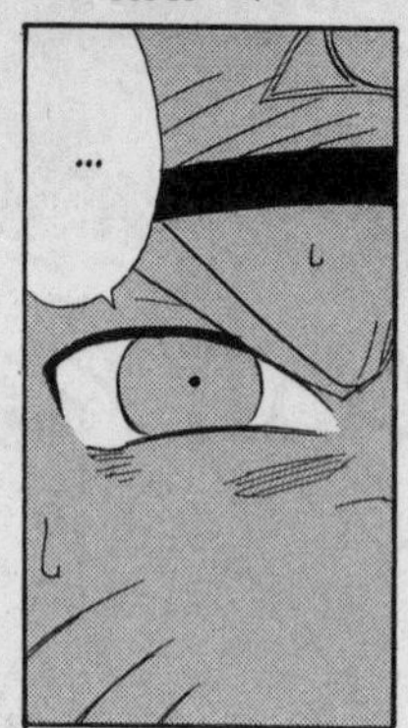
...

...

WAIT... WHAT AM I SUPPOSED TO BE SEEING?!!

HO HO HO...
ON FIRST GLANCE, IT MAY *LOOK* LIKE I'M JUST HOLDING THE BALLOON IN MY HAND...

BUT LET ME SHOW YOU WITH MY LEFT HAND WHAT'S *REALLY* GOING ON!

SO WHAT'S...
HAPPENING INSIDE THE BALLOON, YOU ASK?
KURL
PLMP

!

SHWRRRR

...WHOA, HIS CHAKRA IS SWIRLING FASTER AND FASTER...!
YET IT'S STAYING IN A CIRCLE... IT'S LIKE...

...A MINI-
CYCLONE!

...AND THE SAME THING'S GOING ON...
...INSIDE THE BALLOON IN YOUR RIGHT HAND?
YUP!

WOW...
GULP

HE'S TURNING SO MUCH CHAKRA, BUT THE BALLOON DOESN'T EVEN MOVE...
...EVEN THOUGH THE CHAKRA'S MORE POWERFUL AND ROTATING FASTER THAN WHEN HE BURST THE RUBBER BALL!

SO YOU SEE...
...IN THE THIRD STATE, YOU PUT OUT EVERYTHING YOU'VE LEARNED SO FAR FULL FORCE, AND THEN...

...CONTAIN IT!

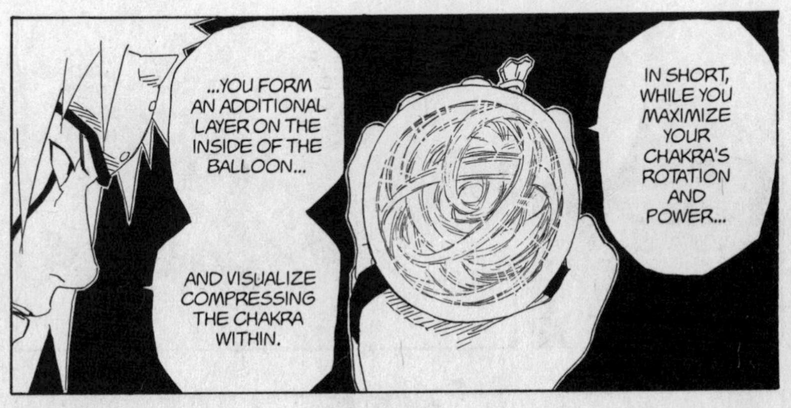
IN SHORT, WHILE YOU MAXIMIZE YOUR CHAKRA'S ROTATION AND POWER...
...YOU FORM AN ADDITIONAL LAYER ON THE INSIDE OF THE BALLOON...
AND VISUALIZE COMPRESSING THE CHAKRA WITHIN.

I GET IT!
SO WHAT YOU'RE SAYING IS KEEP THE SAME ROTATIONS I HAD IN THE SECOND STATE...
...BUT INSTEAD OF BURSTING THE BALLOON, I NEED TO FOCUS ON NOT BREAKING IT!
HEY NOW! YOU CAUGHT ON QUICK THIS TIME!
HEH HEH...!
...

...HMM ...?
...SO WHY DO I NEED TO LEARN HOW TO DO THAT?!
...HMPH.

WELL.
TWRL
WATCH CLOSELY! UP THROUGH THE SECOND STATE, THIS IS WHAT YOU CAN DO...
PLOP

SHF
SWRRRL
FLASH
HAH!!

NOW, IF YOU MASTER THE THIRD STATE!
PFFT
...WHOA!
SHF

!
SWRRRRL

PSSST

...!

IF YOU CAN KEEP THIS MINI-CYCLONE IN YOUR PALM, IT WILL STAY TOGETHER...
ROTATIONS WILL SPEED UP, THE POWER WILL COMPRESS, AND IT WILL BE THAT MUCH MORE ULTIMATELY DESTRUCTIVE!

...

ALL RIGHT!! I CAN DO THIS...!

WHOO
FEELS GOOD...
...NOW!
WHOMP
WHOMP
WHOMP
NOW CONTAIN IT!!

TWITCH
TWITCH

TWITCH
TWITCH

CONTAIN...

POP

NO, NO HOLDING BACK!

YOU HAVE TO CONTAIN THE POWER WHILE ROTATING FULL FORCE!

YOU'RE KIDDING, RIGHT...? I DON'T HAVE THAT KIND OF CONTROL OVER MY CHAKRA...

NO WONDER... IT TAKES THREE STATES.

THIS IS ON A TOTALLY DIFFERENT SCALE THAN THE OTHER TWO...

I TOLD YOU...THAT THIS WAS HIGH DIFFICULTY...
AN A-RANK SUPER-ADVANCED NINJUTSU...

READ
THIS
WAY

...

NOW, NO MORE SHOP TALK!
GO AHEAD AND TRY IT WHILE WE WALK.

...
HEY...WHAT'S YOUR HURRY? CAN'T WE SLOW DOWN...?
WE'VE ALREADY SPENT ONE WHOLE DAY WAITING FOR YOU TO RECOVER.

THERE'S NO GUARANTEE TSUNADE'S GONNA STICK AROUND THAT TOWN.
HEY...!!
KRNCH
WHRL

IT'S NOT LIKE AN OLD FRIEND'S GONNA CONVENIENTLY SHOW UP AND CHAT HER UP ABOUT THE OLD DAYS...
LET'S GO!

...
AW, ALL RIGHT...

LONG TIME NO SEE...
OROCHI-MARU.

I'VE SEARCHED LONG AND HARD FOR YOU, MY DEAR.
WHAT BUSINESS COULD YOU POSSIBLY HAVE WITH ME?
DON'T EVEN TRY TO TELL ME YOU JUST WANNA CATCH UP...

READ
THIS
WAY

ACTUALLY, I HAVE A SMALL FAVOR TO ASK OF YOU.

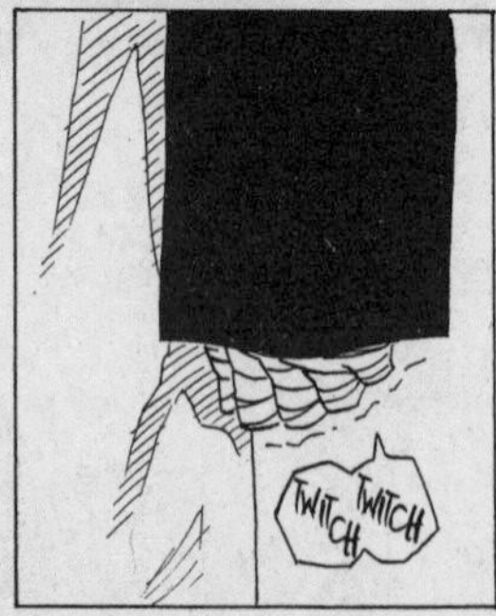
TWITCH TWITCH

...
HIS HEART RATE'S ERRATIC... FROM HIS COMPLEXION, HE HAS A HIGH FEVER AND HE'S BEEN IN A STATE OF EXHAUSTION FOR A WHILE... AND HIS ARMS...

LADY TSUNADE... YOU PROBABLY ALREADY KNOW.

GO ASK SOMEONE ELSE.
I QUIT MEDICINE A LONG TIME AGO.

BUT WE CANNOT... YOU MUST UNDERSTAND THE SEVERITY OF HIS WOUNDS...
NO ONE ELSE CAN HEAL HIS ARMS.

NO ONE EXCEPT YOU.
YOU WHO GAINED FAME AS A MEDIC SPECIALIST...
ONE OF THE THREE GREAT SHINOBI OF LEGEND, PRINCESS TSUNADE.

...
...HIS ARMS... THOSE ARE NO ORDINARY INJURIES...
SOME SORT OF CURSE MARK OR SOMETHING...
WHAT HAPPENED TO YOU, OROCHI-MARU?

NOTHING REALLY...
JUST A MINOR INCIDENT WHEN I KILLED THE THIRD LORD...

!!

!!

HUMPH... NO NEED TO SCOWL, PRINCESS...

YOU...DID WHAT...?

ALL THINGS EVENTUALLY COME TO AN END...
AS DO PEOPLE...

YOU OUGHT TO KNOW...

FOR YOU LET THE TWO PEOPLE...
GRRR
...YOU LOVED MOST IN THE WORLD DIE...

Number 156: The Offer

...
...SHE LET TWO PEOPLE WHO SHE LOVED... DIE...!?

...I SEE NOW. YOU ARE MOST CRUEL...

CACKLE CACKLE...

YES INDEED...
THOSE WERE SUCH BRUTAL DEATHS...
BLUR
SLLP
!
TWWNGG!
SWISH-WISH-WISH-WISH
DISH

THKK
THKK
PLNK PLNK
THKK
THKK

...POISON... THESE NEEDLES ARE LACED...

STAND DOWN, SHIZUNE.

READ THIS WAY

HUF
HUF

HER COMPANION...! SHE'S GOOD...

SIGH...

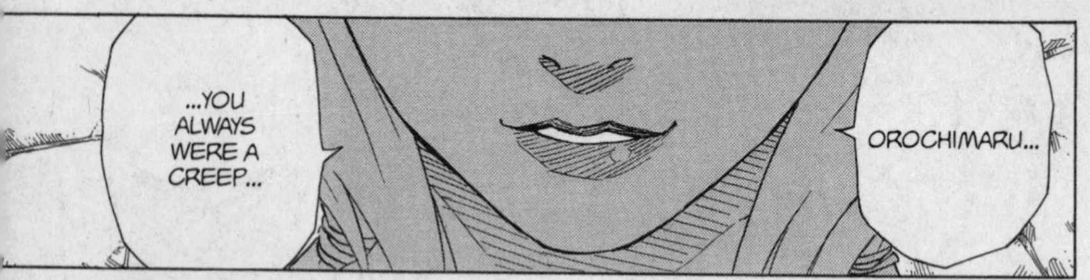
OROCHIMARU...
...YOU ALWAYS WERE A CREEP...

?!

BUT YOU OUGHT TO KNOW ME BETTER THAN THAT...
YOU MOCK ME...

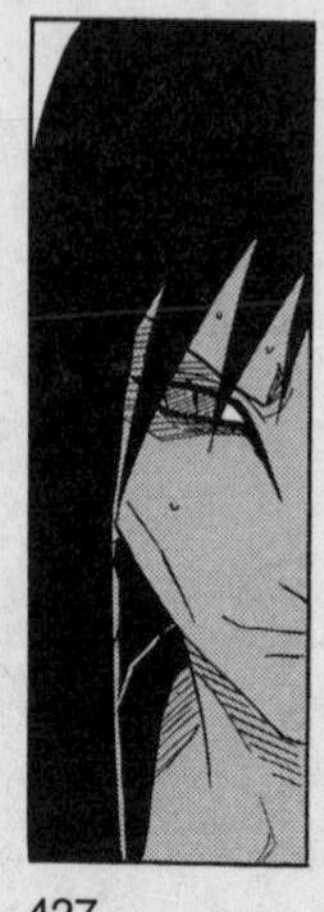

...AND I'LL KILL YOU!
OKAY?!

KRVOOOSH
AND... SCARY...
I BET SHE'S SINGLE... I'D PUT MONEY ON IT...
...
...SHE'S STRONG...!

POPPP
WAAH!

(Sign: Tanzaku Town)

TSUNADE'S IMPATIENT AND SHORT-TEMPERED...
SO I HOPE SHE'S STILL AROUND...
OWW...!

WE DID NOT COME HERE TO FIGHT YOU...
WE WOULD MERELY LIKE TO STRIKE A DEAL WITH YOU.

READ
THIS
WAY

I THOUGHT I JUST TOLD YOU.
GET LOST!
YOU ARE THE ONLY ONE WHO CAN HEAL LORD OROCHI-MARU'S ARMS.

WE'RE *NOT* ASKING YOU TO DO IT FOR FREE.
WON'T YOU CON-SIDER... OUR OFFER?

I'M GOING TO GIVE YOU A COUNT OF FIVE...
GET LOST BEFORE I FINISH!
OR ELSE I'LL ERASE YOU.

PLEASE CALM DOWN...
I REALLY DON'T THINK YOU'LL BE DISAPPOINTED BY THE TERMS...
5
4

SIGH...
3
2
...
1

I'VE LEARNED THE FORBIDDEN JUTSU...

...I CAN REANIMATE YOUR BELOVED LITTLE BROTHER AND YOUR LOVER BOTH...

...!
FLCK

READ THIS WAY

...!

SNORT?

...

DOES THE FACT THAT WE'RE STILL STANDING HERE WHOLE AND HALE...

...MEAN OUR OFFER IS ACCEPTABLE?

...

大
人
ばくち
半
丁

AAH...!
I THINK I KNOW THAT LADY...

I BELIEVE SHE SAID SHE WAS HEADING THERE...
TO TRY TO WIN BACK THE MONEY SHE LOST HERE.
THERE? WHERE'S THERE?

LOOKIE HERE, BOY.
IF YOU ADD THE PIPS ON THE DICE AND GET AN EVEN NUMBER, THAT'S CHÔ.
IF YOU GET AN ODD NUMBER, THAT'S HAN.

SHUT UP! CAN'T YOU SEE I'M BUSY HERE?! LEAVE ME ALONE!

KLIK
KLIK

SWSH

CLOMP

HEY, THERE'S NO FREE ANYTHING AT A GAMBLING HOUSE. LET'S MAKE A DEAL.
IF YOU WIN, I WON'T CHARGE YOU FOR THE INFORMATION... BUT IF YOU LOSE, IT'LL COST YOU 1,000 RYO*. HOW'S THAT?

(*1,000 ryo is roughly 10,000 yen, or $100.)

...ALL RIGHT!

WELL THEN, PICK CHÔ OR HAN.
SURE!
POOF
LET'S SEE...

HMM...

HOW ABOUT...
SINCE I JUST TURNED 50...
...CHÔ!

WHICH MEANS HAN SHALL WIN IT FOR ME...
...
ULP
SO... HERE WE GO!

!
SH... SHOOT...! 2+5=7, HAN!

WAH!
POPP
!

TICK

NICE, NARUTO!!
HO HO...IT LOOKS LIKE I WON!
OH!

!

READ
THIS
WAY

DARN! FOILED AGAIN!

SQNT SQNT
SHEESH, SHE AIN'T HERE!
SRCH SRCH

!

POINK

IS THIS WHERE I PUT IT IN...?
RSTL RSTLE

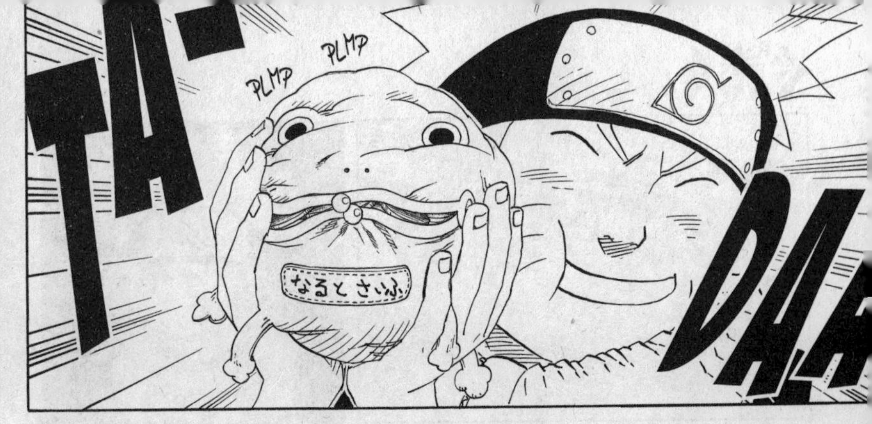
TA-
DA
PLMP
PLMP
なるとさいふ

YOU ARE SO MUCH CUTER WHEN YOU'RE FULL.♡
RBB RBB
LA-DI-DA
...
I CAN'T BELIEVE HE GOT THAT FAR WITH JUST ONE COIN!
HE'S GOT GOOD GAMBLING INSTINCTS...
EVEN THOUGH HIS TALENT FOR JUTSU STINKS!

...BUT MORE IMPORTANT...
...WHERE'D THAT TSUNADE TAKE HER-SELF...?
SHE COULDN'T HAVE GOTTEN TOO FAR, NOT IN THIS SHORT A TIME...

...WELL, IT CAN'T BE HELPED... WE'LL HAVE TO GO SOME-WHERE HIGH UP AND LOOK FOR HER THE OLD-FASHIONED WAY...
IF I REMEMBER RIGHT, THIS IS A CASTLE TOWN...WE CAN GET UP THERE AND...
KSHNK

LET'S GO, NARUTO.
THIS WAY!
OKIE DOKIE!

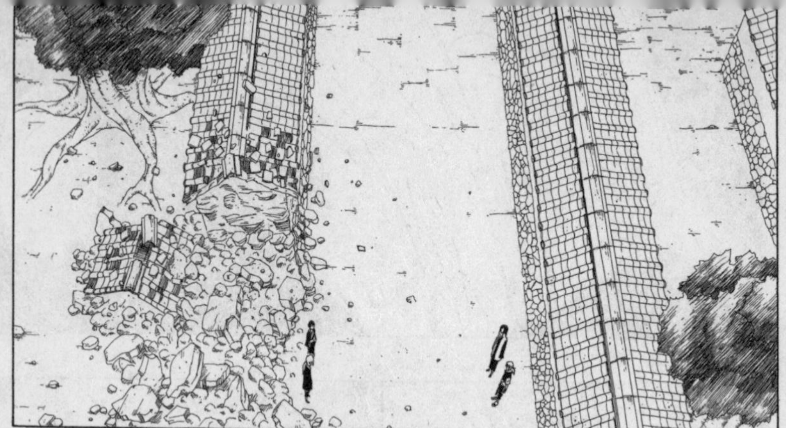

...

DON'T YOU WANT TO SEE THEM AGAIN, TSUNADE...?

...

...DAN...
...NAWAKI...
...

...SUPPOSE I FIX THOSE ARMS...
WHAT ARE YOU GOING TO DO?

SSS

I HATE LIES...
...SO I'LL BE SQUARE WITH YOU...

...ALONG THE WAY OF CLAIMING THAT WHICH I DESIRE...

HEY! WAIT!
SO WHERE'S THIS CASTLE?
?!!
...THIS TIME I ANNIHILATE KONOHA ONCE AND FOR ALL.

THE WORLD OF KISHIMOTO MASASHI
MY PERSONAL HISTORY, PART 27-B

I LIKE OIL PAINTING, DON'T GET ME WRONG, BUT WHAT I LEARNED IN COLLEGE WAS FINE ART, SO IT WAS PRETTY USELESS. I WAS TAUGHT THAT ONE SHOULD CREATE WHATEVER ONE FELT LIKE, EXPRESSING SOMETHING THAT WAS INSIDE ONESELF IN A WAY THAT IT COULD BE APPRECIATED BY THE VIEWER, AND YET IT SEEMED TO ME THAT MOST WORKS WERE SO ABSTRACT THAT THE VIEWER HAD TO RELY ON THE TITLE OR THE ACCOMPANYING BLURB, AND NOT ON THE PIECE ALONE. ONCE, MY INSTRUCTOR BROUGHT IN PHOTOS OF OILS HE HAD PAINTED HIMSELF, AND WAS BOASTING ABOUT HIS SOLO EXHIBITIONS AND HOW HE HAD SOLD HIS ART, BUT ALL I COULD THINK TO MYSELF WAS "IF YOU WANT YOUR STUFF TO BE ACKNOWLEDGED MORE, BE A BETTER ENTREPRENEUR!" IT WAS ALWAYS INSTRUCTORS LIKE HIM THAT WOULD RIDICULE MANGA, AND TRY TO IMPOSE A RANKING SYSTEM UPON THE ART WORLD. THEY WHO ELEVATED FINE ART AND DENIGRATED ENTERTAINMENT WERE THE ONES WHO WANTED TO SELL THEIR OWN WORK OR BE ACKNOWLEDGED THE MOST. I THINK IF THEY REALLY WANT TO CREATE FINE ART, THEY SHOULD AIM FOR SELF-SATISFACTION. BECAUSE WORKS THAT THEY PAINT HOPING TO RELAY AND EXPRESS THEIR EGO, NO MATTER IF THEY FIT WITHIN THE REALM OF FINE ART, ONCE THEY DECIDE THEY WANT TO MAKE A LIVING FROM SELLING SUCH WORKS, THEY'VE ALREADY MOVED IN THE DIRECTION OF ENTERTAINMENT.

THE WORKS OF THOSE WHO WANT TO MAKE A LIVING AS PAINTERS BUT WHO CAN'T LIVE OFF OF THE SALE OF THEIR PAINTINGS SO RELUCTANTLY FIND EMPLOYMENT AS ART TEACHERS AND DENIGRATE MANGA (I.E. ENTERTAINMENT) ARE THE LOWEST FORM OF ENTERTAINMENT.

I THINK MANGA IS AN AMAZING MEDIUM BECAUSE NOT ONLY IS IT LOW-COST IN TERMS OF PRODUCTION, DEPENDING ONLY ON INK PRICES, BUT IT IS HIGH-QUALITY ENTERTAINMENT WHERE IT IS EASY TO CONVEY ONE'S SELF-EXPRESSION THROUGH THE USE OF DIALOGUE, STORYBOARDING, AND CHARACTERS.

...I LOVE FINE ART, DON'T GET ME WRONG. AND I REALLY ADMIRE THOSE WHO PRODUCE FINE ART. IT'S JUST THAT I AM WARY OF THOSE ARTISTS WHO TRY TO JUDGE FINE ART AGAINST ENTERTAINMENT. IT IS THOSE ARTISTS WHO ARE NEITHER ARTISTS NOR ENTERTAINERS, BUT JUST PLAIN CRUD. ♡

...HUH, I HADN'T REALLY INTENDED TO WRITE ABOUT THIS... BUT I GUESS OLD RAGE DIES HARD...A-HA-HA.

Number 157:
Tsunade's Answer...?!

...
...

WHAT'S... GOING ON...?
BEATS ME...

HUF
HUF
SHFFF
!

HO THERE, STRANGER! HOLD ON JUST A MINUTE!
WHAT THE HECK WENT DOWN HERE?
!

...!
YOU ALL OUGHT TO RUN TOO!
THERE ARE MONSTERS UP THERE!

READ THIS WAY

...
MONSTERS ?!

WHAT DO YOU MEAN?
...WHAT SORT OF MONSTERS ?!

A...A GIANT SERPENT!
IT DESTROYED THE CASTLE IN AN INSTANT!

...

?!

HOW BIG WAS IT?

I'VE SEEN ONE BEFORE TOO! IN MY VILLAGE...

I WAS ATTACKED BY THIS HUMONGOUS SNAKE...

WHRRL

!

C'MON, NARUTO!

METHINKS THIS SNAKE...IS THE SAME FELLA YOU MET ONCE...

...
ANNIHILATE KONOHA?!

...

READ THIS WAY

...YOUR ANSWER?

LADY TSUNADE!

NO! YOU MUSTN'T BE TAKEN IN BY THEIR SWEET TALK...!
NEITHER YOUR LITTLE BROTHER NOR MY UNCLE WOULD WANT THIS!

I KNOW IT!
THAT NO MATTER WHAT YOU SAY, YOU STILL, DEEP DOWN...

HAVE YOU FORGOTTEN THEIR WISHES... OR EVEN MORE SO...
...HAVE YOU FORGOTTEN YOUR WISH... YOUR DREAM, LADY TSUNADE?!

BE STILL, SHIZUNE!

...

...

...YOU NEED NOT GIVE US YOUR ANSWER THIS VERY MINUTE...
HOWEVER, WE WOULD LIKE A RESPONSE IN ONE WEEK'S TIME.

...OH AND JUST SO YOU KNOW, THIS FORBIDDEN JUTSU REQUIRES LIVE SACRIFICES...
SO PLEASE HAVE TWO PEOPLE PREPARED ON YOUR END...
LADY TSUNADE !!
LET'S JUST KILL THEM RIGHT HERE AND NOW! OROCHIMARU'S WEAKENED!
IT'S OUR BEST CHANCE! LADY TSUNADE... TOGETHER WE CAN TAKE THEM ON...!
...
LADY TSUNADE...
...
TWITCH
TWITCH
KRNCH
PT-PTT

!!
SHVV SHVV
SQZZZE!

READ THIS WAY

?!

GRR... DARN...
AS ANOTHER OF THE PRODIGAL THREE... HE KNOWS ABOUT *THAT* TOO, HUH...

I MAY BE WEAKENED... BUT...
...I KNOW TSUNADE'S WEAKNESSES, TOO...

IT HASN'T FADED YET, EH...
...YOUR FEAR OF BLOOD...

HEMO-
PHOBIA
...?!
...!

...

...SHALL WE GET GOING, KABUTO?
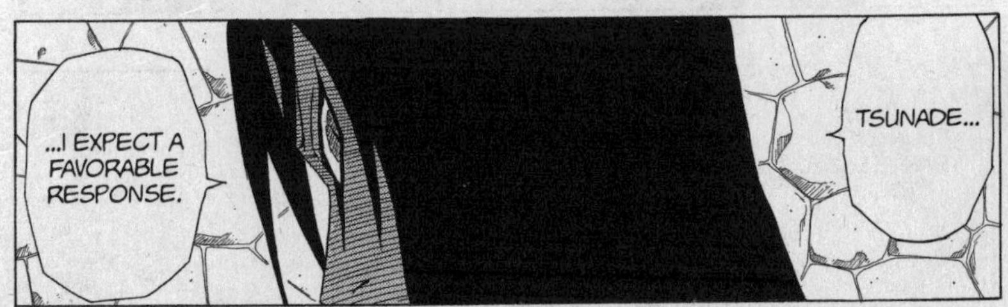
TSUNADE...
...I EXPECT A FAVORABLE RESPONSE.

BLRR
BLRR

...

SHVV SHVV

KLNCH

KLAKK

VOOSH
VOOSH

油
!

SCREEEEECH

...
LOOKS LIKE WE MISSED THE PARTY...

HMM, DID THE SNAKE DO THIS TOO?!
C'MON, NARUTO, LET'S GO.

酒
居酒屋
百楽
百楽
酒
WEL-COME!

BZZ
YAK
YAK
BZZ

READ THIS WAY

YO, MISTER! 'NOTHER!
LADY TSUNADE... YOU'VE HAD ENOUGH ALREADY!
SHOOKA-SHOOKA

URP...
...

...LADY TSUNADE...

...WELL, EITHER WAY, LET'S GRAB A BITE HERE FIRST...
WHAT...?! BUT ISN'T THIS A DRINKING ESTABLISHMENT?

KID...THIS IS THE BEST PLACE TO GATHER NEWS...

OH!
!

TSUNADE!

JIRAIYA ...?!

!

!

WHAT...
...THE HECK ARE YOU DOING HERE...?

WHA... THAT LADY'S TSUNADE ...?!
SHE'S SERIOUSLY 50...?!!
WHAT A CON!
SIGH...
I'VE FINALLY FOUND YOU!

HOW UNCANNY... TO RUN INTO BOTH OF THE OTHER PRODIGAL THREE IN ONE DAY...

READ THIS WAY

'BEEN SEEING A LOT OF FAMILIAR FACES TODAY.

...OROCHI-MARU, RIGHT? ...SO WHAT'S UP?

GRRRR

NUTHIN', REALLY...
JUST WANTED TO SAY HI, I GUESS.

...

THEY SAY SHE'S A FEMALE NINJA WHO CAN HEAL ANY INJURY... IS IT REALLY TRUE?
SCARF SCARF

SO WHAT'S UP WITH YOU... WHADDAYA WANT FROM ME?

I'LL LAY IT STRAIGHT.
TSUNADE... THE VILLAGE REQUESTS YOU ACCEPT THE TITLE OF FIFTH HOKAGE.

URG!!

...!

!

READ THIS WAY

F...FIFTH HOKAGE?!!
HACK! GUGH!
THUD THUD
...! WHERE THE HECK DID THAT COME FROM?!! WHAT'S GOING ON?!

DID YOU HEAR ABOUT THE THIRD LORD?

LORD THIRD... SO IT WAS TRUE...

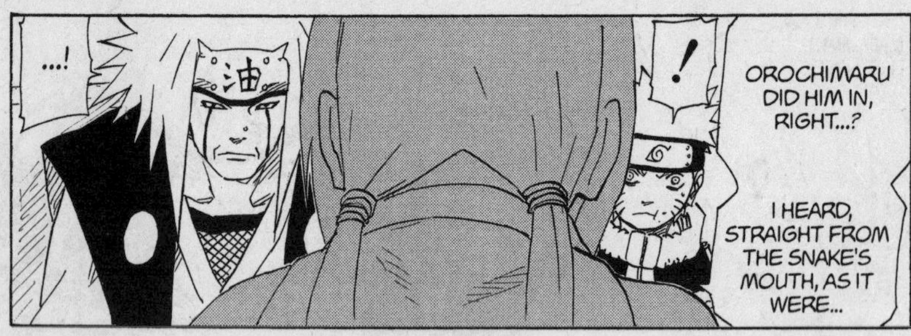
OROCHIMARU DID HIM IN, RIGHT...?
I HEARD, STRAIGHT FROM THE SNAKE'S MOUTH, AS IT WERE...
!
...!

...?!!
...OROCHI-MARU DID IT...?

OROCHI-MARU...?!
HE KILLED THE THIRD HOKAGE ?!

WHO THE HECK'S OROCHI-MARU?!

...THE THIRD MEMBER OF OUR PRODIGAL THREE.

WHAT?!

BUT I THOUGHT THE THREE GREAT SHINOBI WERE ALL FROM KONOHA!

SO WHY?!

...

JIRAIYA, WHO IS THIS BRAT?

GRR

...
THIS IS UZUMAKI NARUTO...
!
SO THIS LAD...HAS THE NINE-TAILS...

...AND WHY HER FOR FIFTH HOKAGE?!
JUST HUSH UP, NARUTO!
...SO!
WELL? DO YOU ACCEPT?

READ THIS WAY

...

...

AARGH
...

...I CAN REANIMATE YOUR BELOVED LITTLE BROTHER AND LOVER BOTH...
...THIS TIME I ANNIHILATE KONOHA ONCE AND FOR ALL.

...

Number 158:
No Forgiveness...!!

WELL, TSUNADE?

...
LADY TSUNADE...

AARGH...

...SORRY...

NO THANKS!

READ THIS WAY

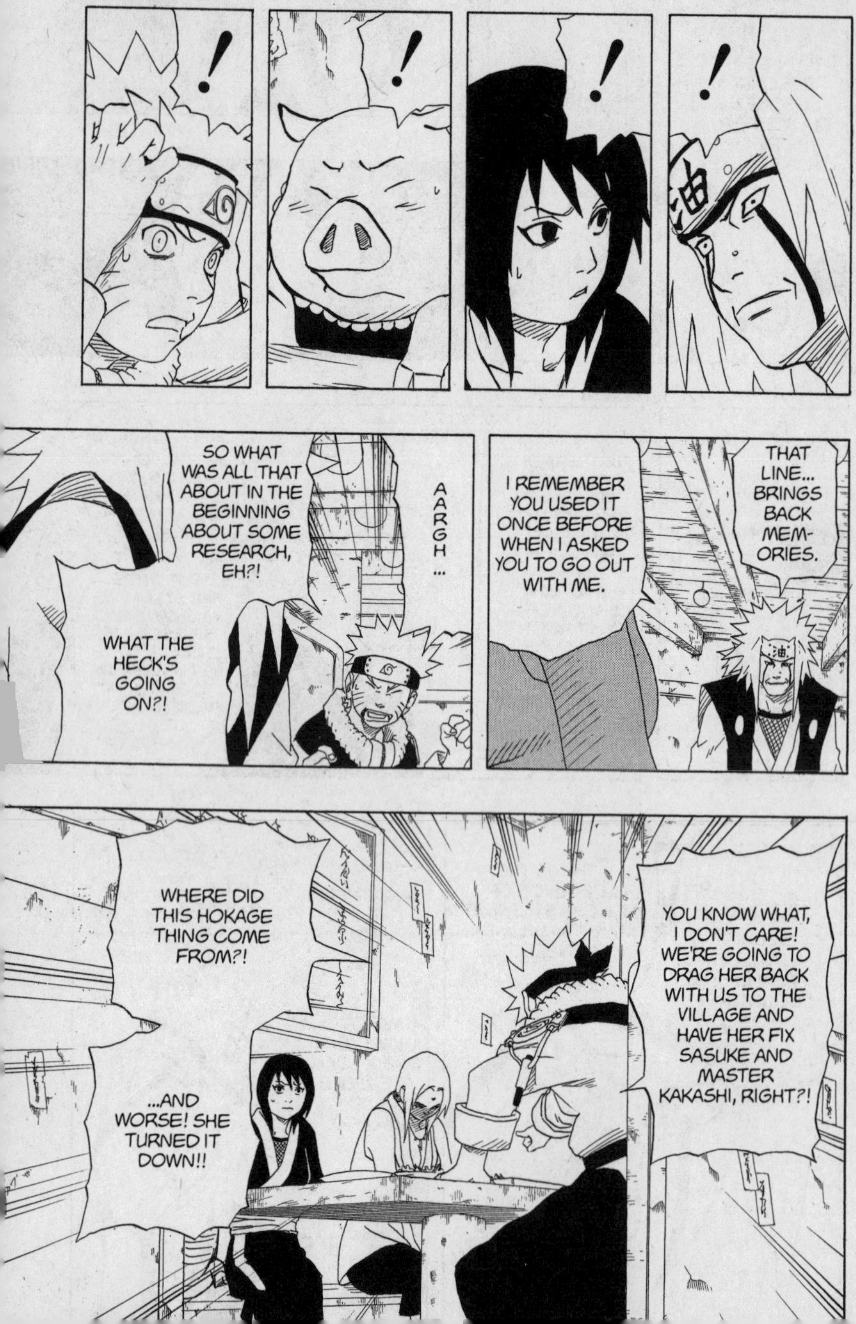

!

!

!

!

THAT LINE... BRINGS BACK MEM-ORIES.
I REMEMBER YOU USED IT ONCE BEFORE WHEN I ASKED YOU TO GO OUT WITH ME.

AARGH...
SO WHAT WAS ALL THAT ABOUT IN THE BEGINNING ABOUT SOME RESEARCH, EH?!
WHAT THE HECK'S GOING ON?!

WHERE DID THIS HOKAGE THING COME FROM?!

...AND WORSE! SHE TURNED IT DOWN!!

YOU KNOW WHAT, I DON'T CARE! WE'RE GOING TO DRAG HER BACK WITH US TO THE VILLAGE AND HAVE HER FIX SASUKE AND MASTER KAKASHI, RIGHT?!

...

CALM YOURSELF.
TSUNADE'S THE ONLY POSSIBLE CHOICE FOR THE FIFTH HOKAGE...

...LADY TSUNADE...
DON'T TELL ME YOU'RE CONSIDERING ACCEPTING OROCHIMARU'S OFFER...

NOT ONLY DID SHE CONTRIBUTE GREATLY TOWARDS KONOHA'S VICTORY DURING THE TURBULENT ERA OF GREAT WAR...
BUT THERE ARE STILL NONE WHO CAN STAND SHOULDER TO SHOULDER WITH HER IN REGARDS TO BATTLE OR MEDICAL JUTSU.
FURTHERMORE, TSUNADE IS THE GRAND-DAUGHTER OF THE FIRST HOKAGE, SO SHE IS A KONOHA SHINOBI OF A MOST WORTHY BLOODLINE...

!

IF SHE WOULD JUST AGREE TO BECOME HOKAGE, WE CAN GO HOME.
AND THEN, LIKE YOU SAID...
WE CAN HAVE HER TAKE A LOOK AT SASUKE AND KAKASHI.

THIS IS THE DECISION OF KONOHA'S HIGHEST-RANKING WILL, THE COUNSELORS.
SO THE OPINIONS OF ONE JUNIOR NINJA DON'T REALLY COUNT...

HMPH

HEH... JIRAIYA.
...UNLIKE YOUR LAST DISCIPLE, THIS KID'S GOT WORSE MOUTH, BRAINS...
AND EVEN MUG.

WHAT ?!
AW, COME ON, EVERYBODY PALES IN COMPARISON TO THE FOURTH LORD.

AS A SHINOBI, HIS CAPACITY WAS UNPARALLELED, A TRUE ONE-OF-A-KIND...
HE WAS OVERFLOWING WITH TALENT FOR JUTSU AND INTELLIGENCE... HE WAS SOCIALLY POPULAR...AND WELL, HE WAS QUITE A LOOKER, JUST LIKE ME.

...BUT EVEN WITH ALL THAT GOING FOR HIM, HE DIED PREMATURELY...

SACRIFICING HIS LIFE FOR THE SAKE OF THE VILLAGE...

油

...

LIFE IS NOT LIKE MONEY...

...

...TO RISK AND THROW IT AWAY SO EASILY...
IS A FOOL'S ERRAND.

THEY SAY BOTH MY GRANDFATHER AND THE SECOND LORD...WANTED AN END TO HOSTILITIES MORE THAN ANYTHING...
AND YET IN THE END, THEY DIED IN VAIN FOR THE VILLAGE, WHILE STILL IN THE MIDST OF PURSUING THEIR DREAMS.

YOU'VE CHANGED, TSUNADE...
I DON'T KNOW IF THESE THOUGHTS HAD BEEN RUNNING THROUGH YOUR MIND THE WHOLE TIME, BUT TO ACTUALLY BE VOICING THEM...
HUMPH... I AM IN MY FIFTIES, YOU KNOW...
TIME CHANGES PEOPLE.

...
SAME THING WITH MASTER SARUTOBI...
IF A TEETERING GEEZER TRIES TO ACT YOUTHFUL, OF COURSE HE'S GOING TO CROAK!
FLCK

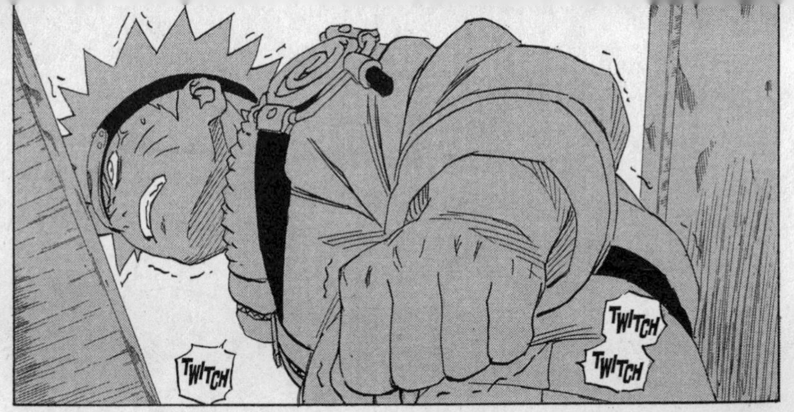
TWITCH
TWITCH
TWITCH

THE TITLE OF HOKAGE'S A JOKE.
ONLY A FOOL WOULD TAKE IT.

KRASH

CHUF
BOING
GGH!

HEYYY
!!!
LEMME GO
!!!
DOWN! THIS IS A PUB.

WH... WHAT'S GOING ON?
CAN I HELP YOU?
LEMMEGO!!

UGH...
LADY TSU-NADE ...!

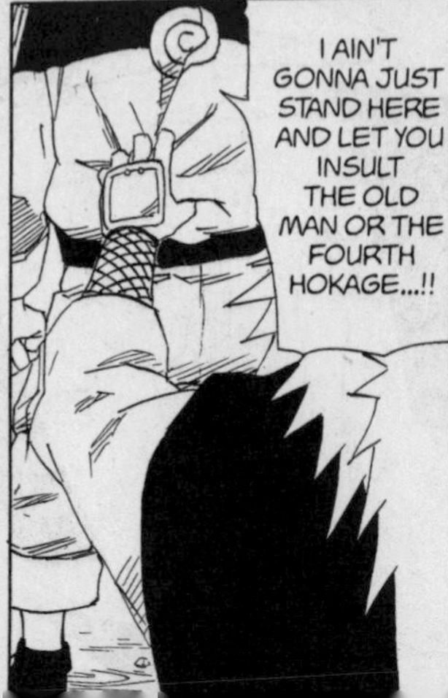
I AIN'T GONNA JUST STAND HERE AND LET YOU INSULT THE OLD MAN OR THE FOURTH HOKAGE...!!

...

I DON'T CARE THAT YOU'RE A LADY!!
I'LL SLUG YOU WITH ALL I'VE GOT!!!
BAM

READ THIS WAY

...

...

...

...

...
YOU GOT GUTS, I'LL GIVE YOU THAT... TO SAY IT TO MY FACE...
FWHMP
COME ON OUTSIDE WITH ME... BRAT.
...LADY TSUNADE!

GRR...!!

...
SIGH...
油

DESPITE HOW I MIGHT LOOK, I WAS ONCE COUNTED AMONG THE PRODIGAL THREE.
I DON'T NEED MY FULL STRENGTH AGAINST A GENIN.

WHAT ?!!

THIS ONE FINGER'LL BE ENOUGH.
JAB

...
SWISH
KLIK
KRNCH

KLAP
GIVE ME A BREAK !!
WHOOSH
SWISH
SLASH
DUKK
JAB
WHPP
OW!
FWP
TWRRL
KLUTCH

WHAPP
UGGH
ARGH!
NRR
!
GAH!

LADY TSU-NADE ...

ZWOOOOSH

UNH...
SHE FLICKED MY FORE-HEAD...?! HOW DARE SHE...!
FHWMP

!
WHOOSH

!!
THOK

KLUNK

...HEY
...KID!
I'VE JUST GOT ONE QUESTION FOR YOU BEFORE YOU PASS OUT.

...!

WHY...
...ARE YOU SO SENSITIVE ABOUT THE TITLE HOKAGE?

...'CUZ UNLIKE YOU...
I WANT THAT TITLE SOMEDAY...!
HUF
HUF

...
FLCK

TO BE HOKAGE IS MY DREAM!

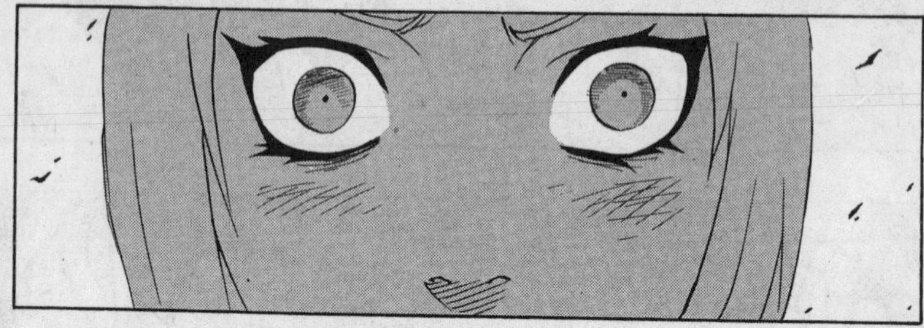

...

THIS CHILD...
...

...GRUNT...

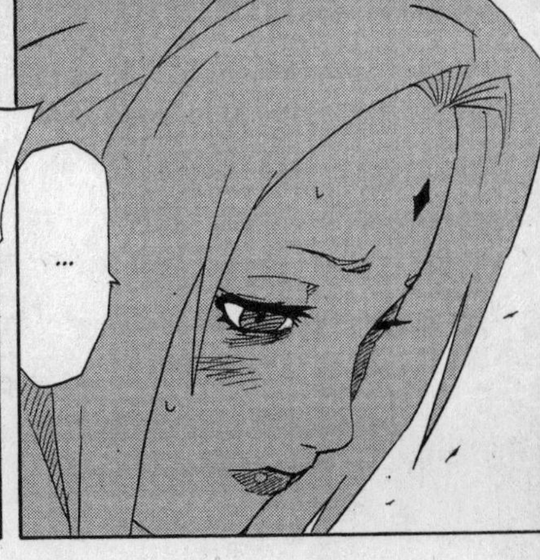
...

?!
WHAT THE?!
...I COULD...!

...I- CAN...
I SHOULD USE THAT JUTSU...!
KURL

FOCUS...!

WHOOSH

READ THIS WAY

GUK GUK GUK

...

HUNH?
!

HAAH !!

!!
WHA...THIS JUTSU'S...!!
TAKE THIS !!

THE WORLD OF KISHIMOTO MASASHI
MY PERSONAL HISTORY, PART 28

RECENTLY, ALL SORTS OF THINGS ARE BECOMING DIGITIZED. THE *NARUTO* COMICS ARE APPARENTLY THE FIRST COMIC BOOK SERIES THAT IS EDITED DIGITALLY.

WHEN I WAS A COLLEGE STUDENT, THERE WAS A PARTICULAR MUSIC VIDEO THAT I REALLY GOT HOOKED ON. IT WAS KEN ISHII'S MUSIC VIDEO, EXTRA. IT CONTAINS THE WORK OF ONE OF MY FAVORITE ANIMATORS, MR. KOJI MORIMOTO. THE VIDEO WAS SHOWN OVER AND OVER ON MTV, AND GOT BIG ENOUGH THAT IT EVEN BECAME A CONVERSATION TOPIC AMONG MY COLLEGE FRIENDS. PRETTY AWESOME, THEY'D SAY!

I HAD SOMEHOW HEARD THAT IT WAS AN ANIME VIDEO PRODUCED BY A JAPANESE ANIMATOR, BUT UNTIL I ACTUALLY WATCHED IT, IT DIDN'T QUITE HIT ME. BUT THEN, I WAS STRUCK WHEN I DID! I GOT SUCKED INTO IT SO MUCH THAT I PLAYED HOOKY FROM SCHOOL AND SAT AT HOME WATCHING IT ALL DAY. THE REASON WHY I GOT SO HOOKED WAS BECAUSE I HAD NEVER SEEN SUCH MIND-BLOWING IMAGES BEFORE! TO USE A MORE CURRENT REFERENCE, IT WAS AN IMPACT LIKE THE SLO-MO FLYING BULLET SEQUENCE IN *THE MATRIX*.

FIRST, EVEN THOUGH THE SUBJECT CHARACTERS AND PERSPECTIVE KEEP RAPIDLY CHANGING, THE BACKGROUND SHIFTS ACCORDINGLY AND IN SYNC. AND THE NARROW SENSE OF SPACE AND DEPTH WAS SO REALISTIC. AT FIRST I WONDERED, HOW DID HE DO THIS? BUT BECAUSE I KNEW HE COULDN'T HAVE DRAWN THE BACKGROUNDS BY HAND, I REALIZED THAT HE MUST HAVE DIGITALLY RENDERED IT USING A COMPUTER OR SOMETHING AND THEN ADDED THE BACKGROUNDS AS TEXTURE LAYERS...I HEARD THEY DID THAT WITH GAMES LIKE *VIRTUA FIGHTER 2*, TOO...SUCH WERE THE GEEKY CONVERSATIONS I WAS HAVING.

NOW THAT ANIME HAS ENTERED THE DIGITAL AGE AS WELL, SUCH MOVING BACKGROUNDS ARE NO LONGER NOVELTIES. IN FACT, THERE ARE WORKS NOW WHERE EVEN THE CHARACTERS ARE RENDERED FROM POLYGONS AND ONE NO LONGER HAS TO DRAW EACH CELL INDIVIDUALLY. JUST...WHEN ONE USES THE COMPUTER, THE LINES ARE TOO CLEAN... IT KIND OF LOSES A LITTLE OF THE ENERGY... OR EMOTIONAL IMPACT, SOMETHING LIKE THAT... I FEEL LIKE SOME OF THE NICE PARTS OF HAND DRAWING HAVE DISAPPEARED (ESPECIALLY IN TERMS OF THE CHARACTERS).

I WISH THIS FEEL-GOOD STUFF COULD BE EXPRESSED BY THE COMPUTER AS WELL; THAT WOULD MAKE THINGS PERFECT... IT SEEMS LIKE MANGA ARE ALSO GETTING MORE AND MORE DIGITIZED, BUT I WONDER IF DIGITAL TECHNOLOGY STILL COSTS TOO MUCH TIME AND MONEY...?

Number 159: The Wager...!!

TH... THIS JUTSU, IT'S?!
OOO
SWISH

VWO
FWHOO
ROOOOAR!!

!!
KLNK
!
WAAH!
FWHMP
GAKK

THUDDD
THUMP
ARGH!!

...I NEVER EXPECTED HIM... TO TRY TO USE THE FOURTH LORD'S JUTSU.
...

...I REMEMBER ONCE GETTING CLOBBERED BY HER AND BEING BLOWN BACK ALMOST 100 METERS...
THAT TSUNADE... STILL GOT MONSTER STRENGTH, EVEN AFTER ALL THESE YEARS, EH...
...

BUT EITHER WAY, NARUTO, YOU GOTTA DO BETTER...
UGH!

HACK... HACK!
ARE YOU ALL RIGHT...?

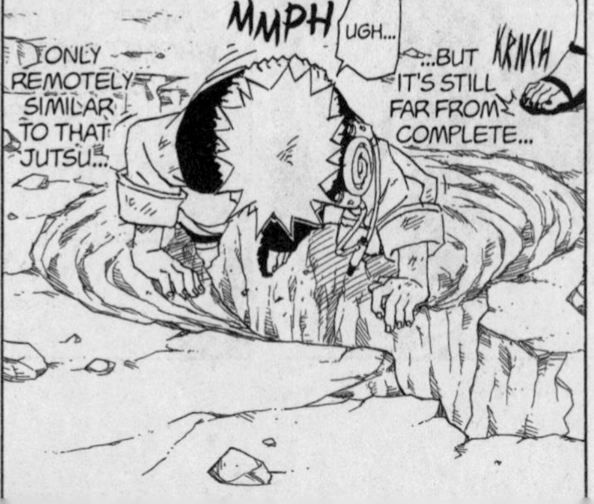
MMPH
UGH...
ONLY REMOTELY SIMILAR TO THAT JUTSU...
...BUT IT'S STILL FAR FROM COMPLETE...
KRNCH

JIRAIYA, WAS IT YOU?
WHO TAUGHT HIM THE RASENGAN?!

I AM HIS MENTOR, YOU KNOW... FOR THE PRESENT...
HUMPH... THE ONLY ONES WHO CAN MANAGE THAT JUTSU ARE YOU AND THE FOURTH LORD.

RASENGAN...?!
TWITCH

PLAYING MIGHTY MENTOR BY TEACHING HIM JUTSU HE HAS NO HOPE OF MASTERING?
...THAT'S PRETTY CRUEL.

THAT'S HOW DREAMY-EYED BRATS GET STARTED ON THE WHOLE *I'M GOING TO BECOME HOKAGE* FARCE!

...
...

IT'S NOT A FARCE!!
SHUT UP! SHUT UP!!

...
GIVE ME THREE DAYS, AND I'LL MASTER THIS JUTSU FOR YOU!!

FEH... NICE WORDS, BRAT...
BUT A MAN DOESN'T BREAK HIS WORD, YOU KNOW!
HEH!

I NEVER GO BACK ON MY WORD...
...THAT'S MY SHINOBI WAY!

...
...
...GRUNT.

...THEN...
...LET'S MAKE A WAGER.

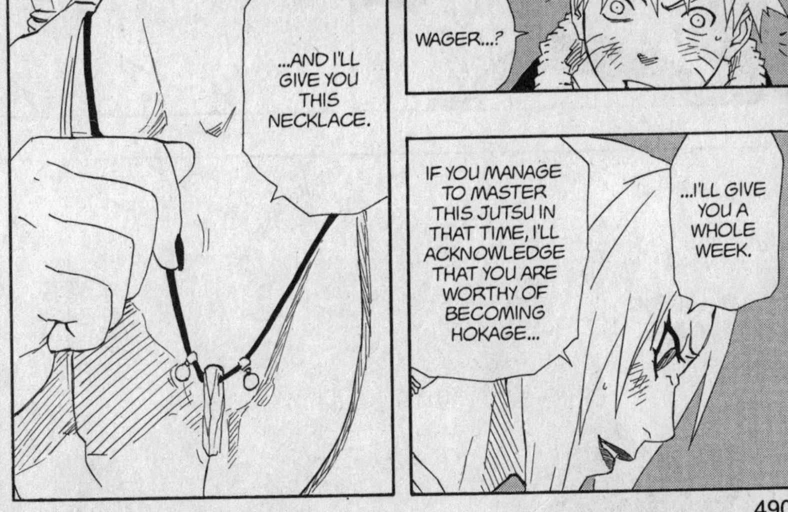
WAGER...?
...I'LL GIVE YOU A WHOLE WEEK.
IF YOU MANAGE TO MASTER THIS JUTSU IN THAT TIME, I'LL ACKNOWLEDGE THAT YOU ARE WORTHY OF BECOMING HOKAGE...
...AND I'LL GIVE YOU THIS NECKLACE.

READ
THIS
WAY

!
LADY TSUNADE?! B...BUT THAT'S...!

!
NO THANKS, I DON'T WANT SOME OLD NECKLACE!

...NOW NOW, DON'T SAY THAT, NARUTO...
IT'S MADE FROM A UNIQUE ORE THAT BELONGED TO THE FIRST HOKAGE.
YOU COULD BUY THREE MOUNTAINS IF YOU SOLD IT...

WH... WHOA...
O...OH... OKAY!
...WHAT A MER-CENARY...

HOWEVER, IF YOU FAIL TO MASTER THE JUTSU BY THE END OF SEVEN DAYS...
YOU LOSE!
AND ALL YOUR EASY CASH IS MINE!!
TA-DAA

HEY! MY FROGGIE!
WHEN THE HECK DID SHE ...?!

...
LADY TSUNADE...

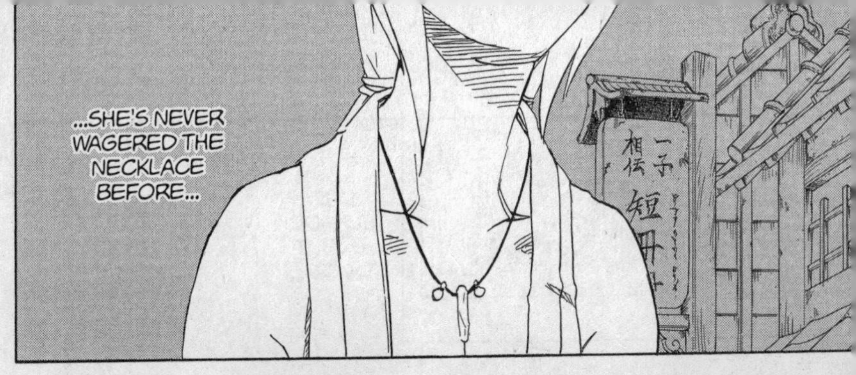
...SHE'S NEVER WAGERED THE NECKLACE BEFORE...

BUT WHY?! THE NECKLACE IS...!
HMPH, IT'S NOT LIKE HE'S GOING TO MANAGE IT...
KRNCH
!

WHRRL
LET'S GO, SHIZUNE!

...YOU NEED NOT GIVE US YOUR ANSWER THIS VERY MINUTE...
HOWEVER, WE WOULD LIKE A RESPONSE IN ONE WEEK'S TIME.

...

TSUNADE... WON'T YOU COME DRINKING A BIT LONGER WITH ME?
FOR OLD TIME'S SAKE...
!

READ THIS WAY

SHIZUNE, COULD YOU TAKE NARUTO WITH YOU AND GO LOOK FOR THE NIGHT'S LODGINGS?
...!
CLOMP CLOMP

...

THAT OK WITH YOU?

...
YES, SIR!
THANK YOU... LORD JIRAIYA...

?

...
THERE YA GO!
KLINK

MAN...YOU'VE GOTTEN EVEN PRETTIER THAN THE LAST TIME I SAW YOU...

...AND YOU HAVEN'T CHANGED AT ALL...
LET ME MAKE THIS CLEAR: I STILL HAVE NO INTEREST IN YOU.
HUMPH! I DON'T GOT THE HOTS FOR YOU NEITHER!

ESPECIALLY SINCE YOU'RE ACTUALLY LIKE AN OLD WOMAN NOW...
...WHAT'D YOU JUST SAY?!
NOTHING...

...

...
...

READ THIS WAY

SO DOES IT BOTHER YOU...?
WHAT?

...NARUTO.

...
WHY SHOULD HE...?

WELL, THAT WAS PRETTY IMMATURE, CHALLENGING A KID LIKE THAT...
YOU KNOW THERE'S NO WAY HE CAN MASTER THAT JUTSU IN UNDER A WEEK.
I WOULDN'T CALL IT A WAGER...

TSK...
...

WHY SO DES-PERATE...?

I'M *NOT* DESPERATE!

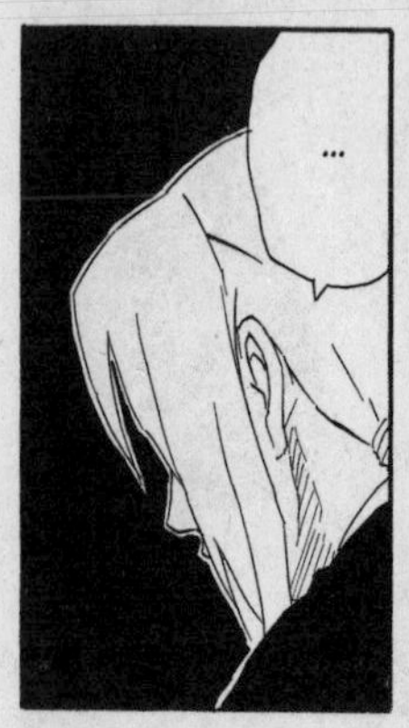
...

YOU MEETING WITH OROCHI-MARU?

...!

I SAW THE LOOK ON SHIZUNE'S FACE.
I DON'T KNOW WHAT KIND OF OFFER HE MADE YOU, BUT...

...JUST DON'T RUSH INTO IT.

OH, AND...
...I GOTTA TELL YOU ONE THING.

...

EVERY ONE OF THE PREVIOUS HOKAGE RISKED THEIR LIVES TO PROTECT THE VILLAGE OF KONOHA AND ALL THOSE WHO LIVE THERE...

...THEY WANTED AN END TO TURBULENT DAYS AND TO SEE THE VILLAGE PROSPER. IT WAS THOSE IDEALS...

...THAT WAS THE DREAM THEY FOUGHT FOR!

I DOUBT THAT YOU DON'T UNDERSTAND OUR PREDECESSORS' FEELINGS.

BUT...IF YOU SHOULD EVER HAPPEN TO DO SOMETHING THAT WOULD BETRAY OUR VILLAGE OF KONOHA...

...

I'LL PERSONALLY HUNT YOU DOWN AND KILL YOU!

...WHY SHOULD I CARE ANYMORE, EH!

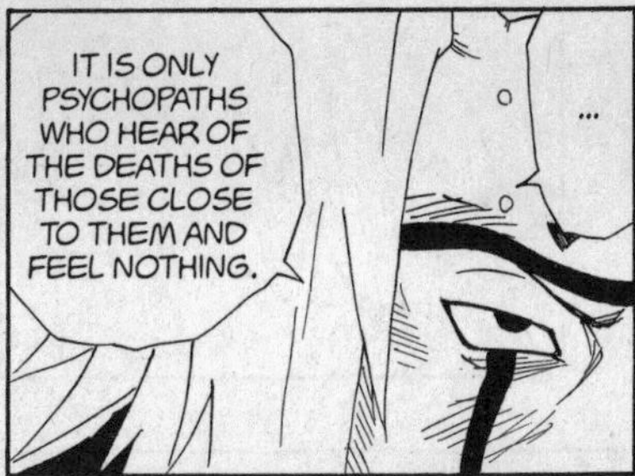
...
IT IS ONLY PSYCHOPATHS WHO HEAR OF THE DEATHS OF THOSE CLOSE TO THEM AND FEEL NOTHING.

...
THAT'S NOT YOU, IS IT?

YOU USED TO BE THE FIRST TO CARE ABOUT THE SAFETY AND WELL-BEING OF FELLOW VILLAGERS...
EVEN THAT DAY...
THAT'S ENOUGH!

...

...

READ THIS WAY

...
WHY... DID YOU BRING ALONG THAT BRAT.

TO BE HOKAGE...
...IS MY DREAM!

...

...
UNCANNY, ISN'T IT? ...HE'S EVEN ABOUT THE SAME AGE...

...

TO BE HOKAGE...

...IS MY DREAM!

SHEESH, ALWAYS TAKING SUCH RISKS...DO YOU WANT TO DIE?!
YOU'RE STILL A GENIN, NAWAKI, SO ON THE BATTLEFIELD, IT'S OKAY TO RUN OFF!

DON'T YOU TELL A MAN TO RUN!!

...
EVEN HIS DREAM... AND HIS DRIVE...

THE TIME LIMIT'S ONE WEEK!
I SWEAR I'M GONNA MASTER THAT WHATEVERITIS-GAN JUTSU!!

KNOK
KNOK

KLIK
SORRY TO BOTHER YOU SO LATE, NARUTO... BUT THERE'S SOMETHING I'D LIKE TO SHARE WITH YOU...

...

Number 160:
The Necklace of Death...!!

IT'S THE MIDDLE OF THE NIGHT... WHAT'S SO IMPORTANT?!
I NEED TO REST UP TONIGHT SO I CAN TRAIN EARLY!

I'M SORRY...
...BUT I DON'T WANT YOU TO MISUNDERSTAND LADY TSUNADE...
...AND I WANTED TO EXPLAIN ABOUT THE NECKLACE, TOO...

HUMPH! WHAT DO I CARE ABOUT THAT OLD LADY?!
LADY TSUNADE ISN'T THE KIND OF PERSON YOU THINK SHE IS!
PLEASE DON'T SAY SUCH THINGS WITHOUT KNOWING ANYTHING!

...

...
I'M SORRY... I DIDN'T MEAN TO RAISE MY VOICE AT YOU...

READ THIS WAY

SHE WASN'T LIKE THAT AT ALL, LONG AGO...
SHE WAS KIND AND COMPASSION-ATE...SHE REALLY LOVED THE VILLAGE...
BUT THEN... SHE CHANGED...

...

...ALL BECAUSE OF THAT DAY.

?
THAT DAY...?

...

WHAT DO YOU MEAN... THAT DAY...?

THE DAY SHE LOST EVERY-THING...
...HER DREAMS, HER LOVE, EVEN HOPE ITSELF!

...ALL THAT REMAINED AFTER-WARDS...
...WAS THE NECKLACE, LOADED WITH MEMORIES...

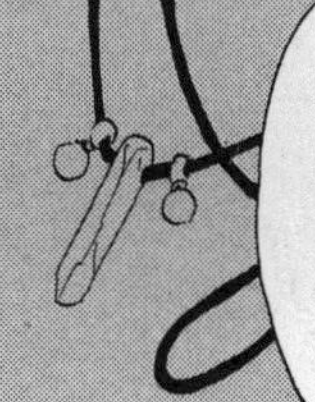

THE NECKLACE IS AS PRECIOUS TO LADY TSUNADE AS HER OWN LIFE...
IT'S NOT SOMETHING SHE WOULD EASILY HAND OVER ON A WAGER...

...?!

HOW WOULD I KNOW THAT?!
SHE'S THE ONE WHO PUT IT ON THE TABLE!

AND...THE NECKLACE IS NOT MEANT FOR YOU!
IT'S NO ORDINARY NECK-LACE...

?

IT ONLY ACKNOWLEDGES LADY TSUNADE...
...IF ANYONE ELSE TRIES TO WEAR IT, THEY ALL EVENTUALLY...

...DIE!!
...?!

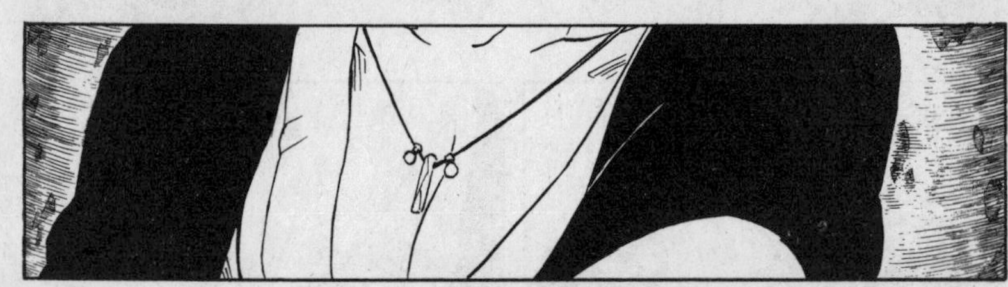

...BUT I CAN'T BELIEVE YOU STILL HANG ON TO THE NECKLACE...
I THOUGHT YOU'D ALREADY LOST IT IN A WAGER.
HUMPH ...

...IT'S A MEMENTO, ISN'T IT...?

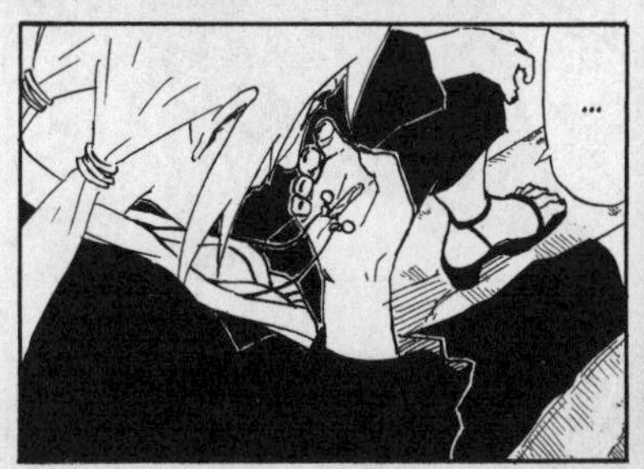
...

NAWAKI!
HAPPY 12th BIRTHDAY!
THWAP
YOU KNOW, I'M NOT A KID ANYMORE!
DON'T KEEP GETTING ME BIRTHDAY PRESENTS!
OH, COME ON!
YOU ARE STILL A KID!
BESIDES, HURRY UP AND OPEN IT!
I BET YOU'RE GONNA LIKE IT!
RIP RIP
?
!
BUT BIG SIS, ISN'T THIS...
YUP...IT WAS THE FIRST HOKAGE'S, OUR BELOVED GRANDFATHER'S, HOKAGE NECKLACE!
I LOVE YOU, SIS!
UNF
I THOUGHT IT WOULD BE BETTER FOR YOU TO HAVE IT.
I MEAN, YOU'VE ALWAYS WANTED IT... SO TAKE GOOD CARE OF IT!

IT'S NOT JUST THIS NECKLACE YOU KNOW
WHOOSH
THE ENTIRE VILLAGE WAS GRANDPA'S TREASURE! AND I'M GOING TO DEFEND IT!
'CUZ I'M THE GRANDSON OF THE FIRST HOKAGE, THE BUILDER OF KONOHA-GAKURE!
HO HO... NICE WORDS, BUT A MAN DOESN'T BREAK HIS WORD, YOU KNOW!
YUP!
I'M GONNA BE STRONG LIKE GRANDPA AND ONE DAY BE GRANTED THE TITLE OF HOKAGE!
'CUZ TO BE HOKAGE IS MY DREAM.
TAKE YOUR HEADBAND OFF, NAWAKI.
SST
?
JUST DO IT. I'VE GOT ONE MORE PRESENT FOR YOU.
A CHARM TO MAKE YOUR DREAM COME TRUE.
FFFT

HUF
HUF
HUF

HUF
HUF
SPLASH...
!
YOU PROBABLY OUGHTN'T LOOK AT THE BODY...
WHY NOT...?
IT'S NOT LIKE SHE COULD TELL JUST BY...
QUIT IT, OROCHI-MARU!
WE *ARE* IN THE MIDDLE OF A WAR, YOU KNOW...
THIS IS THE INEVITABLE END FOR A SHINOBI, SINCE THERE ARE NO MEDICS ON THE BATTLE-FIELD.
SWISH SWISH
...BUT... CHILDREN ARE SO EXCITABLE, AREN'T THEY...
I MEAN, THE VERY NEXT DAY AFTER GETTING PRESENTS.

READ THIS WAY
CLENCH
IT'S NOT JUST THE NECKLACE, YOU KNOW!
THE ENTIRE VILLAGE WAS GRANDPA'S TREASURE!
AND I'M GOING TO DEFEND IT!
...FIRST AND FOREMOST, FOR THOSE FOUR-MAN CELLS THAT WILL BE SPENDING...
...EXTENDED TOURS IN ENEMY TERRITORY, ON MISSIONS REQUIRING AUTONOMOUS ACTIVITY...

...I FEEL THAT ASSIGNING A MEDICAL SPECIALIST AS ONE OF THE FOUR UNIT MEMBERS...
...WOULD GREATLY INCREASE BOTH THE MISSION SUCCESS RATE AS WELL AS THE UNIT SURVIVAL RATE.
THUS, I BELIEVE THAT THE CULTIVATING OF MEDIC NINJA POSSESSING ADVANCED MEDICAL KNOWLEDGE AND THE FURTHER DEVELOPMENT OF MEDICAL NINJUTSU...
...THE ESTABLISHMENT OF SUCH A SYSTEM OUGHT TO BE OUR TOP PRIORITY!
MMM...
FOR SURE, THE NEED IS THERE, AS YOU SAY...
...BUT WE ARE CURRENTLY IN THE MIDDLE OF A WAR... IN ORDER TO ACTUALIZE A MEDICAL INSTITUTION, NOT ONLY DOES IT TAKE TIME, BUT WE LACK TOO MUCH KNOW-HOW AT THE PRESENT TIME AS WELL.
THE ENEMY IS *NOT* GOING TO WAIT AROUND FOR US TO...
HEY, LISTEN UP, GEEZER!
BAM
SO WHEN ARE WE EVER GONNA...
!
I AGREE WITH HER COMPLETELY.

I DO NOT WANT TO WASTE THE DEATHS OF THOSE SHINOBI WHO HAVE ALREADY SACRIFICED THEIR LIVES.
WE OUGHT TO LEARN SOMETHING FROM THEM.
...
U...UM... THANKS FOR EARLIER.
!
...
YOU ARE CORRECT, YOU KNOW.
...
UM...
IT'S GETTING LATE... YOU WANT ME TO ESCORT YOU HOME...?
HUH?
REALLY? BUT WHERE DO YOU LIVE...?
IN THE OPPOSITE DIRECTION.
THEN DON'T WORRY ABOUT IT.
...NO, REALLY... I WANTED TO TALK TO YOU ANYWAY...

THIS WAS THE STREET I USED TO ALWAYS TAKE ESCORTING MY LITTLE SISTER TO THE ACADEMY.
IT'S MY FAVORITE PATH.
AND BESIDE
THIS MAN... HE'S JUST LIKE ME...
TOMORROW, OUR MISSIONS WILL TAKE US TO THE FRONT LINE...
TO FIGHT AND LOSE THOSE WE LOVE...
...ISN'T THE ONLY JOB OF A SHINOBI, YOU KNOW.
IT'S BECAUSE I LIVE IN THE WORLD OF SHINOBI, CONSTANTLY SHADOWED BY DEATH...
THAT I WANT TO STAKE MY LIFE ON PUTTING AN END TO THIS ERA OF CONFLICT.
I LOVE THIS VILLAGE, AND ALL OF MY FRIENDS...
THAT'S WHY I WANT TO DEFEND IT.
...I KNOW...
SINCE THE DAY MY LITTLE SISTER DIED...
THIS THOUGHT IS THE ONLY THING THAT'S BEEN KEEPING ME
THAT'S WHY I WANT TO BECOME HOKAGE...

BECAUSE TO BECOME THE PROTECTOR... THE HOKAGE, IS MY DREAM.
...!
DAN...
CLENCH!
I WANT YOU TO...
...ACCEPT THIS...

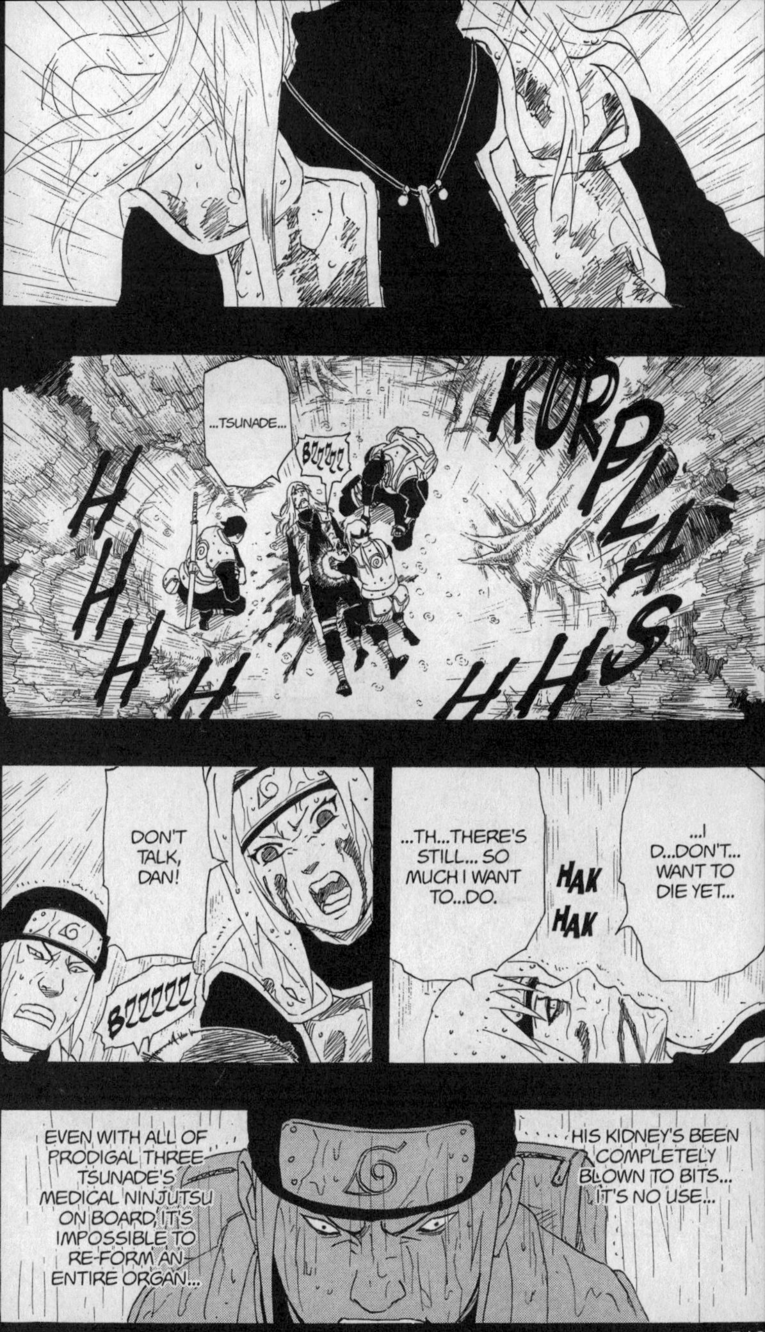
KORPLASHHH
...TSUNADE...
BZZZZZ
HHHH
DON'T TALK, DAN!
BZZZZZ
...I D...DON'T... WANT TO DIE YET...
HAK HAK
...TH...THERE'S STILL... SO MUCH I WANT TO...DO.
....HIS KIDNEY'S BEEN COMPLETELY BLOWN TO BITS... IT'S NO USE...
EVEN WITH ALL OF PRODIGAL THREE TSUNADE'S MEDICAL NINJUTSU ON BOARD, IT'S IMPOSSIBLE TO RE-FORM AN ENTIRE ORGAN...

...I...CAN'T AFFORD...TO DIE...HERE...
DON'T WORRY, I'VE STOPPED THE BLEEDING!
...YOU'RE IN THE CLEAR NOW... YOU'LL HEAL, DAN!
...REALLY...? OH, GOOD...
...
BZZZZZZZ
UGH ...!
UNH...
BZZZZZ
ZPURT
ZPURT

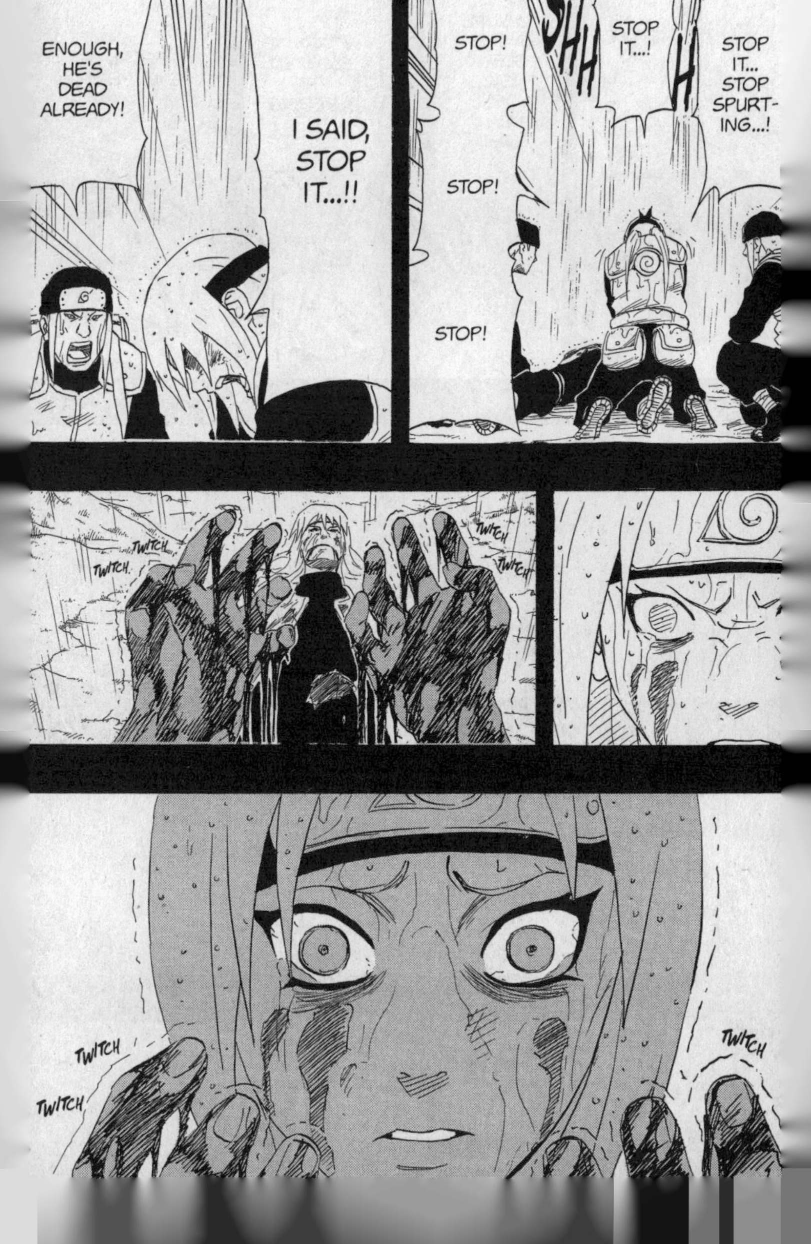
SHHH
STOP IT...!
STOP IT... STOP SPURTING...!
STOP!
STOP!
STOP!
I SAID, STOP IT...!!
ENOUGH, HE'S DEAD ALREADY!
TWITCH
TWITCH
TWITCH
TWITCH
TWITCH
TWITCH
TWITCH

SHMP

民宿

SO PLEASE UNDER-STAND, NARUTO...
SINCE THAT DAY, LADY TSUNADE'S... BEEN TORN.
SWSH

KLAK

?!
NARUTO ...?

I'M GONNA GO...
...TRAIN!!

THE WORLD OF KISHIMOTO MASASHI
MY PERSONAL HISTORY, PART 29

I FEEL LIKE I GEEKED TOO MUCH IN MY PERSONAL HISTORY PARTS 27 AND 28, SO I THINK I'LL WRITE AN EMOTIONAL STORY THIS TIME.

IN ANY CASE, IMMEDIATELY FOLLOWING MY MANGA *KARAKURI* WINNING THE HOP☆STEP AWARD, MY ASSIGNED EDITOR MR. YAHAGI ASKED ME TO DRAW A DRAFT (KIND OF A ROUGH SKETCH OF A MANGA) OF A STAND-ALONE STORY. WHEN HE SAW *WANDERING DETOUR*, THE BIG MISTAKE OF A MANGA THAT I JUST DREW WILLY-NILLY, MR. YAHAGI SIMPLY SAID, THIS...ISN'T SHONEN MAGAZINE MATERIAL! A-HA-HA-HA. AND I WAS THE MASOCHISTIC NEWBIE WHO REPLIED, SO IT'S A REJECT... HUH ACTUALLY REVELING IN THE REVERBERATION OF THE WORD REJECTION AND EVEN HAPPILY SELF-PROCLAIMING THAT IT WAS A REJECT (SEE VOLUME 4, PAGE 26'S KISHIMOTO MASASHI'S FIRST MANGA REJECT SPECIAL).

LATER ON, MR. YAHAGI ENCOURAGED ME WITH WHY DON'T YOU DRAW A MORE SHÔNEN-STYLE BATTLE EPIC! SO I EQUALLY EAGERLY REPLIED, RIGHT! AND WANTING TO MEET MR. YAHAGI'S EXPECTATIONS, I IMMEDIATELY SET OUT TO THINK UP A NEW VERSION OF MY WINNING WORK, *KARAKURI*. OF COURSE THE STORY OF AN ELEMENTARY SCHOOL KID AND HIS MISADVENTURES ON THE WAY HOME FROM SCHOOL ISN'T ENTERTAINING! WHAT A FOOL I HAD BEEN! I HADN'T UNDERSTOOD ANYTHING! AND THE REGRET WENT ON... SO I QUICKLY DREW AN ALTERNATE VERSION OF *KARAKURI* AND MAILED IT IN...THIS TIME, FOR SURE...

MR. YAHAGI SIMPLY SAID, ER...I DON'T UNDERSTAND IT AT ALL! A-HA-HA-HA. SO AGAIN, I SELF-PROFESSED, ...WHICH MEANS...IT'S REJECTED, RIGHT...AND ONCE AGAIN, I HADN'T MET MR. YAHAGI'S EXPECTATIONS. ...THIS TIME, I LOST MY EAGERNESS. I BECAME QUITE DEPRESSED, IN FACT. ...REALITY IS HARSH. ...THEN ONE DAY, I RECEIVED A LETTER FROM MR. YAHAGI. WHEN I EXAMINED IT, I REALIZED IT CONTAINED TWO FULL PAGES OF POINTERS ABOUT HOW TO DRAW MANGA AND OTHER ADVICE. AND, WHEN I GOT TO THE END OF THAT LETTER...MY EYES STARTED WELLING A BIT WITH TEARS. HERE'S WHAT IT SAID...

"YOU DO HAVE TALENT. PLEASE KEEP TRYING."

EVEN IF IT WERE A LIE OR FLATTERY, IT STILL MADE ME HAPPY! I HAD BEEN DEPRESSED, BUT IT RENEWED MY DETERMINATION! IMMEDIATELY, I STARTED DRAWING A DRAFT. AND THEN, WHEN I FOUND OUT THAT MR. YAHAGI HIMSELF WAS PLANNING TO PAY ME A PERSONAL VISIT TO MY HOUSE (IN KYUSHU) TO GO OVER IT, I PUT GREAT DRIVE INTO MY DRAFT, AND WENT TO MEET MR. YAHAGI AT MY LOCAL MISTER DONUT. I'M NOT GOING TO WASTE THOSE TEARS I SHED, I SWORE TO MYSELF! I PUT GREAT ENERGY INTO THIS DRAFT! THIS TIME FOR SURE!

HE TOOK A LOOK AT THE MANGA, THEN UTTERED, "THIS ISN'T REALLY MANGA..."

I DIDN'T KNOW WHAT TO SAY ANYMORE...SINCE THEN, I'VE GOTTEN DEPRESSED COUNTLESS TIMES, BUT EACH TIME I WOULD PULL OUT THAT LETTER AND REREAD IT TO THE END AGAIN...IT'S A PRECIOUS LETTER THAT I STILL PEEK AT FROM TIME TO TIME EVEN NOW.

Number 161: Tsunade's Choice!!

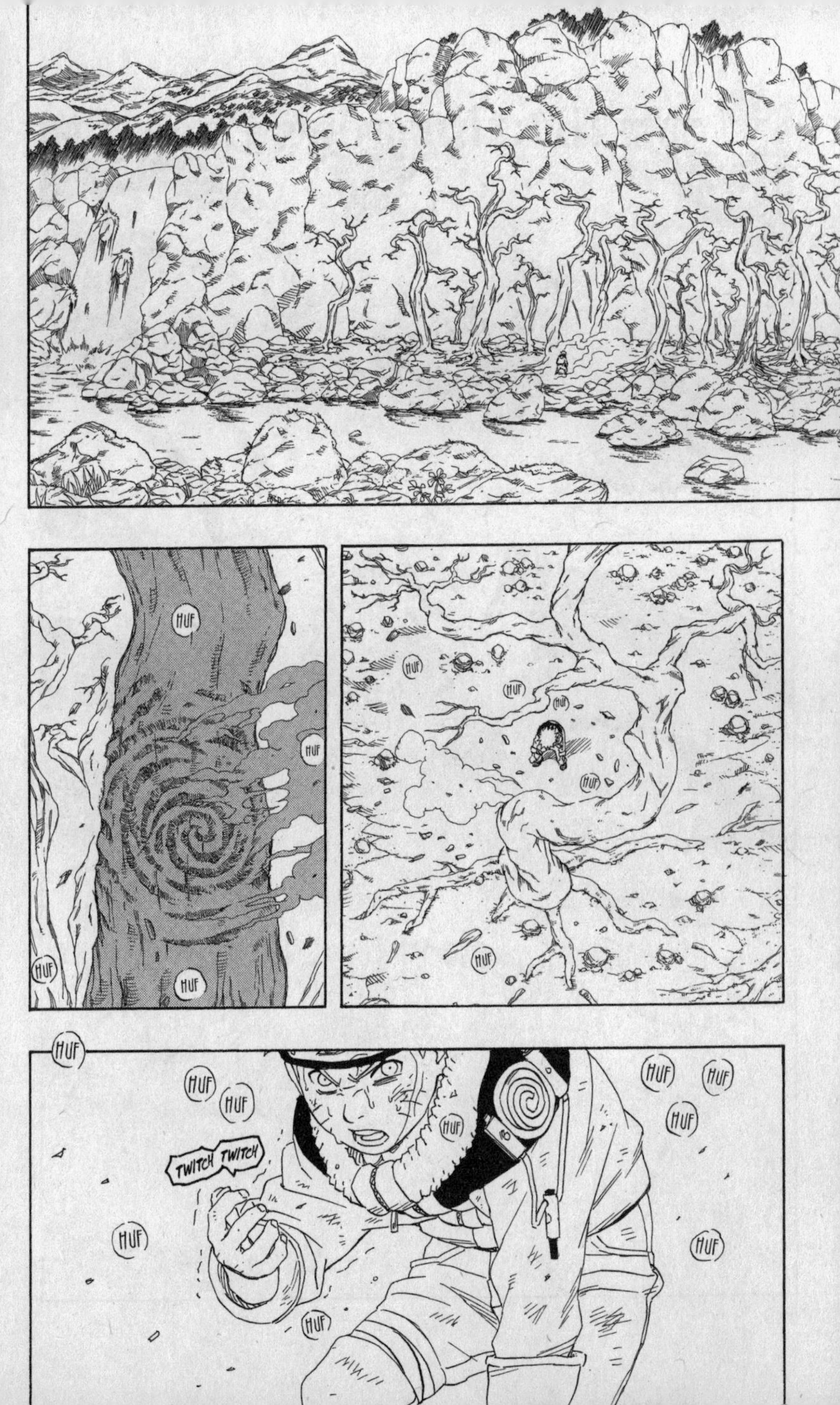
HUF
HUF
HUF
HUF
HUF
HUF
HUF
HUF
HUF
HUF
HUF
HUF
HUF
HUF
HUF
HUF
HUF
HUF
HUF
TWITCH TWITCH

READ THIS WAY

民

YAAWW... OWW, MY HEAD...
IOWW
THAT TSUNADE... I FEEL ROTTEN!

...
SCRITCH SCRITCH
THAT NARUTO... IT SEEMS HE NEVER CAME BACK LAST NIGHT, HUH...

KLAT
...
KLAK-KLAK

HE'S SUCH... A FOOL.

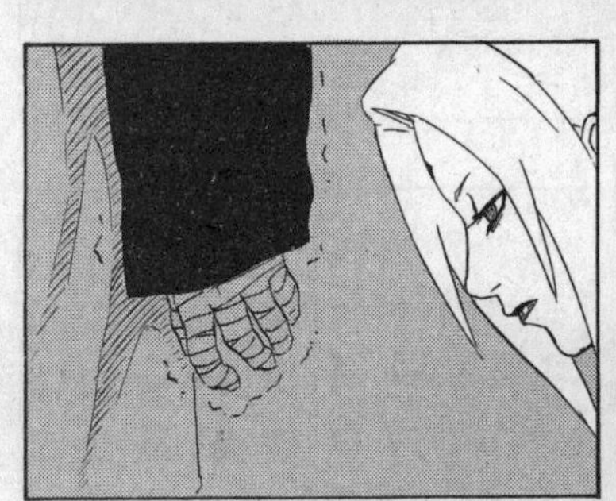

WON'T YOU CONSIDER... OUR OFFER?

...I CAN REANIMATE YOUR BELOVED LITTLE BROTHER AND LOVER BOTH.
I'VE LEARNED THE FORBIDDEN JUTSU...

DON'T YOU WANT TO SEE THEM AGAIN, TSUNADE...?

KLINK
KLINK
KLINK
KLINK

...SUPPOSE I FIX THOSE ARMS...WHAT ARE YOU GOING TO DO?

THIS TIME I ANNIHILATE KONOHA ONCE AND FOR ALL.

NO! YOU MUSTN'T BE TAKEN IN BY THEIR SWEET TALK...!
HAVE YOU FORGOTTEN THEIR WISHES... OR EVEN YOUR WISH... YOUR DREAM, LADY TSUNADE?!

I'LL LAY IT STRAIGHT, TSUNADE...
...THE VILLAGE REQUESTS THAT YOU ACCEPT THE TITLE OF FIFTH HOKAGE.

EVERY ONE OF THE PREVIOUS HOKAGE RISKED THEIR LIVES TO PROTECT THE VILLAGE OF KONOHA AND ALL THOSE WHO LIVE THERE...
...THEY WANTED AN END TO TURBULENT DAYS AND TO SEE THE VILLAGE PROSPER. IT WAS THOSE IDEALS...
...THAT WAS THE DREAM THEY FOUGHT FOR!

...

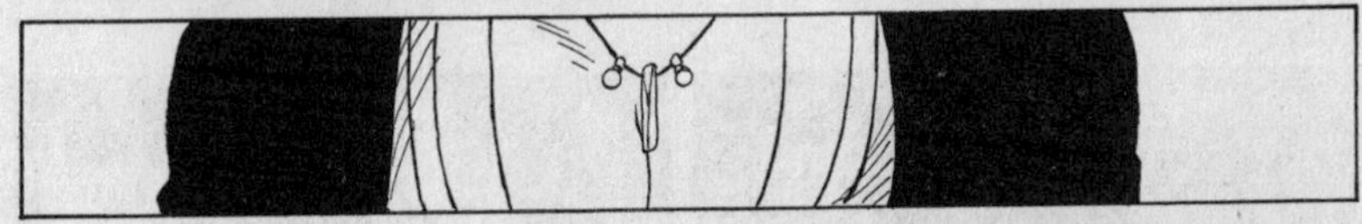

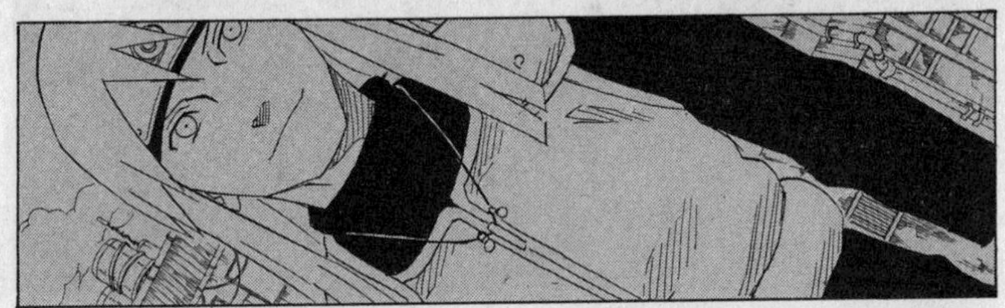

KLINK-KLINK

READ
THIS
WAY

THE SECOND NIGHT AFTER THE WAGER WITH TSUNADE...
HUF
HUF
HUF
HUF

IT'S NO USE!
HUF
HUF
HUF
UNGH!
HUF
I SWEAR, TOMOR-ROW, I'LL GET IT...!!

HUF
HUF
HUF
HUF
HUF

...

...YOU NEED NOT GIVE US YOUR ANSWER THIS VERY MINUTE... HOWEVER, WE WOULD LIKE A RESPONSE IN ONE WEEK'S TIME.
...OH AND JUST SO YOU KNOW, THIS FORBIDDEN JUTSU REQUIRES LIVE SACRIFICES... SO PLEASE HAVE TWO PEOPLE PREPARED ON YOUR END...

丁
半
ばくち

SO! WHICH WILL IT BE?!

WELL?! CALL IT!
...

READ THIS WAY

I WONDER WHICH IT WILL BE...

IF SHE ACQUIESCES TO OUR TERMS, THEN YOUR ARMS WILL BE HEALED AND YOU CAN RESUME OPERATION DESTROY KONOHA IMMEDIATELY, LORD OROCHIMARU...
PLUS, SHE WILL BE REUNITED WITH THE TWO PEOPLE SHE LOVES MOST.
HOWEVER... IF SHE SHOULD DECLINE...

...EVEN IF BY FORCE...
...I'LL MAKE HER FIX MY ARMS...

DO YOU THINK IT'LL GO SO EASILY...?
I'VE GOT YOU...

LEER

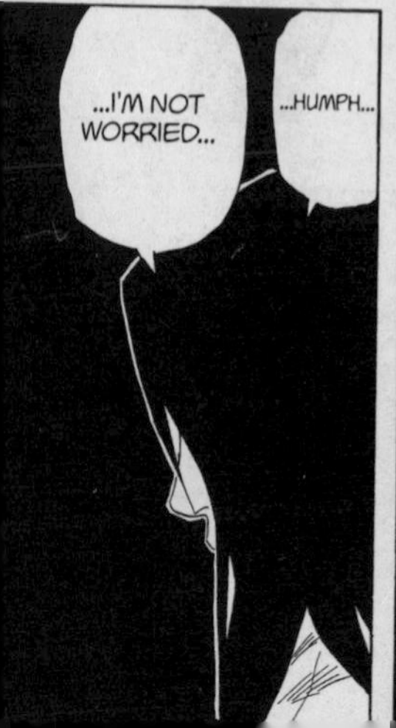
...HUMPH...
...I'M NOT WORRIED...

I KNOW HER BETTER THAN SHE KNOWS HERSELF...!
I ALSO KNOW HER GREATEST WEAKNESS.
MAKE NO MISTAKE, SHE WILL SWALLOW OUR TERMS.
YOU CAN COUNT ON IT...
AND SO...THE MORNING OF THE THIRD DAY...

HAH!
ZWWRL
THUDDD
ZWOOOOSH

HUF

HUF

SO YOU SEE, IN THIS THIRD STATE, YOU PUT OUT EVERYTHING YOU'VE LEARNED SO FAR FULL FORCE, AND THEN... CONTAIN IT!

IN SHORT, WHILE YOU MAXIMIZE YOUR CHAKRA'S ROTATION AND POWER, YOU FORM AN ADDITIONAL MEMBRANE ON THE INSIDE OF THE BALLOON AND VISUALIZE COMPRESSING THE CHAKRA WITHIN.

HUF

HUF

HUF

HUF
HUF
I UNDERSTAND THE PRINCIPLE OF IT IN MY MIND...
HUF
HUF

SWSH

...BUT I CAN'T SEEM TO COMPRESS MY FULL CHAKRA AND CONTAIN IT IN THE SHAPE OF A PERFECT SPHERE...

GLARE

WHAPWHAP

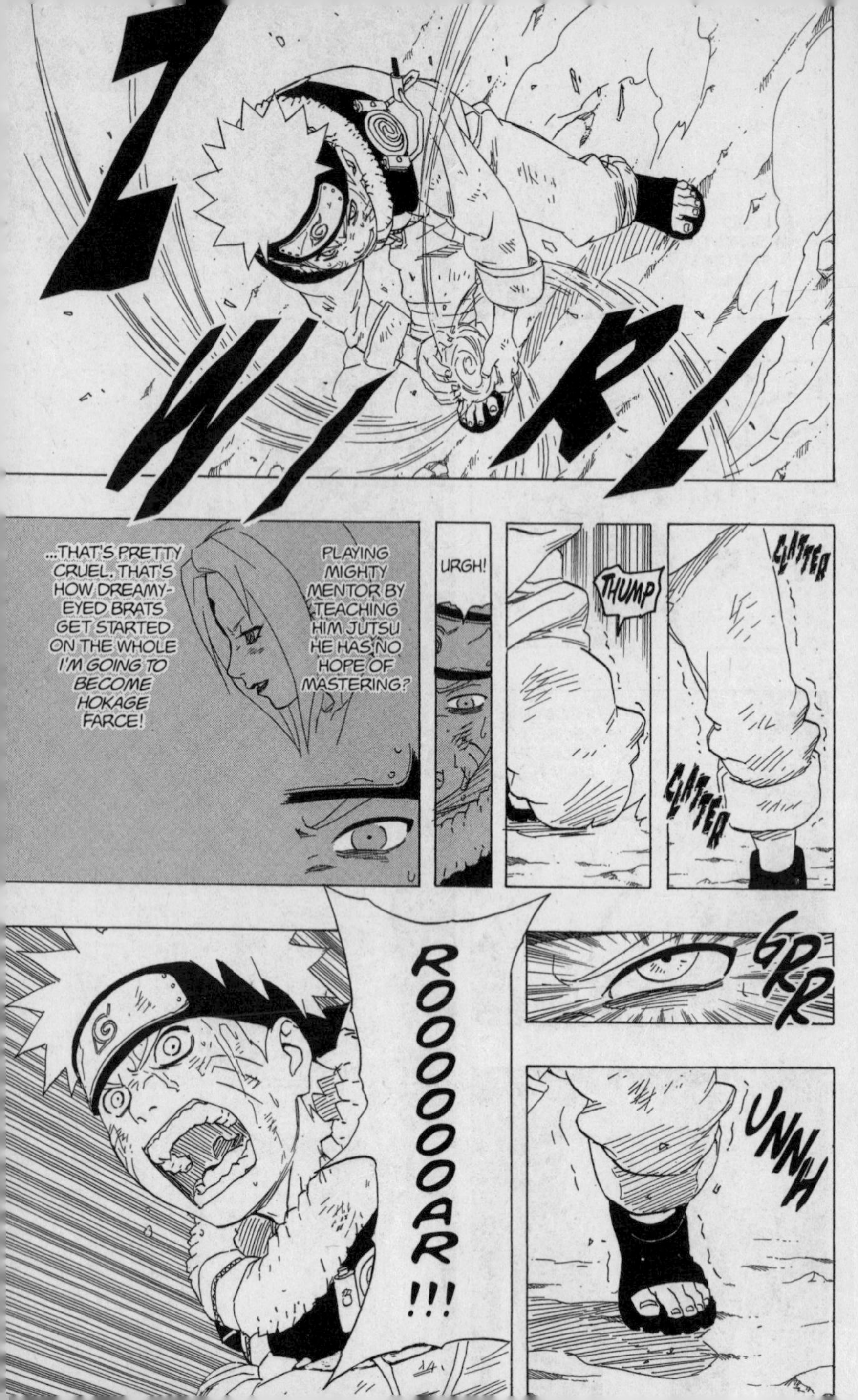
WHIRL
CLATTER
CLATTER
THUMP
URGH!
PLAYING MIGHTY MENTOR BY TEACHING HIM JUTSU HE HAS NO HOPE OF MASTERING?
...THAT'S PRETTY CRUEL. THAT'S HOW DREAMY-EYED BRATS GET STARTED ON THE WHOLE I'M GOING TO BECOME HOKAGE FARCE!
GRR
UNNH
ROOOOOOOAR!!!

THE SIXTH NIGHT...

...TO-MORROW'S THE DAY, HUH...

もちや
...

FROM THE DEGREE OF TSUNADE'S AGITATION...
...HE MUST HAVE OFFERED SOME-THING HUGE...

THERE'S SOMETHING ABOUT THE ONE WEEK THAT'S GNAWING AT ME...

READ THIS WAY

...

NARUTO'S BARELY BEEN BACK AT THE INN THIS WHOLE TIME.

PERHAPS I SHOULD LEAN ON TSUNADE ONE MORE TIME...

...
IT'S USELESS... BUT WHY...?

I'M RUNNING OUT OF TIME...
AT THIS RATE, I'M NOT GOING TO MAKE IT...

POP
!

!!
WH... WHAT THE...?!

WH...WHAT HAPPENED, NARUTO?!!

おてんや

WHAT DO YOU WANT NOW?

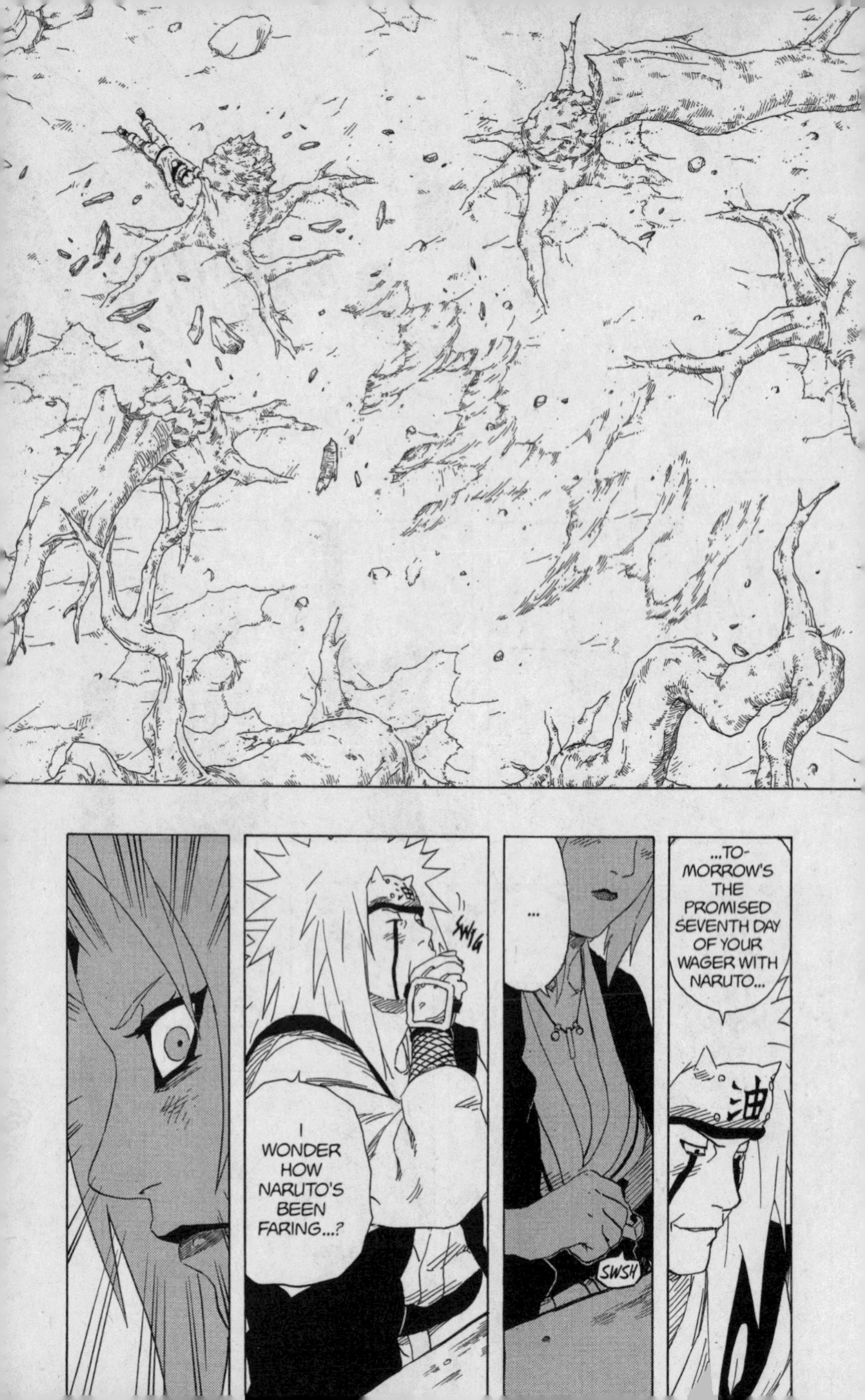

...TO-
MORROW'S
THE
PROMISED
SEVENTH DAY
OF YOUR
WAGER WITH
NARUTO...

...
SWSH

SWIG
I
WONDER
HOW
NARUTO'S
BEEN
FARING...?

WHISK
SKISH
SKISH

SWSH

TAP

TEP
KLNK

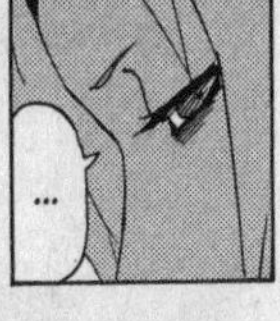
...

HERE YA GO!

GLUB GLUB

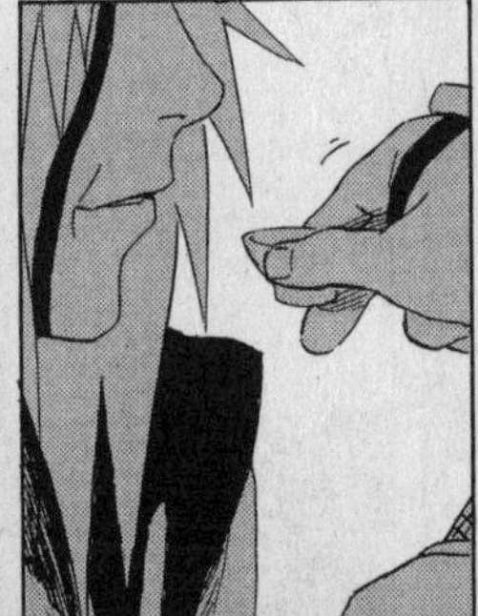

THE DAIKON RADISH'S READY!
AAH! NICE, LOOKS DELICIOUS!
TAP

MMM!
油

SST

OH YEAH, OH YEAH!
MMM MMM

GULP

...!

Number 162: A Vulnerable Heart...!!

MISTER! IT'S MORNING!
WAKE UP ALREADY, WILL YA!!

...
...YEESH.

HEY?!
BMP BMP
KRNCH

M... MISTER?!
ARE YOU ALL RIGHT?!!
THUD

SLMP

Number 162:
A Vulnerable Heart...!!

NARUTO
-ナルト-

LADY TSUNADE ...?!
HE'S SEVERELY EXHAUSTED...
...AND HIS RIGHT PALM'S BEEN BURNED BY CHAKRA...
SWOO SWOO
AT THIS RATE, HE...PROBABLY WON'T WAKE UP UNTIL THE DAY AFTER TOMORROW.
...IT'S JUST AS JIRAIYA SAID...
I CAN'T BELIEVE I MADE SUCH A SILLY BET.
...
HO HO...I SHOCKED MYSELF WITH MY OWN PASSIONATE REACTION...
I WAS SUCH A FOOL.

...
PLEASE...
...
...DO NOT GO TOMORROW!
WHY?! WHY WON'T YOU SAY ANYTHING?!
...LADY TSUNADE! DON'T BE SILENT! PLEASE SAY SOMETHING!

IF...YOU INSIST ON GOING...
EVEN IN EXCHANGE FOR MY LIFE...
...I WOULD STOP YOU!
...
...WHAT WOULD YOU DO ABOUT IT?
SHIZUNE...
GRR
DON'T YOU DARE USE THAT TONE WITH ME...!
SWEAT
SKREE
HUH?

KLOD
VOOSH

READ
THIS
WAY

IT WOULD BE MOST BOTHERSOME TO BE INTERRUPTED DURING OUR NEGOTIATIONS...
...!

...
...WHAT WOULD YOU HAVE ME DO?

THAT ATTENDANT OF TSUNADE'S...
...IT MIGHT NOT BE A BAD THING FOR YOU TO KILL HER.

SWISH

SCREEECH

ZWISH

HEY!
HEY YOU!

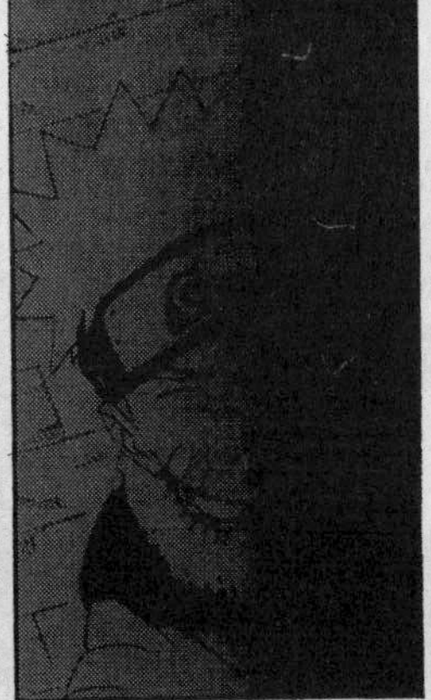

...NARUTO...?

AT THIS RATE, HE... PROBABLY WON'T WAKE UP UNTIL THE DAY AFTER TOMORROW.
...

WHOA!
O... OH NO!!
WH... WHAT DAY IS TODAY?!
UH...IT'S MONDAY...

...

WHAT?!
YOU FEEL OKAY?
SWSH

EVER SINCE I WAS A KID, I'VE BEEN ABLE TO RECOVER FROM PRACTICALLY ANY INJURY AFTER ONLY A SINGLE NIGHT'S SLEEP!!

THAT'S RIGHT... WE'VE GOT NO TIME TO LOSE!

BUT NEVER MIND ME...
WHERE'S THAT ANNOYING OLD LADY?!
TODAY'S THE PROMISED DAY!
I MAY NOT HAVE PERFECTED IT IN TRAINING YET, BUT THERE'S NOTHING LIKE GAME DAY PRESSURE...

THAT'S RIGHT... THIS BOY HOSTS THE NINE-TAILED...
CRACK
OWW...

!!
DASH
NARUTO, YOU STAY HERE!!

THKK
!
WHAT...?!
POP
YOU'RE...!

HUF
HUF
...HOLD UP, SHIZUNE...!
HUF
TSUNADE DRUGGED MY DRINK...!
NOT ONLY CAN I NOT CALL UP MY CHAKRA PROPERLY, BUT MY BODY'S SO NUMB I CAN'T EVEN HOLD CHOPSTICKS RIGHT!

READ THIS WAY

YOU, WHO KEEPS BRAGGING ABOUT HOW GREAT A NINJA HE IS?!
SO WRONG, MAN!!
DID YOU FALL FOR SOME PERVY ATTACK OR SOME-THING?!
SHUT UP!

SHE MAY BE RUSTY, BUT SHE'S STILL A MEDIC SPECIALIST...

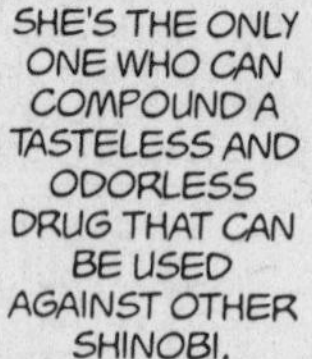
SHE'S THE ONLY ONE WHO CAN COMPOUND A TASTELESS AND ODORLESS DRUG THAT CAN BE USED AGAINST OTHER SHINOBI.

...ALTHOUGH I CAN'T BELIEVE SHE WAS ABLE TO SLIP IT TO ME, NO MATTER HOW DRUNK I WAS!

...

...I WOULD NEVER HAVE GUESSED THAT LORD JIRAIYA HIMSELF WOULD SHOW UP HERE...
粉吹屋
...NOW THIS IS REALLY GETTING TROUBLESOME...MY BEST COURSE IS WITHDRAW AND REPORT TO LORD OROCHIMARU!...

EVEN YOU, NARUTO...
...ARE HERE... INTERESTING...

SWSH

油
!

...
SO, SHIZUNE!
...

READ THIS WAY

WHY DON'T YOU START SPILLING IT?
WHAT ALL YOU'VE BEEN CHATTING WITH OROCHIMARU ABOUT.

OROCHIMARU ?!

...
I WANTED TO TRUST LADY TSUNADE... THAT'S WHY I DIDN'T SPEAK UP SOONER.
BUT NOW...

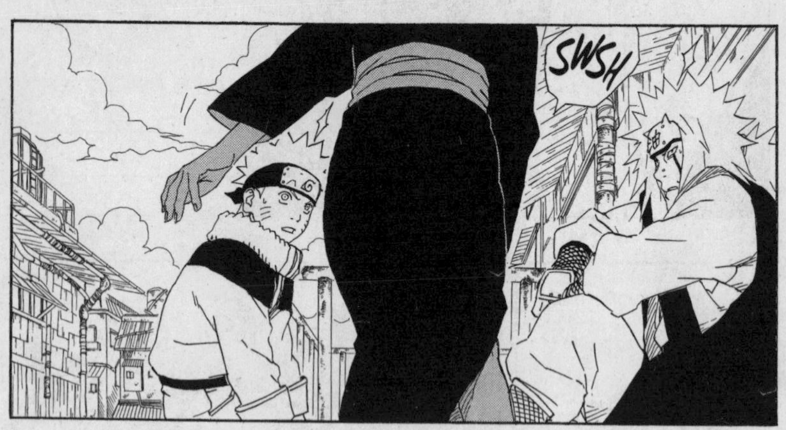
SWSH

THERE'S VERY LITTLE TIME... PLEASE COME WITH ME!
I'LL EXPLAIN EVERYTHING ON THE WAY!!
SURE THING!
I'M COMING TOO!

FFT

...YOUR RE-SPONSE?

THIS COULD BE BAD...

OF COURSE SHE'S GOING TO SAY NO!
ZWISH ZWISH ZWISH

READ
THIS
WAY

TSUNADE'S PROBABLY...
...STILL GRASPING ON TO THEIR MEMORY...

DEPENDING ON THE CIRCUM-STANCES...
...I MIGHT HAVE TO KILL TSUNADE!

...

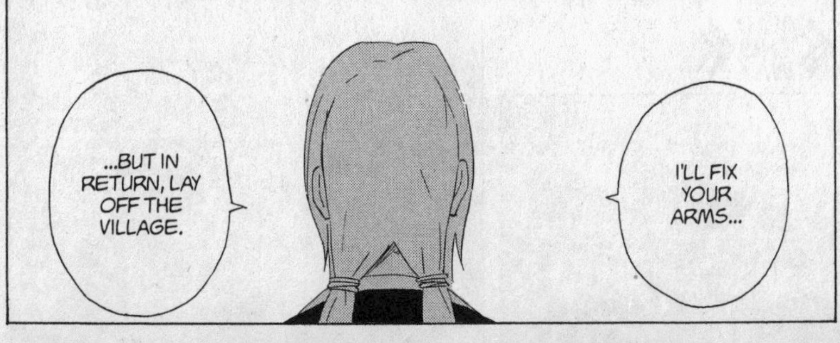
I'LL FIX YOUR ARMS...
...BUT IN RETURN, LAY OFF THE VILLAGE.

...
...CACKLE CACKLE... VERY WELL.

READ THIS WAY

WAFT...

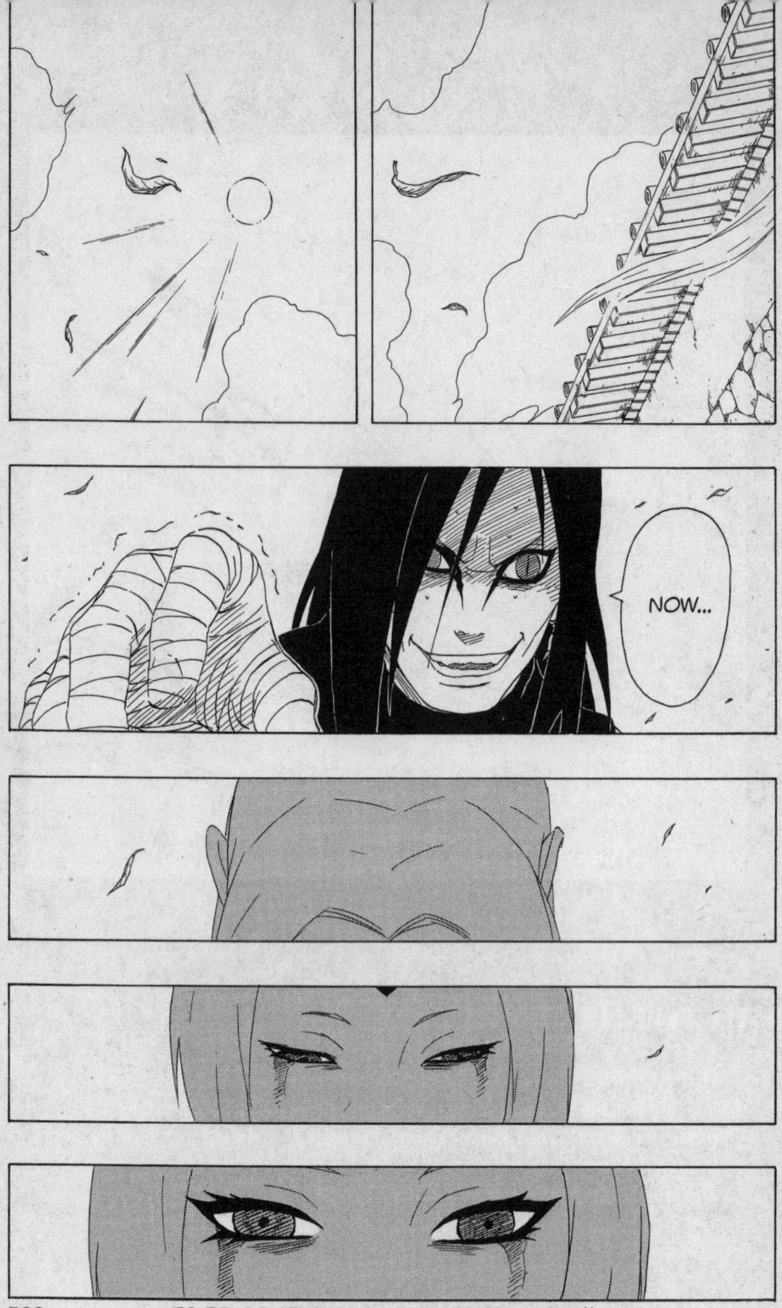

NOW...

TO BE CONTINUED IN *NARUTO* VOLUME 19!!

N THE NEXT VOLUME...

THE PROMISE

t's all-out shinobi war as Naruto, Tsunade, Jiraiya and Shizune take on
Drochimaru and Kabuto in battle, but Tsunade's darkest fears may be her
downfall. When a recovered Sasuke sees how strong Naruto has become,
ne challenges him to fight, and Sakura is caught in the middle! Then Sasuke
nakes a decision that may tear the friends apart forever, unless Naruto,
Shikamaru and the others can stop him!

NARUTO 3-IN-1 EDITION VOLUME 7 AVAILABLE NOW!

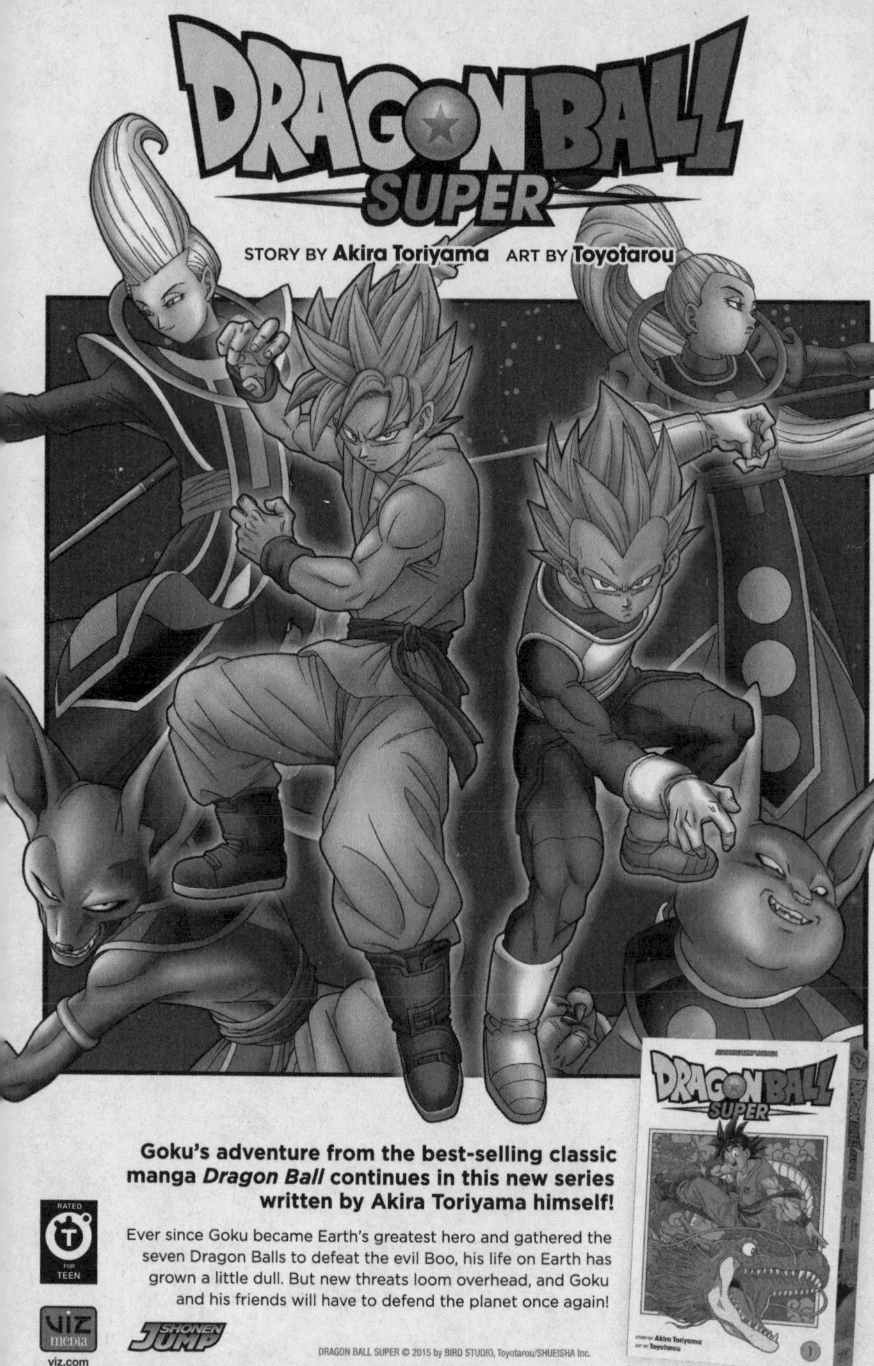
DRAGON BALL SUPER
STORY BY Akira Toriyama ART BY Toyotarou
Goku's adventure from the best-selling classic manga *Dragon Ball* continues in this new series written by Akira Toriyama himself!
Ever since Goku became Earth's greatest hero and gathered the seven Dragon Balls to defeat the evil Boo, his life on Earth has grown a little dull. But new threats loom overhead, and Goku and his friends will have to defend the planet once again!
RATED T FOR TEEN
VIZ media
viz.com
SHONEN JUMP
DRAGON BALL SUPER © 2015 by BIRD STUDIO, Toyotarou/SHUEISHA Inc.
DRAGON BALL SUPER
Akira Toriyama
Toyotarou
1

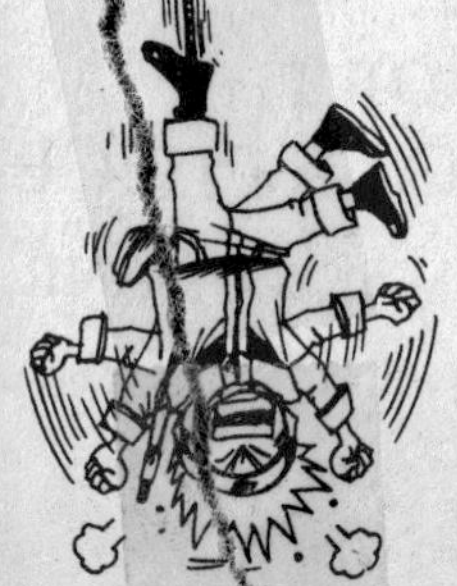

You're Reading in the Wrong Direction!!

Whoops! Guess what? You're starting at the wrong end of the comic!

...It's true! In keeping with the original Japanese format, **Naruto** is meant to be read from right to left, starting in the upper-right corner.

Unlike English, which is read from left to right, Japanese is read from right to left, meaning that action, sound effects and word-balloon order are completely reversed...something which can make readers unfamiliar with Japanese feel pretty backwards themselves. For this reason, manga or Japanese comics published in the U.S. in English have sometimes been published "flopped"—that is, printed in exact reverse order, as though seen from the other side of a mirror.

By flopping pages, U.S. publishers can avoid confusing readers, but the compromise is not without its downside. For one thing, a character in a flopped manga series who once wore in the original Japanese version a T-shirt emblazoned with "M A Y" (as in "the merry month of") now wears one which reads "Y A M"! Additionally, many manga creators in Japan are themselves unhappy with the process, as some feel the mirror-imaging of their art alters their original intentions.

We are proud to bring you Masashi Kishimoto's **Naruto** in the original unflopped format. For now, though, turn to the other side of the book and let the ninjutsu begin...!

—Editor

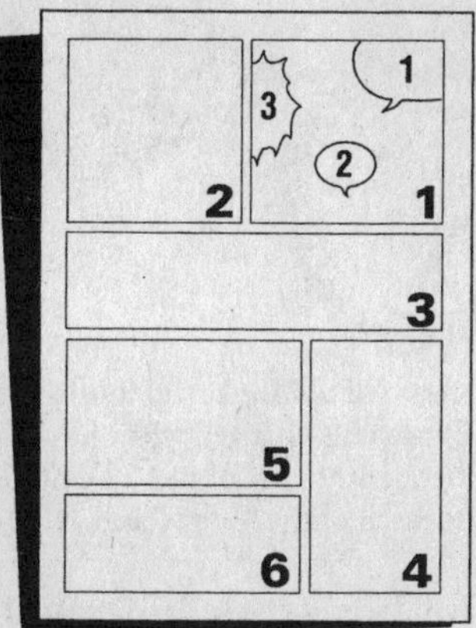
1
2
3
1
2
3
5
6
4